THE MINNESOTA

LIBRARY

ON AMERICAN WRITERS

LEONARD UNGER
AND GEORGE T. WRIGHT,
EDITORS

THE SEVEN *essays which appear in this book were first published separately in the series of University of Minnesota Pamphlets on American Writers and, together with the other pamphlets in the series, are intended as introductions to authors who have helped to shape American culture over the years of our colonial and national existence. The editors of the pamphlet series have been Richard Foster, William Van O'Connor, Allen Tate, Leonard Unger, Robert Penn Warren, and George T. Wright.*

Seven American Women Writers
of the Twentieth Century
An Introduction

Edited by MAUREEN HOWARD

UNIVERSITY OF MINNESOTA
PRESS □ MINNEAPOLIS

55.5567

Library of Congress Catalog Card Number 77-072905
ISBN 0-8166-0796-6

Contents

SEVEN AMERICAN WOMEN WRITERS

OF THE TWENTIETH CENTURY

MAUREEN HOWARD

Introduction

THIS BOOK collects for the first time seven essays on American women writers which were published not because the writers are women but because they are literary figures worthy of our study. No doubt these essays will fit nicely onto the shelf with recent studies in women's literature, but the reader will not find here any thematic interpretation that deals exclusively with the female sensibility. We find — refreshingly, I believe — that in place of ideology there are compact, illuminating chapters that attempt to lead us through the career of each woman and open to us particular stories or novels. If there is a feminine vision of the world to be discovered, say, in the landscapes of Cather and Glasgow and the southern idiom of Flannery O'Connor and Eudora Welty, it will be revealed to us as a part of the work; for the particular problem of being a woman is no more or less difficult for a real artist than problems of place or diction — or for that matter the problem of being an American or an accurate reflection of one's time. To my mind this is the most egalitarian manner in which to study women's literature — to presume that these women are artists first and do not have to be unduly praised or their reputations justified on grounds of sex. All but one of these essays are written by men, a note which may jar some devout feminists, but again I feel this is a good approach: the intention when Louis Auchincloss wrote on Ellen Glasgow and Ray B. West on Katherine Anne Porter was to write a critical appreciation of an American author without either consciously examining the work of a woman or self-consciously addressing an audience of women.

3

Read together these essays reveal an impressive range and high degree of professionalism that is characteristic of our best women writers. It is dazzling to look down the list of publications by Ellen Glasgow and Edith Wharton, to find that Mary McCarthy and Willa Cather were theater critics, book reviewers, working journalists of the first rank. And it is equally impressive to discover that the seemingly guarded spirits of Katherine Anne Porter and Flannery O'Connor responded with rage to the political and moral issues of their time. Ellen Glasgow with her string of pearls and fine manners brought the suffragette message to Virginia and didn't care a ladylike hoot what Richmond society thought of her. Set side by side these women writers appear to be a fearless company who took on the big themes of modern literature; innovative when it served them, sure of their craft — and if the reader can discern a similarity of feminine consciousness or a woman's point of view in their works it will add a depth of pleasure, a degree of insight that we may have slighted in the past.

In introducing these essays I would like to suggest to the students of women's literature that they attend to the women characters in *My Ántonia* or *Memories of a Catholic Girlhood* — that the female image or self-image reflected in the works they will read is a legitimate area of concern, bearing in mind that complex works of literature will not answer to oversimplified or unfair demands. Thus we cannot ask that the thread of female self-denial or oppression run through every novel or expect a "special sensitivity" in the writing of McCullers, Welty, and Porter, a sop which is often thrown to women as a substitute for real respect. The dimension of female concern and response is there for us, but please no favors: a laundry list of feminist grievances is as harmful to any serious study of women's literature as the critical contrivance of politely rushing to open doors

4

for the ladies. Each woman is engaged in a private artistic vision, not the vision of a cause, and her work is in response to an entire social and cultural milieu of which her sex is but one part. The rules of the game that I set forth may seem scrupulous but in the end our honesty in dealing with the texts of these American women writers is our greatest tribute to their work.

Of all the women we will consider in this collection Ellen Glasgow is the most slighted talent, the most faded reputation. Her masterpiece — and it is a splendid work of American fiction — *The Sheltered Life*, is not in print. Her delightful comedy of manners, *The Romantic Comedians*, is cast aside as though it were no more memorable than any best seller of the 1920s, yet it is as entertaining, bright, and witty as the Spencer Tracy-Katharine Hepburn movies that we have come to savor as art in film courses, lingering over the repartee and smart decor. The ironies of *The Romantic Comedians* are enduring: the January-May marriage that is the central metaphor in this novel is managed with skill. The situation is a comic cliché and Glasgow knows it. She plays with her plot and with her characters — the refined, upright, old southern gentleman, the foolish, modern coquette. They exist much as the stock heroes and heroines in the plays of Bernard Shaw and Oscar Wilde, to be put through their paces and to make what is, in the end, a serious statement about the folly of romance, the emptiness of lives dedicated to worn-out ideals.

All the feminine roles in *The Romantic Comedians* are mocked: the old judge's perfectly suitable wife who is remembered by him dishonestly after her death as a paragon of dry domestic virtue; his old love Amanda Lightfoot, so chaste and high-minded, is a parody of southern womanhood, her vision misted over with idealism. Amanda's life is a constant holding action, a model of self-denial to preserve the image of herself as sweet girlhood incarnate. As a woman who understood the Old South, Ellen Glasgow knew how destructive the idealization of women could be, how many lives were laid waste in catering to this myth of fragility and purity in women which is unfortunately still with us. The last page of *The Romantic Comedians* is hilarious considering all the heartbreak the old judge has gone through with his errant young wife. He mistakes the trim young nurse who moves about his bed for his mother comforting him as a child; then he sees the figure of a pretty girl and having learned nothing at all from his disastrous experience falls back at once to fixed ideas: "Fresh, spotless and womanly in her white uniform, with the competent hands of a physician and the wise and tender touch of a mother. . . ." " 'There,' the old fool thinks, 'is the woman I ought to have married.' There, sympathetic and young, obeying her feminine instincts in every exquisite gesture, was the woman he ought to have married." Ellen Glasgow must have enjoyed her final irony and repeated it triumphantly: that is what he wanted, to be treated like a sick child, to be tucked in by everlasting sympathy and youth, of course youth, and then that gentle scorn of the phrase "obeying her feminine instincts": women are pleased, delighted to serve.

The Romantic Comedians holds up nicely. The humor is apparent but so is the anger, a woman's anger turned to mockery and a display of wit, much as Glasgow herself built "a wall of deceptive gaiety" around her life in Richmond. In her autobiography, *The Woman Within*, she wrote: "Only on the surface of things have I ever trod the beaten path." What she says of her life is also true of her best work and what may seem to us now fairly traditional historical novels were conceived as an enormously ambitious project, an entire social history of her native Virginia. She is dismissed as a regionalist and too glibly accused

6

of mourning the passing of old aristocratic values. In our continuing insecurity we take to heart Anthony Powell's novel
Dance to the Music of Time, a meticulous chronicle of Britain
between the two World Wars, and ignore the energy of our own
natural product.

In *Barren Ground* Ellen Glasgow has created an overwhelming female character, Dorinda Oakley, a woman of great strength
who, like Willa Cather's Ántonia, feels a religious commitment
to the unyielding land. Dorinda cannot be thought of as an exaggeration: though she is an example of Glasgow's indominitable
women, she is also flesh and blood. We see her first as a passionate girl, desperate to escape the confines of poverty and a provincial life yet wed to her home duties and already caught in a
lifelong preservation of the land. Her goodness is the brittle
goodness of disappointment and service. In New York, where
she flees after a degrading love affair, she makes a career of caring
for others but she is always an alien in the city, always unfulfilled. "That woman," she says enviously of a passerby in the
street, "looks as if she lived without love, but she doesn't look
unhappy. She must have found something else." Dorinda Oakley
is a brilliant portrait of the female role of renunciation, the
substitution of work for sexual fulfillment. An abandoned
woman, she feels that she "belongs to the abandoned fields."
she breeds life out of the land by herself. Glasgow's description
of Dorinda's happiness is chilling: "At twenty, seeking happiness,
she had been more unhappy, she told herself, . . . than other
women; but at fifty she knew that she was far happier. The difference was that at twenty her happiness had depended upon
love, and at fifty it depended upon nothing but herself and the
land. To the land she had given her mind and her heart with
the abandonment that she found disastrous in any human relation."

The price of Dorinda's success is awful. "I may have missed something, but I've gained more," she thinks smugly, "and what I've gained nobody can take away from me." As Glasgow knew, this is hardly contentment but a grim satisfaction built on fear. For all her pioneer heroism Dorinda Oakley is constrained and sterile. The old romance eats at her until in the end she rejects even the bitter dream of lost love and can only exist in her mythic role united with the earth and the seasons. When marriage is suggested once again at the end of the novel, Dorinda's reply is one of the iciest ever uttered by a woman in fiction: "Oh, I've finished with all that. . . . I am thankful to have finished with all that."

The Sheltered Life is by far Ellen Glasgow's most controlled novel: it is a carefully sustained performance, a polite structure imposed on a seething story of raw sexuality. Jenny Blair is a little girl when the novel opens, reading *Little Women* against her will. She is mildly rebellious yet tractable from the start, surrounded by women who have sacrificed their lives to a grotesque masquerade of feminine beauty and romance. I can think of no other American novel in which the falseness of the postures between the sexes is so brilliantly delineated. Jenny's mother is a fey widow, given to eternal mourning, her aunt is a dotty recluse wounded forever by a lover's rejection, and Eva Birdsong, the legendary beauty of the town, forced like a fading actress to hide any sign of age or despair, is the most pathetic of them all. It seems inevitable, given Jenny's protected life, that the lovely Eva will appeal to the innocent girl as a friend and model: deceived by manners and grace, Jenny grows up believing in the myth of Mr. and Mrs. Birdsong's perfect love. *The Sheltered Life* is, as Louis Auchincloss points out, a complex work: the strains of destructive myth and harsh reality are handled deftly. The three male roles are as fully realized as the female ones: the aristocratic old gentle-

8

man, General Archbald, the young realist, John Welch, and the weak, handsome Don Juan, George Birdsong. George, who uses women in the crudest way to bolster his own male pride, is a fine portrait of the sentimental brute, as perfectly conceived as Tom Buchanan in Fitzgerald's *The Great Gatsby*.

Jenny Blair stays in her city in Virginia to witness the passing of the old order: this was the world Glasgow understood as closely as Proust understood his Combray. The moral problems of *The Sheltered Life* are far-reaching and Glasgow's insights are no more hampered by her class than are Virginia Woolf's in *Mrs. Dalloway*. It is a passionate novel, a work that is absolutely unsheltered in its knowledge of sex. Eva Birdsong, diseased, dying, her beauty sapped, says to Jenny, "What they [women] value most is something that doesn't exist. Nowhere. Not in my part of the world. Not in the universe." She has let her life become a trashy romance, of no more value than the pulp novels that incited Emma Bovary, the lethal love stories that are still turned out and read by millions of women each year. For Eva the terrible charade is over, no longer does she have to paint herself and cater to the gentlemen. She kills her worthless husband not so much in vengeance but as an act of negative redemption. She is lost but Jenny Blair, his newest conquest, can be saved from George's shallow and corrupting romantic ideas.

In *The Woman Within* Ellen Glasgow presents herself as a southern grande dame, demure about personal details yet self-regarding, given to defensive overevaluations of her work and then spilling the beans of self-doubt much like Norman Mailer. While we take delight in Mailer's excessive performance we have limited Ellen Glasgow to the role of corseted southern belle that she mocks in her novels. We can hardly accuse her of being a lady of Virginia any more than we can accuse Jane Austen of not being

George Sand. She felt deeply and wrote well about the dishonesty of both sexes.

Willa Cather, though honored indeed, is another woman writer who deserves a serious reconsideration: she is often treated as a piety or, like Glasgow, as a regionalist (a category which has become as meaningless in criticism as the term genteel). Cather is one of the subtlest and most intelligent of American writers. I have come to believe that the fluency of her style, her strong but easy voice as storyteller, has led to oversimplifications. Lionel Trilling, one of the finest critics of American literature was capable of writing: "[Cather's] women always stand in the mother or daughter relation to men: they are never lovers." On the contrary, she portrayed women in novel after novel who come to the role of mother or daughter after they have been betrayed by a great love. In *A Lost Lady*, Marian Forrester, one of Cather's most intricate women, is first a daughter-wife to Colonel Forrester, the old pioneer railroad builder, and comes to mother him in his decline — but she is sensuous, more alive than a symbol of civilization on the prairie or than the queenly role she plays for the wealthy men who dine at her table. Her early life and her last years are mysterious, perhaps even scandalous, to the narrator of the book who never quite understands that her needs as a woman go beyond the confines of his version of her story. Marian Forrester is "lost" to young Neil, the narrator, because he idealized her and loved her as a "lady." Cather's ironies undercut any mourning for the past, for the old days of vigor on the plains when the American dream was still possible: she suggests that Marian Forrester survived her gracious role and was able to live other lives not as a lady but as a real woman, while Neil Herbert "never found the promise of wild delight" that her eyes held and he would never know whether she "really found the ever-blooming, ever-burning, ever-piercing joy or whether it was all fine play-acting." Fatuously, Neil and an old childhood friend agree they are pleased that Marian Forrester not only survived but prospered. Never having known adventure, Neil is one of life's voyeurs. His last remark is old maidish, filled with a pity Mrs. Forrester would never have asked for: "So we may feel sure that she was well cared for to the very end."

It is a great love, too, that is the theme of one of Cather's strongest works, *My Mortal Enemy*. Myra Driscoll leaves fortune and privilege behind to marry Oswald Henshawe. Their story is one of high romance and the pursuit of freedom after the moment of glory is past: it is a story of consequences and regrets, of love turned to confinement and hate. Cather was always conscious of how much the strong-willed must give up to attain freedom for love or art. Myra Henshawe's heroic break with her uncle means that she will be denied financial security and routine social acceptance. To a degree she succeeds. Myra has her Oswald, her exquisite drawing room in New York, the glittering friendship of celebrities. She creates, in fact, the stage she needs to play out the role of prima donna and like a great lady of the theater she is demanding, stagey, costumed — bigger than life. The story of Oswald and Myra Henshawe, their loyalty and mutual ruin, is a powerful sexual theme close to the love bound with guilt that we find in Strindberg. Oswald in his honest summing up pays the greatest tribute to his wife that a lover can: "I'd rather have been clawed by her, as she used to say, than pelted by any other woman I've ever known. These last years it's seemed to me that I was nursing the mother of the girl who ran away with me. Nothing ever took that girl from me. She was a wild, lovely creature. . . ."

In another distortion of Cather's women, Ántonia Shimerda, her most famous heroine, has been read as an earth-mother figure of such proportions that it is presumed she can not hold our attention as a real woman. As a novel *My Ántonia* is more complicated than this view allows: Ántonia is played off against Lena Lingard (a sensuous, distracting girl) and she withdraws into her safe motherly role only after she has been betrayed by love. The Ántonia of the novel is *my* Ántonia, in great part the creation of the narrator, Jim Burden, who must idealize her as he has idealized his own past. The final scenes are an elegiac acceptance of the present by Jim and Ántonia: battered by life, they honor the past but are not diminished by it. As for the indomitable woman behind the plough, the earth-mother image that has been pinned on the heroines of Glasgow and Cather, I think it is profitable to see these women as housewives, all their tidiness and care taking let loose on the land. For women like Dorinda Oakley and Ántonia Shimerda the unconquered stretch of "country still waiting to be made into landscape," is a challenge as the rooms of an empty house challenge lesser women. Their sexual natures are concentrated on the land. They are wedded to the soil that they nurture and shape.

Willa Cather was a writer with great stamina. The novels of her best years (1918–26) were written out of her own loves and disappointments. Her understanding of the women who give up a private life for artistic ambition was rich and personal. When her finest novels were done she was able to go back to her original strength as a storyteller and with expert craftsmanship brought vitality to the historic novel in *Death Comes for the Archbishop* and *Shadows on the Rock*. One of the nicest appreciations of Willa Cather is by the historian Henry Steele Commager who places her for us as a traditionalist and gives her high marks as an American moralist. In her techniques, however, she could be innovative — breaking off one theme to introduce a complimentary strain, framing her stories ingeniously with a narrator. She knew what felt right and each of her major works creates its own distinct structure.

Cather was boyish when she was a girl. Later in life she became, like many women intellectuals and artists (Lillian Hellman, Doris Lessing), a resourceful woman who did not flinch at taking on the traditional masculine role of a full-scale career. Having decided from her first days as a journalist in Nebraska that she was "one of the boys," she was suspicious of the soft and sentimental in art. In 1895, when she was still in the university town of Lincoln, she wrote: "I have not much faith in women in fiction. They have a sort of sex conciousness that is abominable. They are so limited to one story and they lie so about that." She went on to praise the women who had overcome what she felt was the burden of their sex — George Eliot, Charlotte Brontë, Jane Austen — and then remarked: "Women are so horribly subjective and they have such scorn for the healthy common place." These are youthful, inexperienced words, yet they represent a real fear on the part of Willa Cather, which we find also in Virginia Woolf, that she might be closed out of a sacred brotherhood of art, that limits imposed on her by our culture might prove fatal to her work. She need not have worried.

"Well, you know, there was a time when I wanted very much to belong to the literary world. I wanted to be respected the way someone like Katherine Anne Porter used to be respected." — Norman Mailer.

We know what Mailer means — that for him literary life in America is a sprawling roustabout business and the desire to be distinguished solely for the purity of one's work seems to him an idyll — the time when he wished for such respect, a season of innocence. No one could have a quieter, more persistently dignified reputation than Katherine Anne Porter. Her finest stories, like those of Chekhov and Joyce, must be considered whenever we discuss the nature of modern short fiction. I think that any young woman reading her now will feel that she wrote (and presumably still writes) with an artistic urgency, a commitment that has nothing to do with the demands of literary fashion. Her work will appear in sharp contrast to much of the women's fiction recently published in response to a ready market. It is interesting to note that in a rare interview in 1952 she seemed not to be conscious of herself as a woman writer per se. She speaks as an artist and as an artist politically engaged. When, in a later interview (1964), she is asked to deal with specifically feminist questions, like Doris Lessing she is able to get to the core of a problem in a few sentences with more emotional accuracy than a sheaf of testimonials: "You're brought up with the notion of feminine chastity and inaccessibility, yet with the curious idea of feminine availability in all spiritual ways, and in giving service to anyone who demands it. And I suppose that's why it has taken me twenty years to write this novel (*Ship of Fools*), it's been interrupted by just anyone who could jimmy his way into my life."

But she is not to be mistaken for an ordinary complainer. From the very beginning Katherine Anne Porter was absorbed in a deeper psychological sense with the problem of femininity and personal freedom. In the title story of *Flowering Judas and Other Stories*, Laura is a study in passivity. Her virginity is guarded out of convention as unfelt as the conventions of courtly love, the flowers and serenades of her young admirer. Nunlike in blue serge with twenty collars all the same, her fastidiousness is destructive, even awesome. The men who assault her with their propositions of love — Braggioni with his selfish male pride and lust for power, (a hero from Zapata's revolutionary army) and the young man with his love songs — are both turned away. She is without desire: all her virtue is negative so that even her normal acts of bravery are reduced to a dispirited lack of fear and performed with no conviction. She teaches small children without love. Her visits to political prisoners are routine fulfillments of corporal works of mercy.

The surface of the story is smooth, dreamlike, dispassionate: Porter's narrative gathers all the details of Laura's life, swiftly passing from politics to religion to sex with a grace that lulls her audience into the final nightmare. During the day Laura had watched a prisoner die from an overdose of pills which she — a perverse ministering angel — had brought to him. Now he comes to her in a dream and for the first time she responds to a man after he has called her murderer. Earlier in the story Porter writes "No one touches her . . . ," but now it is Laura who wants to take the dead man's hand. *She* is called the "poor prisoner." We see that this is true — her emptiness is more confining than the prisoner's boredom in jail. In a black-mass communion she drinks the blood of the flowering Judas tree and her dream of death holds more enchantment than waking to the death that is her own life. Porter makes it clear that Laura is a lost soul, an exile from love.

The girl named Miranda who appears in many of Katherine Anne Porter's stories is an autobiographical creation much like Stephen Dedalus in Joyce's *Portrait of an Artist*. The facts of her life make the story, but Miranda is a character freshly and appropriately imagined in each sequence. She is constructed with an artistic decorum that puts the demands of craft ahead of personal outpouring. In "Pale Horse, Pale Rider" Miranda is the woman who escapes death, a precursor of Sylvia Plath's "Lady Lazarus." "Lazarus, come forth," she thinks. "Not unless you bring me my top hat and stick." For the rest of her days Miranda will perform with paint and powder like the tacky vaudeville dancer whose performance she had given a bad review. She has survived not only the great influenza epidemic of World War I but her own romance — a love story too fine for this world. Her lover, a handsome young soldier, is named Adam and they are, in the way that first love makes the world new, the first man and woman in an untried universe. But Miranda is, in her ordinary life, cynical, a modern working girl living on her own, hardly fit for a prelapsarian role. She is more worldly and sophisticated than Adam and yet she is swept into their romance. Here Porter takes a great risk: the style in the scenes given to Adam and Miranda is sentimental. There is a rush of ardor, of sweetness in the prose. Adam is innocent and beautiful. The world is seen at a distance from their perfect enclosure, but the weight of "Pale Horse, Pale Rider" pulls away from the love story: their love becomes an event of Miranda's life. That is the tragedy. It is over like the war. In contrast to the spontaneity and the wild desire to be caught up in life (the automatic "yes, yes" to drinking, eating, dancing that Miranda feels on her last day with Adam), the rest of her life, we now understand, is willed.

The Miranda of "Old Mortality" is rebellious. She has broken with her family, married too young in a defiant, romantic gesture of freedom. Two women in her family are given to her as threatening models. Cousin Eva is a plain and bitter feminist and Aunt Amy is a legend, a girl who dramatized herself as an eccentric self-destructive beauty and died young. Miranda must reject the programmatic freedom of Cousin Eva which, for all its suffragette courage, is tied to dry theories, as well as the wild freedom of Cousin Amy which offers only a decadent tag-end romanticism. Warning Miranda against romantic distortions, Cousin Eva says, "Knowledge can't hurt you." But Eva's knowledge is filtered through grievance and a sense of failure in the traditional feminine roles. In "Old Mortality" Miranda is presented with her life as a reality and with the hope that she can live her own story, not bound to the past. It is a hope that Porter undermines delicately in the final phrase — "At least I can know the truth about what happens to me, she [Miranda] assured herself silently, making a promise to

herself, in her hopefulness, her ignorance." She has already revealed herself as being part Eva, part Amy and the struggle for
freedom, for a viable balance of freedom will be continued for the
rest of her life.

In writing about "The Grave," a particularly rich story, Robert
Penn Warren remarks that it concerns Miranda's "destiny as a
woman." Never straining for effect, "The Grave" is so *symboliste*
that it yields to overinterpretation, but Warren's phrase gets to
the true nature of the piece. Katherine Anne Porter is always writing quite naturally as a woman and often consciously about female
sexuality but never so subtly as in "The Grave." Scandalous, un-
conventional, the little girl Miranda wears boys' clothes. She does
not like her dolls but prefers to wander the fields hunting with
her brother. Openly written, this is almost too easy for the reader
to construe. As Cleanth Brooks points out: "This matter of clothes,
and the social sense, and the role of women in the society are
brought into the story unobtrusively, but they powerfully influence its meaning. For if the story is about a rite of initiation, an
initiation into the true meaning of sex, the subject is not treated
in a doctrinaire polemic way. In this story sex is considered in a
much larger context, in a social and even philosophical context."

The last paragraph of "The Grave" accomplishes intricate cuts
that we are used to in film but seldom find so effortlessly done in
fiction. Miranda, a grown woman now, stands in a foreign marketplace and is reminded by the dead animals that are for sale of that
day in her childhood when she and her brother played in the family
graves and shot a rabbit. She looks at that time "in a frame upon
a scene that had not tired or changed since the moment it happened, the episode of that far off day leaped from its burial place
before her mind's eye." Thus her memory is an uncovered grave,
mingling "sweetness and corruption." The colorful marketplace,
her troubled memory of "the time she and her brother found

treasure" are constructed as a montage and "the dreadful vision" instantly fades and is replaced by the more comfortable impression of her brother "whose childhood face she had forgotten, standing again in the blazing sunshine, again twelve years old, a pleased sober smile in his eyes, turning the silver dove over and over in his hands." The technique is like that of Ingmar Bergman in *Wild Strawberries* but lighter, more resonant. Then there is the haunting ironic suggestion that Miranda's brother may have got the best of the treasure that day, the screwhead from a coffin, which she traded with him for a wedding ring.

Katherine Anne Porter has written a small body of critical work distinguished by an easy wit and an accessibility that we might never suspect from her closely written stories. Her truly imaginative essay on Gertrude Stein is presented partly as appreciation, partly as parody, and partly as bitchy critique. It is an artist's response to an infuriating legend. Her attack on the sentimental use of four-letter words in D. H. Lawrence's *Lady Chatterly's Lover* is perceptive, angry, and downright hilarious. By contrast to Lawrence (who *did* write powerfully of sex, there can be no dispute), her own precision of language in a story like "María Concepción" is unself-consciously poetic yet intensely sexual. An essay that should be required reading for all intelligent contemporary women contemplating marriage is "The Necessary Enemy": it speaks directly and sympathetically of her own ambivalence to commitment. In a short appreciation of Virginia Woolf she writes: "She lived in the naturalness of her vocation." Katherine Anne Porter, a great natural herself, would discern through all the pain of her work that true feeling of vocation.

It comes as an encouraging bit of extraliterary detail that Porter was generous to Eudora Welty when she first started to write and that she detected what was special and knowing in Flannery O'Connor — "there was almost no way for her knowing the difficulties of human beings," Porter writes, "and her general knowledge of this was really very impressive because she was so very young and you wondered where — how — she had learned all that. But this is a question everybody always asks himself about genius." Flannery O'Connor spent much of her adult life confined to her farm in a small southern town and her range of women may be narrow but her knowledge of female psychology is deep. Mothers and daughters, the hateful dependency of that relationship, is a central theme. She has created the most horrifying mothers in our literature, women who do not exist outside of the social claims made upon them. In "Everything That Rises Must Converge," the mother is doomed by her own rattling tongue: her beliefs in white supremacy and the finer days of the past are no more than hysterical fears of an empty, pretentious woman. O'Connor lets the mother and housekeeper of "Good Country People" damn themselves by their meaningless social mumblings, an amusing yet horrendous exchange of clichés. Even the dotty old Georgia hick in "The Life You Save May Be Your Own" wants marriage, the sine qua non of a tidy acceptable life, for her idiot daughter. Both the girlish Joy of "Good Country People" and the Wellesley girl in "Revelation" are ugly, maimed daughters, unable to perform the slightest gesture of normal human commerce. Their hatred of the conventional women around them is pointlessly cruel and self-defeating. I can think of no more terrifying or revelatory portraits of female self-hatred than these in Flannery O'Connor. Joy, the wooden-legged Ph.D. in "Good Country People," thinks up the cheap trick of changing her name to Hulga — an accurate and unpleasant reflection of her blighted life. Her sex scene with a con artist is a parody of a roll in the hay. Lucynell, the simpleton in "The Life You Save May Be Your Own," goes off on a marriage trip which is a mockery of the real thing. Both girls are humiliated and abandoned. The men who desert them, find them less valuable than the objects — cars, money — that fulfill their needs. Both these daughters are innocent, childish-looking women who at the age of thirty can pass for girls in their teens. They are emotionally retarded, but our hearts do not break for these unlovely creatures: O'Connor never lets us forget that they are either idiotic or truly awful.

The voice that we hear in Flannery O'Connor is a heavy southern drawl. A backwoods posture was easy for her to assume and there is much of the oral tradition in her macabre humor. If we listen carefully, the violence, bloody murder, and criminal high jinks of her work sound like tall tales, the exaggeration of folk literature. As a woman she seems to have found her position grotesque, but she saw her world as outrageously funny and thus, as an artist, life was made endurable.

We find adolescent heroines in Carson McCullers, too, and, as Lawrence Graver points out, a good deal of feminine self-pity. Both Frankie in *Member of the Wedding* and Mick in *The Heart Is a Lonely Hunter* are driven to fantasy. In their dreams they play roles in which they are attractive and successful, but, more significantly, roles that bring them into the company of adults with grace. These boyish, presexual girls in Carson McCullers are never given the dimensions of time and memory that Katherine Anne Porter or Willa Cather use to set off the dislocation of youthful imaginings. There is something slightly perverse in the loving portrait Carson McCullers paints of female adolescence, a sense that grown-up womanhood is tainted and corrupt and that the pain of being powerless and innocent is preferable to maturity.

This fear of adult female sexuality is so extreme that her grown women are grotesque. In *Reflections in a Golden Eye* Alison Langdon, the woman who is sensitive, sympathetic, cultured, is a sexual failure, so full of self-loathing that she mutilates herself, significantly cutting off her nipples with a garden shears — a hideous denial of her womanly nature. She loves and nurtures a strange little homosexual servant. She is all quivering ineffectual soul without body, while Leonora Penderton, her husband's mistress, is body without mind, a beautiful animal, sexually free but a moral idiot. Leonora, who is barely literate, is as contemptible as Alison is pitiful and refined. Women of sensitivity are freaks, compensating for their shameful natures by the most tortured adjustments to the world. As Ellen Moers points out in *Literary Women*, Alison's love for her servant might be drawn from the queer attachment of Isak Dinesen for her black boy in *Out of Africa*, both examples of "frustrated maternal love." But I think the fear of full adult sexuality, heterosexual or homosexual, goes deeper in McCullers. The men in *Reflections in a Golden Eye* are paired off in quite the same way as the women — Major Langdon being sexually competent but stupid and Captain Penderton being brilliant, precise, dandified but blocked from all insight about his own homosexuality. The poor private soldier who stares at Leonora's body in a mystic trance each night is a martyr to the warped marriages of the Langdons and the Pendertons. Even the soldier's lust is blocked by a perverse religiosity.

In studying McCullers, O'Connor, and Welty we will inevitably find that they are often grouped as regional writers, a category which is misleading. Like Faulkner, these women have all said at one point or another that they do not consider themselves "southern" writers. The South is their material. We may run across a repeated concern with the dying of an old order, but it is one concern among many. This is true of their bond as women and we cannot force the point: it is their material. Eudora Welty,

MAUREEN HOWARD

as deeply southern as O'Connor or McCullers, recreates myth
(*The Robber Bridegroom, The Golden Apples, The Bride of the
Innisfallen*) as a means of dealing with the extremes of southern
life. In another more realistic mode she is interested in the gift
of feminine feeling. Here she is closer to the urban, sophisticated
approach of Mary McCarthy, psychologically exact. The attractive young woman from Ohio in the story "No Room for You, My
Love" lets herself be picked up by a man from the North whom
she meets at lunch in a New Orleans restaurant. Together they
travel to the end of the Louisiana Bayou country, a sweltering
mosquito-plagued ride to no place, out of civilization, beyond his
marriage and her love affair. What they need from each other is
sexual reassurance: ". . . they were like a matched team — like
professional Spanish dancers wearing masks. . . ." Except for
their physical contact which is a stylized perfection, they remain
masked and closed to each other. She never gets the drink of water
she asks for in the seedy Cajun cafe. Their dance to the jukebox
music provides only a temporary relief from her hopeless and
mysterious love affair. The man leaves her off at her hotel just
when the sounds of New Orleans are heading into evening, re-
minding him of his youth when "the shriek and horror and unholy
smother of the subway had its original meaning for him as the lilt
and expectation of love." "No Place for You, My Love" is written
with a hard-edged reality but there are swift lyrical passages reminiscent of Katherine Anne Porter. At the end the man says "forgive me" because the woman expects the social formality, a polite-
ness that makes sexual encounters permissible.

In *Delta Wedding* and *The Optimist's Daughter* Eudora Welty
creates women much like Ellen Glasgow's who represent a finer
sensibility and who are confronted with Snopes-like upstarts determined to claim their place in the sun. Wanda Fay McKelva in
The Optimist's Daughter is a vulgar, scrappy woman. She stands

22

opposed to her stepdaughter Laurel Hand, who is a gentle, cultured soul. Laurel, as Patricia Meyer Spacks points out in her splendid book *The Female Imagination,* has the "gift of feeling." The novel is melodramatic in an admirable sense. Fay, grasping and whining, is a dreadful villainess — while Laurel, whose much-loved father had married this horror in his old age, is increasingly sensitive. There is no easy resolution: Welty challenges Laurel's "gift of feeling" and does not dismiss Fay's strengths:

But of course, Laurel saw, it was Fay who did not know how to fight. For Fay was without any powers of passion or imagination in herself and had no way to see it or reach it in the other person. Other people, inside their lives, might as well be invisible to her. . . . She could no more fight a feeling person than she could love him.

The reader will empathize with Laurel: she is our heroine and yet we are made aware of her limitations. Her fineness is crippling. She lives with memories, bows to society's conventions, and while priding herself on an interior life has lost personal force in the outside world. *The Optimist's Daughter* seems a puzzling title, but Laurel's father was indeed a hopeful man, letting a creature like Fay, a brash prediction of the future, into his life. This awful woman, this cruel stepmother is an odd legacy to the daughter he loved. It is from Fay that Laurel will learn to relinquish the past and live in the present with a hard, long look at herself.

No woman writer in America has looked at herself more clearly and consciously than Mary McCarthy. Her work is invaluable to the student of women's literature, a necessary corrective to all the self-pity, self-justification, and hypocrisy of so many autobiographical fictions that have been issued since the resurgence of the feminist movement in the 1960s. In the two central works of her career, *The Company She Keeps* and *Memories of a Catholic Girlhood,*

Mary McCarthy is unrelenting in her search for an honest appraisal of herself as a modern American woman. Margaret Sargent, the heroine of *The Company She Keeps*, is defined by her society, by the men with whom she is involved, by her education, her politics, her work. In the midst of fluctuating values she must discover herself, to what degree she plays sexual and intellectual roles to get approval in life and, more difficult, to save herself from being a reflection of others. Self-discovery becomes the drive behind the loosely joined narrative of Margaret and the company she keeps. The final story "Ghostly Father, I Confess" is an intricate, controlled performance in which Margaret realizes that no matter how painful self-knowledge and her own perceptions may be they are the lifeline to individuality and freedom. After a visit to the psychiatrist, the modern priest to whom she confesses, "for the first time she saw her own extremity, saw that it was some failure in self-love that obliged her to snatch blindly at the love of others, hoping to love herself through them, borrowing their feelings, as the moon borrowed light."

It is a hard judgment that Mary McCarthy levels at her heroine who is but a thinly disguised version of herself. That nervous search for approval, for confirmation of the self is destructive to Margaret Sargent and, Mary McCarthy implies, to many women: Margaret is fragmented, directionless, driven to playing the roles of wife, adulteress, intellectual, divorcée rather than establishing her own reality. Yet Margaret can hold on to the precious idea that "she still could detect her own frauds." "Oh my God," she cries, "do not let them take this away from me. If the flesh must be blind, let the spirit see. Preserve me in diversity. . . ."

The reliance on reason as against feminine sensibility in McCarthy can also be found in the English novelist Doris Lessing and in the playwright Lillian Hellman's autobiographical work: it is a drive for truth and that truth becomes the proof of one's existence as a mature though flawed woman. While Lessing in her recent novels has turned to psychic experience as an alternative reality, McCarthy in her political reporting on Vietnam and Watergate has kept to the facts, which are more outrageous than fiction, to fulfill her own artistic needs. Often her insistence on the cognitive has led her to want something from the arts which cannot rightfully be asked for: in her criticism she often denies a play or a novel the aesthetic space to make its own statement through the emotive. Many of her theater reviews and her assessments of our culture are overly articulated. She displays a puritanical resistance to the sensuality of words in O'Neill's *The Iceman Cometh* and takes a pristine academic delight in Nabokov's *Pale Fire,* a novel which is deeply moving.

In Mary McCarthy's beautiful autobiography, *Memories of a Catholic Girlhood,* her talent as a *raisonneur* is joined to true emotion. Here we find a fictionalized autobiography, the reverse of *The Company She Keeps*: her identity as a writer is assured and her life can be used without disguise, without fear of exposure, for she controls the fabric of reality which is her art. *Memories* is an amazing book built on the great tradition of autobiography yet unique in its revelations about that mode. McCarthy plays with the idea of Rousseauian confession and her Augustinian conversion is to secularism. In part it is an intellectual autobiography full of wit and an understanding of her culture. I have read *Memories of a Catholic Girlhood* a dozen times and can still be affected by the death of her parents, the cruelty of the bad uncle, the bare bones of the story of her life, and simultaneously enchanted by the careful unfolding of moral detail — blame and praise, irony and straight emotion — an artistry which imitates her journey to an uneasy maturity.

"Ask Me No Questions" is the last episode of *Memories,* a clear-headed but loving portrait of her grandmother structured on self-revelation: the older woman grows more and more dependent on her femininity, nursing the myth of past beauty, the wounds that life has dealt her and an ultimate passivity. Like Miranda in Katherine Anne Porter's "Old Mortality," the granddaughter must dishonor past stories in order to honor her own life. Mary McCarthy's understanding of herself as an artist and a woman is opposed to her grandmother's useless feminine narcissism. "Ask Me No Questions" is impassioned, a cautionary tale for us all. Primping for death, the grandmother's request for a mirror is horrifying and wonderfully apt, the appearance of things being at the center of her stunted life to the very end.

Students of women's literature must be bold in their demands and expect nothing but the best of themselves as readers for we have a heritage of importance and lasting value to which we must attend. At one extreme there will be women who feel they must consider literature without subjecting it to the odd angle of feminine sensibility, admittedly a partial view, and at the other extreme there will be women who claim that only women are privileged to understand even the greatest work written by another woman. Ideologues are not artists nor can they respond to art. The critics who wrote the essays in this book were free to give us their reading of the texts without bias, to evaluate these American writers — they happen to be women — without political or sexual allegiance. In this introduction I have tried to reread some of the novels and stories by these women, paying particular attention to their creation of female characters: the desire for a real identity that is not constructed on outmoded romantic notions or is not a response to the dictates of society seems to be a consistent concern in these self-portraits or fragments of the self turned into character. Another concern of what we may fairly call the feminine domain is a drive for self-acceptance. From Dorinda Oakley to

Ántonia Shimerda to Margaret Sargent, we can trace the unending search for maturity. Literature instructs us, true, but its function is also to please. Read a story by Katherine Anne Porter with an eye to the sensuality of her prose. Laugh out loud at Flannery O'Connor. Talk back to Mary McCarthy: she begs for our argument.

As women we must go by our finest instinct, knowing that we have more than feminine instincts going for us, and bear in mind Willa Cather's admonition: "If you hate what is cheap in life you must love the good with equal passion."

In judging a college contest of recent fiction written by students at Barnard, a woman's college, I found that there were several entries written on the models of commercially successful women's books featuring the familiar list of grievances and/or a smashing breadth of sexual experience. There were just as many entries that were honest efforts, free of cant, and to my mind these stories had a new assurance. They were never ladylike nor needlessly tough nor enchanted with the idea of a feminine sensibility. In the tradition of our best American women writers, they held promise of a professional commitment, a commitment to language and even, in a few cases, to art. What more can one hope for? "The truth," Emily Dickinson has told us, "must dazzle gradually or every man be blind."

MAUREEN HOWARD

Editor's Note on Edith Wharton and Gertrude Stein

Edith Wharton (1862–1937) is discussed in *Seven Modern American Novelists: An Introduction*, edited by William Van O'Connor, University of Minnesota Press, Minneapolis, 1964. She is, indisputably, one of our most distinguished American writers. At the age of twenty-nine she published her first work of fiction. At the start she was almost apologetic about her writing, for a career of any sort was not considered "nice" for a woman of her grand position in society. Over the next ten years she wrote a handful of stories and a restrained book on the decoration of houses, a sincere interest but also a repudiation of her mother's taste. After this tentative beginning she wrote thirty-two volumes of fiction, a travel book, a memoir, a voluminous correspondence, and a beautifully composed passage of female erotica which has recently appeared in R. W. B. Lewis's *Edith Wharton: A Biography*.

From a young married woman whom we see to be restless and unfulfilled, writing stories that cry out softly against the restraints of her society, we come, through her mature fiction, to know a committed artist who could write to a troubled friend: "I believe I know the only cure, which is to make one's centre of life inside of one's self, not selfishly or exceedingly, but with a kind of unassailable serenity to decorate one's inner house so richly that one is content there, glad to welcome anyone who wants to come and stay but happy all the same in the hours when one is inevitably alone."

28

Editor's Note on Edith Wharton and Gertrude Stein

Like many women, Edith Wharton knew that the claims of the outside world, of marriage and the woman's duty to home and society could be merciless and that the inner life could become a source of strength. The best of her novels are like inspired rooms, places which she creates for us with a completeness of moral and psychological detail. Lily Bart, the doomed heroine of *The House of Mirth*, Wharton's finest novel, is conscious that she is a "decoration," a visual effect in the fashionable houses she visits. Her failure to accept that role leads to her destruction. In a mood of independence, Lily goes to the rooms of Lawrence Selden, a charming dilettante for whom she has a great affinity. There, in the midst of his collection of pictures and books — a little humanistic enclave — he proposes to her rather falsely and rhetorically that there is "a republic of the spirit," a private place of refuge that can be created outside of society. But Lily Bart's fate, unlike Selden's — he has a career, financial independence — is bound completely to the outside world. She is a beautiful woman with no options, no resources, and her quest for freedom ends in suicide in a miserable rented room, the first and last room of her own.

Ethan Frome, probably the most widely read of Wharton's novels, we now know to have been written when, as a woman in her forties, she experienced her one passionate love affair. Though she was living as an expatriot in France, the scene — so close in fact to her own unhappy marriage and illicit love — is transposed to a New England farmhouse. Every detail of the poor farmer's kitchen is recorded. A chair scrapes. The doorknob turns. The characters move about in an unadorned emotional confinement. Gone the parlors and verandas of high society. For this strict moral tale she went back to her American roots, to the fabalistic strain of Hawthorne and Melville, even to the snowbound Berkshire Hills where *Ethan Frome* is set. It is extraordinary the way in which we feel the plain run-down house as part of the story, each creak and whisper penetrates the silence as the adulterous desire of Ethan Frome and Nattie Silver builds under the eyes of his dour wife, Zenobia.

Edith Wharton's range was considerable. *The Custom of the Country* is broad satire. Here, Undine Spragg, a voracious American beauty, begins her devastating social climb in a showy hotel suite and ends in a French ballroom which has been purchased out of insatiable greed and transplated to New York. Rooms again — the many houses of imagination that contained Edith Wharton's knowledge of her women. It seems naive now that she was admired in the past as merely a novelist of manners and that her tales of New York Society were thought of as historically interesting, minor Henry James, limited to the drawing room scandals of another time. The decor in Edith Wharton's novels does not detract from the architectural strength.

Millicent Bell has written a good critical book, *Edith Wharton and Henry James.* Much illuminating new material on Wharton has become available to us in R. W. B. Lewis's definitive book, *Edith Wharton: A Biography,* Harper and Row, New York, 1975. An excellent new critical study is *A Feast of Words: The Triumph of Edith Wharton,* Cynthia Griffin Wolff, Oxford University Press, New York, 1977.

Gertrude Stein (1874–1946). (A chapter on Stein is included in *Seven American Literary Stylists from Poe to Mailer: An Introduction,* edited by George T. Wright, University of Minnesota Press, Minneapolis, 1973.) She is the most difficult of all American women writers to assess, not only because her writing is difficult but because it tends to lead the reader into discussions of theory rather than discussions of the text. Her studies at Harvard with the psychologist William James led her to take a scientific approach to writing and the study of literature: she was convinced of a continuous psychological present as a precept in her work. In this continuum the writer, Gertrude Stein, is a constantly talking, thinking, rethinking, saying voice. Except for some of her early, more accessible works — *Matisse, Picasso, and Gertrude Stein, Three Lives, Lucy Church Amiably,* and *The Making of Americans* — she is the center of all her art. She establishes herself in Paris in 1903 and was greatly influenced by the symbolists and by the cubist painters, many of whom she knew and entertained. Again, with Stein there is always a great deal of talk about the influences on her — *Tender Buttons* is written according to cubist principles — and her influence on twentieth century writers.

Her main artistic response was to theory and like a scientist supporting her theories, she seems to have found all her experimentation equally interesting. In *Lectures in America* she tells her audience that she has gobbled up *all* of English Literature and has now transformed the art of writing:

And now, the paragraph having been completely become, it was a moment when I came and it had to do more with the paragraph than ever had been done. So I thought I did. And then I went on to what was the American thing the disconnection and I kept breaking the paragraph down, and everything down to commence again with not connecting with the daily anything and yet to really choose something.

In this passage — I will not dare call it a paragraph — I think we get the worst and best of Stein. Her overwhelming egotism — "and when I came" — must be seen with generosity and humor. She created herself as Gertrude Stein, savior, seer, a great literary presence with a force of personality that she believed in. We can read the constant "I" of her work and her life as a truly modernist testing of the self, an extension of the Cartesian "I think therefore I am" altered into "I brag therefore there is more of me." In her work she proclaims not so much the expected "I write therefore I am" as "I experiment therefore I am." She believed religiously in newness so that her insistence on discontinuity in language and the desire to "commence again" without the ordinary historical or emotional reference is a firm restatement of modernist credo. The worst aspect of the passage quoted above is a flatness of style, characteristic of too much of Stein's prose, and a simplistic argument for modernist theory.

The difficulty with Gertrude Stein's scientific approach to the problems of literature is that she asks her audience to be equally interested in every project, never admitting that in science there are many failures on the way to success and end results are the new and beautiful statements, the only things of publishable value. Since Stein herself forces the comparison to modern painting, I feel it is only just to observe that the giants of modern art, Matisse, Picasso, Duchamps, for example, went *through* periods of experimentation and took what was useful to them for their art. Matisse and Picasso moved on: Duchamps, having made only the new that came naturally to him as a good modernist, would not repeat himself and after an early success played chess for the rest of his life. Gertrude Stein had a fine original mind but she was an inflexible woman: having committed herself to "the complete actual present," she would not budge and became a handmaiden to her own theories. While she repeated the modernity that she championed it was assimilated into the work of Proust, Joyce, Eliot, Pound.

The questions that Gertrude Stein raised are of continuing importance — the nature of communication, the life of words, the magic of language — its look on the page, its sound. In an ingenious essay in *Fiction and the Figures of Life*, William Gass discusses her emphasis on "the esthetic significance of style." Gass's piece is titled "Gertrude Stein: Her Escape from Protective Language" and to me his mind proves far more supple than his subject matter. In terms of our inquiry into the female image in women writers we might be able to say that Stein constructed herself of words. What she put on the page was to be, continually, herself, and in that way writing is a distancing process. As Gass puts it "The desire to gain by artifice a safety from the world — to find a way of thinking without the risks of feeling — is the source of the impulse to abstractness and simplicity in Gertrude Stein as it is in much of modern painting where she felt the similarity of aim. Protective language names. It never renders." I think that Gass is right: her artifice denies feeling, but in much visual art the intention of abstraction is to establish a simplicity that will open the emotional dimension of objects, color, composition.

In *Art by Subtraction: A Dissenting Opinion of Gertrude Stein*, B. L. Reid finds that her creative work is "practically worthless," the narrow product of a determined eccentric. Reid's book is brilliant. He outwits Stein and her supporters easily. In reducing her to a perverse, self-created curiosity he refuses to be taken in by the myth of Gertrude Stein but is, perhaps, too harsh. Katherine Anne Porter discovers at the core of Stein's artistic drive the wish for celebrity. I think there was a great conflict between the private vision and the public persona in Stein, and the public won hands down. Her belief in the processes of the mind led her to mistrust all but herself. She did not believe in her own limitations: her intelligence became an enclosure. In dealing with definitions of the modern we are often led back to Vico — ". . . when a man understands he extends his mind and takes in the things, but when he does not understand he makes the things out of himself and becomes them by transforming himself into them." Gertrude Stein is a dominant modern figure, one of the objects of our time.

Having been led into too much theory, as a postscript I must say that Stein is fun to read. The games of dislocation that she plays with words are a good experience, the sounds often delightful. I like the plays, the early prose works that I have mentioned, and *The Autobiography of Alice B. Toklas*. There is always an excitment in our reaction to Stein: some will find "the deep clear bottom" that William Gass claims and some will stumble in the shallows.

Bridgman, Richard. *Gertrude Stein in Pieces*. New York: Oxford University Press, 1971.

Gass, William. "Gertrude Stein: Her Escape from Protective Language," in *Fiction and the Figures of Life*. New York: Knopf, 1970.

Reid, B. L. *Art By Subtraction: A Dissenting Opinion of Gertrude Stein*. Norman: University of Oklahoma Press, 1958.

Ellen Glasgow

Ellen Glasgow's parents combined the qualities that gave to both antebellum and reconstructed Virginia its stubborn romanticism and its peculiar strength. Her father, of Valley stock, was an ironworks executive and a Scotch Presbyterian in every nerve and sinew; he gave his children all the things they needed but love, and in eighty-six years never "committed a pleasure." The best his daughter could say of him was that he had not hurt anyone for the mere satisfaction of hurting. Her mother, on the other hand, descended from Randolphs and Yateses, was a flower of the old Tidewater, who, smiling in the constant sadness of her tribulations, would have divided "her last crust with a suffering stranger." Miss Glasgow attributed the lingering, undiagnosed malady of which her mother ultimately died to the exhaustion of bearing ten children and the hardships of war and reconstruction, but it was more probably the result of the same nervous temperament that her daughter inherited. "Born without a skin," the young Ellen's Negro mammy, shaking her head, used to say of her charge.

But in 1873, the year of her birth, the worst, at least financially, was over. The Glasgows had, in addition to a town house in Richmond, the farm of Jerdone Castle where their daughter could range over wide fields, the greater part of which were left to run wild in broomsedge and scrub pine and life-everlasting, and cultivate the love of natural things and the sense of kinship with birds and animals that were never to leave her. Too nervous to go regularly to any school, she educated herself by reading all the books in the family library, science and history as well as fiction and poetry. An older sister's husband, a scholar, made her study *The Origin of Species* till she knew "its every page." According to her posthumous and by no means modest memoirs, she seems as a young woman to have had her cake and swallowed it, for she "won all the admiration, and felt all the glorified sensations, of a Southern belle" while at the same time making acquaintance with the squalor of Richmond slums as a worker for the City Mission and becoming a "Fabian Socialist." One can assume, at least, that she was no ordinary debutante.

When her mother died in 1893 she was so prostrated with grief that she tore up the uncompleted manuscript of her first novel, *The Descendant,* and a year passed before she was able to turn back to writing. Something of the same paralyzing prostration was to follow, in later years, the deaths of her sister Cary and of the man described in her memoirs as "Gerald B———." Miss Glasgow always regarded herself as a uniquely sensitive and unhappy person. Answering the question of how she had liked her life in 1934 she replied: "not one day, not one hour, not one moment — or perhaps, *only one* hour and one day." It was true that on top of the nervous headaches and attacks of her youth was loaded the burden of increasing deafness, but she was given the compensations of looks, wit, charm, gaiety (she was never one to wear her melancholy on her sleeve), friends innumerable, and a talent that was to grow in power through a long life almost to the end. She never married, but this was for no lack of opportunity. She broke two engagements and recorded that the maternal instinct, sacred or profane, had been left out of her nature.

Nor was she neglected by the reading public. Again and again she was a best seller. But the delay in the serious critical recognition to which she regarded herself as entitled rankled deeply. Believing that she was leading a literary crusade away from a sterile romantic tradition toward the presentation of the South in a realist manner, lightened by irony, she found it hard to be crossed off as a sentimental regionalist. That she obviously loved her native state and that her books sold by the thousands were perhaps enough to make her seem to the casual eye like the very thing that she abominated. And when she did break through the literary barriers with *Barren Ground* in 1925, she was already in her fifties and beginning to have a nostalgic eye for the old state of society against which she had rebelled. If she shuddered at Thomas Nelson Page, she shuddered more at *Sanctuary*. She might almost have said at the end, like that disillusioned Victorian, Rhoda Broughton: "I began life as Zola; I finish it as Miss Charlotte Yonge."

From the beginning she never wavered in her conviction that her role in life was to write novels — important novels. She kept a sharp eye on every development of her career, including all steps of publication, to ensure the unhampered growth of her reputation as a major novelist. She left Harper, which had published her first two novels, without a qualm (so far as appears in her correspondence) when she decided that Walter Hines Page at Doubleday would do a better job on the third, and after Doubleday had published sixteen of her titles (including a volume of poetry and another of short stories) she left it for Harcourt, Brace because she concluded that much of the Doubleday promotion which had helped to make her famous was "cheap." Similarly, although never rich, she did not hesitate, in the depths of the depression, to turn down an offer by *Good Housekeeping* of $30,000 to serialize *The Sheltered Life,* and she made a habit of seeking out critics to have the chance to present her literary case personally and to make perfectly clear what her books were about. In short, she was Ellen Glasgow's own best agent, as Amy Lowell had been Amy Lowell's.

Her first two novels, *The Descendant* (1897) and *Phases of an*

Inferior Planet (1898), bristle with the young liberal's determination to be shockingly realistic and seem a bit jejune to modern eyes, but it should not be forgotten what a determined step away from romantic fiction, particularly on the part of a young woman gently bred, they must have represented to her contemporaries. If a southern lady produced novels at all, they were expected to deal with plantation life, either in its antebellum splendor or in heroic and picturesque decay. Miss Glasgow's first two tales may seem as far from Faulkner as the sentimental tosh from which they were a reaction, and she herself in later years came to regard the so-called "honest" school of southern literature as a combination of everything that was "too vile and too degenerate to exist anywhere else," but there was nonetheless a strong historical link between the two.

It is a pity that she chose to lay the scene of both these novels in New York which she knew then only as an occasional visitor. Even later, when she had lived in the city for several years in succession, she never caught its flavor as she caught that of Williamsburg, Petersburg, and Richmond. She objected to being labeled a Virginia writer, and, indeed, her truths were universal, but it was still the case that they were better seen against a Virginia background. This, however, was to be no serious limitation, for hers was a diverse state, and she knew it thoroughly, its cities and its rural areas, its aristocrats and its businessmen, its politicians and its farmers. If she was a regionalist, she was a regionalist on a Trollopian scale.

The style of these early books combines the epigrammatic with the sentimental in a way that suggests a mixture of Meredith and Charlotte Brontë. Clever sentences like "Conscience represents a fetich to which good people sacrifice their own happiness, bad people their neighbors' " are to be found with such others as "It was the old, old expiation that Nature had demanded and woman paid since the day upon which woman and desire met and knew each other." Even more awkward is the intrusion into the supposedly free and easy life of the young bohemian characters of certain undiscarded standards of the author's Richmond upbringing. The radical hero of *The Descendant*, who preaches against marriage, is nonetheless still chaste when he meets and falls in love with an emancipated virgin to whom he protests: "I am not worthy to touch the hem of your garment." And Algarcife in *Phases of an Inferior Planet*, who loses his job in a women's college because of his articles on the "origin of sex," can still condemn his wife to bitter need rather than let her supplement the family income by taking a role in light opera. In bitter need, too, be it noted, they still have a "slipshod maid of work."

The important thing, however, to be observed about these forgotten little books is that, for all their crudenesses, they demonstrate a flow of narrative power and a vitality that show a young writer bound to make her mark. *The Descendant*, published anonymously, was by many attributed to Harold Frederic, which seems a greater compliment today than Miss Glasgow thought it at the time. In her middle twenties she was already established and could write Mr. Page about her third novel: "If the gods will it to be my last I don't want people to say 'she might have done big things,' because I am writing this book not to amuse, or to sell, but to *live*, and if it does so I shall be content not to — after it is finished."

The Voice of the People (1900), indeed, marks the real beginning of her career as a novelist. She had already conceived her master plan of writing "in the more freely interpretative form of fiction" a social history of Virginia from the decade before the Confederacy. Possibly using a bit of hindsight and showing that passion to see a lifework as centralized that characterizes the great French novelists, she later classified her fiction as fitting into the

LOUIS AUCHINCLOSS

following categories and covering the following chronological
periods:

History: *The Battle-Ground*, 1850–65; *The Deliverance*, 1878–
90; *The Voice of the People*, 1870–98; *The Romance of a Plain
Man*, 1875–1910; *Virginia*, 1884–1912; *Life and Gabriella*, 1894–
1912.

Novels of the country: *The Miller of Old Church*, 1898–1902;
Barren Ground, 1894–1924; *Vein of Iron*, 1901–33.

Novels of the city: *The Sheltered Life*, 1910–17; *The Romantic
Comedians*, 1923; *They Stooped to Folly*, 1924; *In This Our Life*,
1938–39.

Actually, the only common denominator of all these novels is
the Commonwealth of Virginia, as the only one that links the
masterpieces of Zola's *Rougon-Macquart* is France in the Second
Empire, but at least Miss Glasgow had the wisdom to rest her case
on geography and did not try to connect her characters through
the branches of an immense and exotic family tree.

The Voice of the People, although third in the history series,
was the first to be published, because, unlike *The Battle-Ground*
and *The Deliverance*, it required no research. Battle Hall might
have been the Jerdone Castle of Ellen Glasgow's own childhood,
and we meet her for the first time as a writer in full possession of
her native materials. She was to make Virginia the setting of all
her subsequent novels but two: *The Wheel of Life* and *Life and
Gabriella*. The first takes place totally in New York and is a total
failure; the second takes place partly in New York and is in that
part a failure. Without the Virginia that Miss Glasgow knew as
a historian and felt as a poet, her characters never become fully
alive.

As one first begins to succumb to the fascination of Battle Hall,
with the visiting aunt who comes for a week and stays for years,
with the miraculous reorganizing domestic powers of Miss Chris,

40

with the friendly darkies and the long, succulent meals, with the rumbling memories in sleepy afternoons of more heroic days, one may start up and ask: How is all this so different from the romantic tradition? Isn't this more of Thomas Nelson Page? Perhaps. Miss Glasgow had a deeply ingrained sympathy for the antebellum aristocracy, but at the same time one begins to perceive the parts of the picture that her realist eye picks out: General Tom sinking into sloth and fantasy and the rigid standards of Mrs. Webb operating to depress and freeze people in their born stations. Nicholas Burr, the hero, of the poor white class, may educate himself, like Akershem in *The Descendant,* and may even rise to become governor of Virginia, and die a martyr's death holding off a lynching mob, but he fails to win Eugenia Battle, and his failure has been foreordained by the blind prejudice of her family.

Miss Glasgow's resolution of the class problem, however, is a bit muddied by her own preconceptions. One is willing to accept the fact that Nicholas Burr, like Akershem, is subject to violent fits of rage, and even to accept his rages as attributes of the uncivilized barbarian lurking in all of us, but one cannot as easily accept Miss Glasgow's complacent assumption that such violence lurks more insidiously in the lower orders. Why would not *any* man explode against a heroine who, without a hearing, blandly condemns him for the seduction of a farm girl who has in fact been seduced by the heroine's own brother? Yet Eugenia appears to have the author's sympathy when she finds in Nicholas' fury a "sinister" reminder of his father. And why sinister? Is his father an evil man? No, simply a vulgar one. Certainly there is here a tendency to equate violence with low birth and sex appeal, for the heroes of these early novels, however ugly of temper, have also some of the attributes of supermen. Later on, after a disillusioning personal experience, the men with whom Miss Glasgow's

41

heroines become involved (no longer heroes by any stretch of the term) are weak, self-indulgent, and faithless. The confusion that exists in *The Voice of the People* was ultimately cleared up, but at the expense of the male sex.

Throughout this initial period of her literary career, Ellen Glasgow's hearing was steadily failing. As her income increased she began pilgrimages all over the world "more hopeless than the pilgrimages to shrines of saints in the Dark Ages," for there was no cure for the hardening in the Eustachian tube and the middle ear. Science had failed her body, she complained, as ruinously as religion had failed her soul, and she had to fall back on a humane stoicism and — ultimately — on golf. Deliberately she built "a·wall of deceptive gaiety" around herself and cultivated the "ironic mood, the smiling pose." There was a surer refuge in mockery, she found, than in too grave a sincerity.

Romanticism, however, was still evident in *The Battle-Ground* (1902) which Alfred Kazin has called a "superior sword and cape romance based on the legend that the Civil War was fought between gentlemen and bounders." It is the only Glasgow novel where the action takes place before and during the Civil War and consequently before the author's own memory, which may explain why the early chapters are so filled with frothy chatter and gallantry, with toasts and boasts ("To Virginia, the home of brave men and of angels"), with loving loyal slaves and proud, high-tempered colonels. Of course, Miss Glasgow may have been deliberately intensifying the cavalier atmosphere in order to heighten the drama of the coming conflict that would sweep it all away. It has become the classic method of handling the opening of the Civil War, as seen in Margaret Mitchell's *Gone with the Wind* (a book which Miss Glasgow admired) and in Stephen Vincent Benét's *John Brown's Body*. It is, indeed, almost a literary convention to show the Confederacy dancing its way into disaster.

She did better, however, in the war chapters. Here she kept away as much as possible from battle scenes, for she never liked to write about things that she had not seen with her own eyes, and she concentrated on pictures, such as that of wartime Richmond, where her own hard research and contemporary knowledge could combine to give a proper focus. The novel ends where her real work in fiction begins: at the end of the war when the South faces the future in defeat. It is here that she establishes herself as totally distinct from those novelists who could only lament what had passed away and sigh over characters who did the same. Dan Montjoy, coming back to the ruins of his ancestral home, wounded and half-starved, can yet reflect that the memory of a beaten slave which used to haunt him need bother him now no more. And his grandfather, Major Lightfoot, who is unable mentally to take in the fact of Appomattox, augurs the postwar southern mental evasiveness about which Miss Glasgow was to have so much to say and to the exposure of which she was to devote her ironic art.

The Deliverance (1904) is her first fully mature work. It is a well-organized centripetal novel about impoverished aristocrats and unscrupulous parvenus in the era of reconstruction. For the first time Miss Glasgow was able to make effective use of the Virginia soil; and the tobacco fields which bring a fortune to Bill Fletcher, the embezzler who has robbed the Blake family of the plantation where he was once overseer, make a perfect setting for the bloody conflict between the still vigorous old order and the already decadent new, and for the terrible revenge of Christopher Blake who deliberately corrupts and destroys the ex-overseer's grandson. Miss Glasgow was to be outdone only by Willa Cather in her handling of rural atmosphere.

In her affection for the Blakes there is still a bit of nostalgia

43

for antebellum days, but the bleak and closely observed present gives the twist of irony to all the memories and stories of that glorious era. The blind Mrs. Blake, whose family and servants together conspire to create in her sickroom the illusion of a victorious South, going so far as to invent names for the Confederate presidents of two postwar decades, is, of course, the symbol of the old South that rejected reality. Her son Christopher, on the other hand, who works in the tobacco fields to support the family, is an example of the aristocrat who has the courage to face and defeat poverty, even though born with the love of ease and the weakness to temptation in his blood, "with the love, too, of delicate food, of rare wines and of beautiful women." Did Miss Glasgow actually believe in the physical transmission of aristocratic characteristics? Evidently so, for Christopher, without education or other advantages, stands out among his fellow farmers as a natural leader. He is another of Miss Glasgow's supermen — he risks smallpox to bury the children of a former family slave — but he is even more irresistible to women than Nicholas Burr because of his noble birth, and when Maria Fletcher sees him, her creator's style slumps suddenly to the level of the lowest potboiler: "All the natural womanhood within her responded to the appeal of his superb manhood."

Maxwell Geismar has pointed out that Ellen Glasgow's novels are among our best sources of information on the southern mind because we can see in them the persistent imprint of primary cultural myths on even a perceptive and sophisticated talent. Miss Glasgow, he feels, for all her compassion and liberalism, could never quite free herself from her admiration of the old aristocracy with all its narrowness and prejudice. It is true. Negroes in her fiction are apt to appear as a carefree, feckless, lovable servant class whose peccadilloes and promiscuities are to be laughed at rather than condemned. In *One Man in His Time* she was actually able to write a whole book on the social problems facing a liberal governor of Virginia without mentioning the Negroes. She belonged, of course, to a generation that was taught to duck the problem in its cradle. But all this does not mean that she was unaware that it existed. Dan Montjoy in *The Battle-Ground* helps an escaped slave; Mrs. Pendleton in *Virginia* forces herself not to see the slave market; Dorinda Oakley in *Barren Ground* is a true friend of her Negro servant; Asa Timberlake in *In This Our Life* defies his family in order to protect a Negro boy from being framed for a crime. In this last episode Miss Glasgow does, if only for a few pages, face up to the fact that otherwise respectable white people may be willing to sacrifice an innocent colored boy to protect a vicious member of their own race. By and large, however, she did not choose to be overly concerned with the problem. She was one who felt that the modern Negro had lost the "spiritual" quality of his forebears, and she evaded the connection between such spirituality and bondage. She had her loves and her loyalties, and even at her most ironical there were certain boats that she was not going to rock.

In 1900 Ellen Glasgow met the man whom she describes as "Gerald B——" in her memoirs, and until his death seven years later she lived "in an arrested pause between dreaming and waking." As with "Harold S——," the other great love of her life, it was a case of opposites attracting. Gerald was a financier and a married man; they could meet only fleetingly and only on her visits to New York. One infers that the relationship was not happy, but it must have had its wonderful moments, and when he died of an inoperable ailment she was completely overwhelmed. If we are to take the relationship of Laura Wilde and Arnold Kemper in *The Wheel of Life*, a novel which she admittedly wrote as an antidote to her sorrow and later confessed to be in part autobiographical, as a picture of herself and Gerald, we thresh up an

45

interesting speculation. Why was this woman, so dedicated to the mind and spirit, twice to fall in love with egocentric and hedonistic philistines? Was *this* what she meant by the indignities of the spirit to which she was so relentlessly subjected? It is difficult to imagine greater ones.

After receiving the news that Gerald was doomed, she records that she went up on a hillside in Switzerland and lay down on the grass where a high wind was blowing. There she had a mystical experience. "Lying there, in that golden August light, I knew, or felt, or beheld, a union deeper than knowledge, deeper than sense, deeper than vision. Light streamed through me, after anguish, and for one instant of awareness, if but for that one instant, I felt pure ecstasy. In a single blinding flash of illumination, I knew blessedness. I was a part of the spirit that moved in the light and the wind and the grass. I was — or felt I was — in communion with reality, with ultimate being. . . ." Something very like this experience was to go into the making of *Barren Ground* and *The Sheltered Life*.

In the terrible years that followed Gerald's death she became engaged to a man with whom she was never in love, but who offered her everything that her love for Gerald missed: "intellectual congeniality, poetic sympathy, and companionship which was natural and easy, without the slightest sting of suspicion or selfishness." Everything, in short, but delight and joy. His letters, those of a poet, stirred in her no greater emotion than gratitude. She asked herself if she had failed because she had preferred the second best in emotion, just as her fellow countrymen so often preferred the second best in literature. Perhaps she had, but the fact that she could see the irony of her situation was the rock on which she would later build her Queenborough trilogy.

In *The Wheel of Life* (1906), conceived in a mystical mood, poet Laura Wilde and her mentor Roger Adams struggle toward

the recognition that man's only valid purpose is to identify himself with God and to lose his ego. The pursuit of happiness, even
in love — love, in Laura's case, for a man, Arnold Kemper, who,
however inconstant, sincerely offers marriage — is simply an invitation to disillusionment and betrayal. This is a theme that will
constantly be met again in Ellen Glasgow's work. The most that
a woman can expect from love is the opportunity to develop her
character by facing inevitable abandonment with fortitude. It is
a dreary credo, and enveloped in the somber atmosphere of *The
Wheel of Life*, it makes for dreary reading. Laura's collapse into
a living death when she discovers that she no longer loves Kemper
is so humorlessly described that it engenders no sympathy. And
worst of all, this quiet little drama of the soul is played out in
New York, with none of the powerfully evoked landscapes of the
Virginia novels. Miss Glasgow could never seem to get interested
in describing Manhattan. It is always a cold, shadowy island seen
only in terms of directions, "east along Sixty-sixth Street," "west
to Fifth Avenue." Nor are even the minor characters indigenous.
Angela Wilde, who never leaves her house, hovering upstairs like
a wraith because she was compromised in her youth, is more
Richmond than New York (we will meet her in later Glasgow
fiction), and her senile brother who likes to play the flute seems
a faded descendant from the gentle family of Dickensian lunatics.

A Virginia setting makes *The Ancient Law* (1908) better reading, but it is again the inferior product of a depressed period.
Novels about saints are apt to be tedious, and Daniel Ordway,
born in the arid tradition of those austere heroes of George Eliot,
Felix Holt and Daniel Deronda, is not made more credible by
having been, like another library model, a convict. The end of
the book seems almost designed as a parody of nineteenth-century
fictional saints. Ordway, having taken upon his own shoulders
the guilt of his daughter's forgery, leaves his home a second time

47

in disgrace and travels back to Tappahannock, the town which under an alias he has redeemed and made prosperous (compare *Les Misérables*), just in time to purchase the steel mills from the villain and save them from destruction by a mob of furious strikers to whom he promises fair hours and wages and by whom he is hailed in a final apotheosis. There was a curious streak of the preacher in Ellen Glasgow, quite at odds with her natural skepticism and ironical humor, that tended to seize upon her in her low moments.

The Romance of a Plain Man (1909) finds her happily back on the main avenue of a career which, almost uniquely among those of American writers, was to improve in quality (except for two long hiatuses caused by mental depression) until her old age. For the first and the last time in a novel she adopted the stratagem of the hero narrator, which disembarrassed the author of all problems as to points of view. She violated, however, the literary principle attached to its use: that everything to be told can be naturally told by the narrator. One does not believe, for example, that Ben Starr, who is announced in the title itself as a "plain man" and who has had to make his way up a rough business ladder from lower middle class rags to upper middle class riches, would describe breezes as being "fragrant with jessamine" or air as "heavy with the perfume of fading roses." Nor does one believe that Miss Glasgow ever intended him to sound as fatuous as he does when he notes that "I, the man of action, the embodiment of worldly success, was awed by the very intensity of my love."

Yet Ben's conquest of Sally Mickleborough's world is well described, and the best thing about it is that he can never make himself realize that he *has* conquered it. He feels that he must go on making money for Sally even when he suspects — or ought to suspect — that she wants only his love. But that, of course, is just Miss Glasgow's point: that he isn't really making money for her, but only to prove to himself that he is as good as her aunts and even as good as the great General Bolingbroke. He has been made to feel too deeply his own social inferiority as a child to imagine that it could ever be hidden by anything but a wall of gold. It is thus that materialism engenders materialism; in the end, when there is almost no hope left for the Starrs' happiness, Ben at last sees that the real division between himself and Sally has come "not from the accident of our different beginnings but from the choice that had committed us to opposite ends." It is Ben who ultimately insists on the importance of class as rigidly as Sally's Aunt Mitty Bland who has contemptuously remarked, when urged to concede the physical strength and stature of her proposed nephew-in-law: "What are six feet, two inches without a grandfather?"

Miss Glasgow was very sensitive to social changes; she saw and took it on herself to record that all over the South, as the industrial system displaced the agrarian aristocracy, men like Ben Starr were forging their way into prominence. She was perfectly willing to welcome them and to give them their due, perhaps even more, for she endows Ben with a touch of her old supermen when he knocks down a man whom he finds beating a horse. But she was handicapped in the business scenes by her ignorance of financial matters. Ben's money dealings are misty, which is again the fault of the narrator technique. He cannot talk about things that his creator did not understand, yet one knows that such a man would never stop talking about his big deals. Perhaps if one saw him through the eyes of Sally, who hated business, this part of the book would be more convincing. Edith Wharton, by showing her tycoons only at parties in *The House of Mirth*, was able to conceal from her reader an ignorance of stock exchange matters as deep as, if not deeper than, Miss Glasgow's. The latter should have done some of the research that Theodore Dreiser did for his Cowperwood novels before letting Ben Starr tell his own story.

If Ben Starr has risen, however, the old order has by no means collapsed. Ben's greatest ambition is to rise only as high as General Bolingbroke, a Civil War hero and aristocrat who has turned in his later years to business to lead the South out of defeat. The General, one of Miss Glasgow's most vivid characters (he cannot allow Miss Matoaca Bland to criticize a politician's immoral life because he cannot allow that she should know that it existed), achieves independence from his own caste by sheer success. Having been exalted in war as well as in peace, having been a leader in the old plantation days as well as the smoky industrial new ones, he, alone of the characters, can see how fluctuating and passable are class lines. He can see what Sally's aunts can never see, that Ben Starr will ultimately change his class with his clothes and that only a few old maids will oppose him to the end.

The Miller of Old Church (1911) marks Ellen Glasgow's coming of age, her advent as a major talent in American fiction. It dramatizes the same rise of the lower middle class as *The Romance of a Plain Man*, but it does so more effectively because the scene is laid in a rural area. Miss Glasgow knew a lot more about millers than she knew about financiers. The drama, too, is intensified by the fact that the upper class here is declining. Ben Starr and General Bolingbroke go forward, so to speak, hand in hand, but the Revercombs on the way up meet and clash with the declining Gays. This makes for a better story, though on a more fundamental level it is the soil, as opposed to the cobblestones of Richmond, that gives the deeper interest. The Revercombs triumph over the Gays because they have stronger roots. We have already seen that rural aristocrats can hold their position only, like Christopher Blake in *The Deliverance*, by turning to the land. In making her point Miss Glasgow occasionally allows us a glimpse of George Eliot and Thomas Hardy looking over her shoulder, and Jonathan Gay's seduction of Blossom Revercomb is a little too reminiscent of both *Adam Bede* and *Tess of the d'Urbervilles.* She was to assimilate more entirely the bleak morality of her great predecessors when she brought her own to its most effective expression in *Barren Ground.*

The Miller of Old Church shows some of the bluntness of style of Miss Glasgow's earlier days, and the omniscient author continues from time to time to obtrude a bit clumsily on the scene. One feels oneself back in the author's workshop on learning, of Abel Revercomb, that "essentially an idealist, his character was the result of a veneering of insufficient culture on a groundwork of raw impulse," or of Molly that "a passing impulse was crystallized by the coldness of her manner into a permanent desire." But in the delineation of Mrs. Gay, Ellen Glasgow was writing as well as she would ever write. It is the revenge of her aristocrats that even slipping they dominate the scene. Mrs. Gay is everything that old Virginia wanted a woman to be — lovely, helpless, indolent, and ignorant, and she conceals behind these qualities an inner force that enchains and destroys all those around her: her brother-in-law, his mistress, her sister Kesiah (a magnificent portrait of an ugly old maid rejected by a world that idolizes beauty), and finally her own son. The last chapter, where after the catastrophe of Jonathan's murder the characters raise their arms in a paean of praise to the wonder of his mother's fortitude, the same mother whose selfishness and prejudice have caused the tragedy, is the first great triumph in Miss Glasgow's use of irony.

The Mrs. Gays of Virginia, however, were not always destructive. Sometimes they were heroic, in which case, poor creatures, they found themselves, by the turn of the century, harmless anachronisms. Such a one is the heroine of *Virginia* (1913), the first of Ellen Glasgow's great tragicomedies. The amazing thing about the character of Virginia Pendleton is that, loyal, sweet, brave, unimaginative, and uncomplaining, she bores everybody but the reader. In this she surpasses Thackeray's Amelia who bores everybody but Dobbin. She is brought up to be the model wife that every southern gentleman was supposed to desire, and may have desired — twenty years before her birth. She admires her husband without comprehending him or without even trying to. She is gentle when a lady should be gentle but capable of a pioneer woman's strength in adversity. Like her old school-mistress, the embattled spinster Priscilla Batte, she is capable "of dying for an idea but not of conceiving one." She is ignorant, pure, and beautiful, a rose of the Tidewater, but fascinating to meet — in a novel.

From the very beginning of this admirable book, Virginia's parents and teachers are perfectly united in their unconscious aim of turning her into a creature bound to be blighted by the world in which she must live. Her only hope would have been to find a husband (and there were such) who had been in his turn educated to appreciate her type. But, ironically enough, it is old Priscilla Batte herself who, incapable of envisaging any nice young man who would not cherish Virginia, deliberately stimu-lates the interest of Oliver Treadwell in this finest flower of her educational garden. From the moment she does so the novel moves as relentlessly to its conclusion as if it had been conceived by Flaubert or Zola. Virginia's undiscriminating adoration ends by driving her husband to New York and another woman, and when he has gone she has nothing to fall back on but the same commodious attic of fortitude that sustained her mother through the dreary years of war and reconstruction. But military defeat is easier to bear than desertion, and Virginia's cup is bitterer than her parents'.

She does, however, have one consolation, her son Harry, who in the last paragraph of the book telegraphs that he is coming back from Europe to be with her. One does not feel that it is quite fair of Miss Glasgow to leave us on this enigmatic note. Might Virginia not become a worse fiend than Mrs. Gay and ruin Harry's life by a possessiveness disguised as unselfishness? Would that not be just the revenge that her type might unconsciously take on a world and a sex that had let her down?

Virginia is addressed to a social problem that had largely been solved at the time of its publication, for Miss Priscilla Batte and her academy for preserving the natural ignorance of young ladies belonged to an earlier generation. Yet it is hard to imagine a more effective illustration of the romanticism and intransigency of the South which had certainly not disappeared in 1913. When asked what the South needed Miss Glasgow once quipped: "blood and irony." The latter she was to supply in increasing doses, but first was to come the second of those hiatuses in her literary development.

The death of her sister Cary in 1911 was followed by a period of depression in which much of *Virginia* was written. Fortunately for that book it had been conceived and commenced before the final blow, and the writing of it acted as a kind of therapy for her grief. But *Life and Gabriella* (1916), having its birth in a time of desolation, is the arid product of a preoccupied imagination. It is as if Ellen Glasgow were saying over and over again with an almost psychotic monotony: "It does not matter what happens to one, so long as one has fortitude, so long as one is not crushed by life." If Mrs. Gay is the weak and selfish Virginia woman and if Virginia Pendleton is the good and crushed one, Gabriella is the Virginia woman triumphant over all obstacles. The obstacles, indeed, bend like rushes before the storm of her resolution.

Her story reads like the outline of a novel with all the author's notes unerased. The very subtitle, *The Story of a Woman's Cour-*

age, suggests a juvenile. Gabriella Carr, after a few vivid chapters describing the desperate life of decayed gentlewomen in Richmond, is captured by the charms of a New Yorker, George Fowler, marries him, and goes to live in his native city. His charms must be accepted because Miss Glasgow insists upon them. They are not otherwise apparent, though his magnetism is faintly suggestive of Arnold Kemper's in *The Wheel of Life* and may have the same source. When we first see Gabriella and George together we are told in the heaviest of asides that "In his eyes, which said enchanting things, she could not read the trivial and commonplace quality of his soul." George, in the now habitual way of Glasgow men, deserts her, and Gabriella, with serene faith in her own capacities, takes over the management of a flourishing dress shop and, after a brief struggle with her old Dominion blood, marries Ben O'Hara, another lowly born superman who has passed the hero's test by rescuing an asphyxiated woman and her small children from a burning house.

Another unfortunate thing about this novel is that the author's snobbishness is among the notes that she failed to erase. Gabriella's difficulties in bringing herself to accept the Irishman are understandable in a woman of her background, but her attitude toward the newly rich whom she meets at Mrs. Fowler's dinners is based on a pride of birth that the author seems to find quite acceptable. To Miss Glasgow as well as to her heroine it is inconceivable that Mrs. Fowler, "with the bluest blood of Virginia in her veins, should regard with such artless reverence the social activities of the granddaughter of a tavern-keeper." If Mrs. Fowler is going to be a snob, in other words, she should go about it in a larger spirit!

American involvement in World War I and Miss Glasgow's infatuation with the "Harold S——" of the memoirs came at the same time, and neither event helped to get her out of the slump of this period. It was obviously humiliating for the possessor of an eye so keen to irony to have to turn it on herself and her lover, but turn it she did in the pages of her memoirs. There is nothing sharper or more devastating in all her fiction than the picture of Harold in *The Woman Within*. Everything that she despised most in life — trivial honors, notoriety, social prominence, wealth, fashion, ladies with titles, the empty show of the world — he adored, and she loved him in spite of it for nothing more than a "defiant gaiety" that piqued her interest. Only when, on a Red Cross mission to the Balkans, he had acted out against a background of war horrors his grotesque parody of a Graustarkian romance with Queen Marie of Romania, was she partially cured of her infatuation. But in the despair that followed this episode she took an overdose of sleeping pills, not caring if she lived or died.

She lived, and there was left the war. Even worse for her fiction than her passion for the "pluperfect snob" was her vicarious suffering over distant carnage. This produced her worst novel — if a political tract full of Wilsonian idealism can be called a novel at all. *The Builders* (1919) grew out of the same shrill war feeling that produced Edith Wharton's *A Son at the Front*. David Blackburn, a waxwork Rochester, harangues his child's nurse, Caroline Meade, a rather testy Jane Eyre, on the sad state of the solid South, the evils of the one-party system, and the need for a league of nations. "The future of our democracy," he writes her in his first love letter, "rests not in the halls of Congress but in the cradle, and to build for permanency we must build, not on theory, but on personal rectitude." Angelica Blackburn's wickedness and her success in playing the injured wife provide what little story there is, but even this is spoiled by the clumsy device of having the reader see her first through Caroline's eyes as a noble, suffering creature. It is so manifest that she is not this that we brand Caroline as a ninny, and the central point of view of the novel is hopelessly discredited.

The almost immediate disillusionment that came to so many after the Armistice came to Ellen Glasgow, and one suspects that she was soon a bit ashamed of *The Builders*. Certainly there is no trace of David Blackburn's exalted idealism in *One Man in His Time* (1922). It is not a good novel, but it is at least a novel, and there must have been those who wondered, after its predecessor, if she would ever write one again. Gideon Vetch, the poor white who has risen to be governor of Virginia, is a man who believes that the end justifies the means, but at least he believes in an end, and he dies, assassinated, the victim of the rising underdogs and the static "haves," the second Glasgow hero to suffer a violent end in this high but evidently dangerous office. For the first time in her fiction Miss Glasgow paid serious attention to her points of view and handled them with some degree of subtlety. Vetch is never seen directly, but always through the eyes of others, hostile or admiring, which lends a needed suspense to his story.

Other than Vetch, however, this book, like *Gabriella* and *The Builders*, is thin. One feels that Miss Glasgow shares Corinna Page's feeling about the hero: "She had a sincere though not very deep affection for Stephen." Stephen Culpeper is too much under the influence of his vapid mother to have been the war hero he is reputed. One does not believe that it took such valiance in 1920 for a young man to marry the daughter of the governor of Virginia simply because Patty Vetch's mother had reportedly been a circus rider. And his awakening to human misery after a single tour of the slums of Richmond is a turgid interruption of the story, as is the melodramatic episode when Patty, who does not know she is adopted and thinks her mother dead, visits her "aunt," actually her mother, now a dope fiend. But at least one feels in the pulse of the novel that Ellen Glasgow

was emerging from the second period of despond in which she
had been so long engulfed.

The best thing about her life was that the best part of it came
after the age of fifty. As she wrote herself: "After those intoler-
able years, all my best work was to come." Her parents were dead,
as were Cary and Gerald, and she was largely cured of Harold.
She was alone now in the old gray Georgian house with the great
tulip poplars at One West Main Street, except for her companion,
Anne Virginia Bennett, who had come as a trained nurse and
stayed to be a secretary. She regretted the absence of literary life
in Richmond, but it was the world in which she had grown up
and from which she drew much of her inspiration. It was home,
and a home, too, where she was increasingly admired and respected. When she went out to parties, she talked, as she described it, of "Tom, Dick, and Harry," but why not? The real
life was within. And what did Tom, Dick, and Harry matter
when she was entering the finest part of her career?

Barren Ground (1925) shows the influence of Hardy at last
assimilated. Egdon Heath is not more part of the lives of the
characters of *The Return of the Native* than is the Piedmont
countryside part of the lives of the Oakleys. Its flatness creates the
illusion of immensity, and the broomsedge spreads in smothered
fire over the melancholy brown landscape to a bleak horizon. The
colors are fall colors from autumnal flowers: the crimson sumach,
the wine-colored sassafras, the silvery life-everlasting. The Oakleys themselves are "products of the soil as surely as were the
scant crops." Joshua looks heavy and earthbound even in his Sunday clothes; for all his scrubbing the smell of manure clings to
him; and when Dorinda walks in the October countryside she
feels her surroundings so sensitively that "the wall dividing her
individual consciousness from the consciousness of nature vanished with the thin drift of woodsmoke over the fields." The

inanimate character of the horizon becomes as personal, reserved, and inscrutable as her own mind.

Even the morality springs from the soil, or rather from man's battle with it. The broomsedge is the eternal enemy, always ready to engulf every new farm and field, and men are graded by how they fight it. "For it was not sin that was punished in this world or the next; it was failure. Good failure or bad failure, it made no difference, for nature abhorred both." Jason Greylock, Dorinda's lover in her youth, is weak, and he is broken and finally in dying becomes a lesser thing than the soil; he is identified with a thistle. Dorinda in her fortitude, a Glasgow fortitude built on Jason's desertion, triumphs over the land and builds a dairy farm where the broomsedge was. After the death of her husband, Nathan Pedlar, married for convenience, and of Jason, Dorinda embraces the land anew. Perhaps Miss Glasgow is a bit carried away by her theme here: "The storm and the hag-ridden dreams of the night were over, and the land which she had forgotten was waiting to take her back to its heart. Endurance. Fortitude. The spirit of the land was flowing into her, and her own spirit, strengthened and refreshed, was flowing out again toward life."

Aside, however, from a few such overladen passages and the old habit of dwelling at too great length on her heroine's suffering in abandonment, *Barren Ground* is her finest work. She achieves a greater unity than in the earlier books by strictly limiting the points of view. The central struggle in the story is between Dorinda and the soil, and we see it entirely through Dorinda's mind except when the author intervenes to supplement our picture of the countryside and Pedlar's Mill. In this the technique is not unlike Flaubert's in *Madame Bovary* where, as Percy Lubbock has pointed out, we have to see only two things: Yonville as it looks to Emma Bovary and Yonville as it looks to Flaubert. Actually, there is much less of the author in *Barren*

Ground because Dorinda, unlike Emma, is a woman of enough perception to give us most of the necessary impressions herself.

Miss Glasgow maintained that the Abernethys (Dorinda's mother was an Abernethy), the Greylocks, and the Pedlars were representative of a special rural class, not "poor whites" but "good people" and descendants of English yeomen, who had never before been treated in fiction. She gains greatly in the vividness of her portrayal by not mixing them with characters of other backgrounds. Everyone we see in Pedlar's Mill belongs in Pedlar's Mill like the broomsedge, and the only chapters that mar the otherwise perfect unity of mood in this beautifully conceived novel are those where Dorinda goes to New York to work for a doctor. Manhattan, which provides the only important non-Virginian settings in Miss Glasgow's fiction, is, as usual, fatal to it.

She now embarked on her great trilogy of Richmond, or "Queenborough": *The Romantic Comedians* (1926), *They Stooped to Folly* (1929), and *The Sheltered Life* (1932). The three books do not constitute a trilogy in the sense that they have a continuous plot or even characters in common, but they share a common setting and class, the latter being the old but still prosperous Richmond families, and a spirit of ironic high comedy. They also share — and this is a fault if they are read consecutively — a hero, at least to the extent that the elderly man who is the principal observer in each has a melancholy sense of having missed the real fun in life. It is confusing that they are so alike yet not the same. Miss Glasgow never hesitated to plagiarize herself.

Turning from *Barren Ground* to *The Romantic Comedians* is like turning from Hardy to Meredith, from *The Return of the Native* to *The Egoist*. It is one of the great tours de force of American literature. "After I had finished *Barren Ground*," she wrote in her preface, "which for three years had steeped my mind in the sense of tragic life, the comic spirit, always restless when it

59

is confined, began struggling against the bars of its cage." Never
was it to escape to greater advantage. Judge Honeywell, surrounded and tormented by women, is surely one of the most
amusing studies in southern fiction. His outrageous twin sister,
Edmonia Bredalbane, who wears her scarlet letter as if it were a
decoration, his old sweetheart, Amanda Lightfoot, the eternally
brave and sweet "good" woman, whose life is a ruin because she
could never face a fact, and his dead wife whose image wears a
halo of oppressive rectitude, would all keep him from the folly
of turning to a girl forty years his junior, but the benighted old
fool has had enough of them (who wouldn't?) and wants one joy,
one real joy of his own, before the end. The reader knows, everyone knows, even the judge, deep down, knows that this joy will
turn to brambles, but he *will* have his way and does. The young
wife, Annabel, is just right, too, for she has all the selfishness of
youth and all its charm, and we expect her to find her marriage
impossible. There is a tragic tone to the book, but it is never
allowed to become heavy. The laughter, even when muted almost
to a compassionate silence, is still there.

Ellen Glasgow was now in her early fifties and beginning prematurely to suffer from the tendency of so many older people to
find youth without standards and to deplore the loss of disciplines
in the world about her. It was the same tendency that spoiled so
much of the later fiction of Edith Wharton. Miss Glasgow's correspondence is now increasingly full of complaints about the
sloppiness and sordidness of modern living and modern literature.
She came to look back on her own past, which she had found so
stultifying as a girl, with increased nostalgia as she saw the effects
of the new liberty of deportment and the new realism of expression that she had herself espoused. Once the note of shrillness,
even of petulance, had entered her fiction it could only be lost
when, as in The Sheltered Life and in the early chapters of Vein

of Iron, she moved her setting back prior to those ills with which she now saw the world inundated.

They Stooped to Folly is the first of her books to suffer from this lack of sympathy with young people. The youthful characters are hard, angular, and unconvincing. Millie Burden, with the monotony of a minor character in Dickens, repeats over and over that she is "entitled to her life." Mary Victoria is so repellently fatuous and egocentric that she has to be kept off the scene if we are to believe, as the author insists that we shall, in her great influence over other people. And Martin Welding is too weak and self-pitying to cause the havoc he is supposed to cause in female hearts.

The novel as a whole seems like a compilation of discarded sketches from the atelier that produced its happier predecessor. Virginius Littlepage is a small, stuffy version of Judge Honeywell, and nothing happens to him except that he loses his unloved but superior spouse during and not before his chronicle. There is no Annabel for him, only a flirtation with a gay widow that makes him ridiculous but never pathetic. It is impossible to believe in his great love for his daughter Mary Victoria, whose meanness he sees as clearly as does the reader, or in his great sorrow over her obviously doomed marriage to a man whom she has ruthlessly torn from another woman. It is difficult, in fact, for the reader not to feel that all of the Littlepages deserve anything they get.

So what is left? Nothing but epigrams, and even these are repetitive. The characters cannot seem to make their points too often. Millie Burden talks only of her "rights," and her mother only of Millie's need for punishment. Mrs. Littlepage keeps insisting that she has never known her husband to be sarcastic, whereas the reader has never known him to be anything else. And what is the theme of it all? That a woman should not be punished all her life for having lived with a man out of wedlock!

What can Miss Glasgow have thought she was up to? Nobody *is* so punished in the book, except Aunt Agatha, and that was in the ancient past. And nobody in the book thinks anyone *should* be so punished except Mrs. Burden, and she is represented as an absurd anachronism. Why then, in 1929, did the author keep flogging so dead a horse? Is it possible that she was beginning to feel that the age of prejudices had at least had standards? That one could only have ladies if one burned witches?

They Stooped to Folly cleared out the author's atelier of all these rag ends, for the last volume of the trilogy, *The Sheltered Life*, is a masterpiece. "In *Barren Ground*, as in *The Sheltered Life*," she wrote, "I have worked, I felt, with an added dimension, with a universal rhythm deeper than any material surface. Beneath the lights and shadows there is the brooding spirit of place, but, deeper still, beneath the spirit of place there is the whole movement of life." It is not a modest statement, but Miss Glasgow felt that she had worked too hard to have time for modesty, and certainly these two novels have a vibration different from all her others.

Into the double, battered stronghold of the Archbalds and Birdsongs on Washington Street, now all commercial but for them, creeps the fetid smell of the neighboring chemical plant. The smell is more than the modern world that threatens them from without; it is the smell of the decadence that attacks them from within. The sheltered life is also the life of willful blindness; the two families resist change and resist facts. Eva Birdsong, keeping up the queenly front of a Richmond beauty, tries not to see that her husband is a hopeless philanderer. General Archbald, dreaming of a past which he understands, avoids the duty of facing a present which he does not, while his daughter-in-law brings up little Jenny Blair to be a debutante of the antebellum era. Etta, the hypochondriac, lives in a fantasy world of cheap novels and heroes, and Birdsong, in the arms of his Negro mistress, imagines that he still loves his wife. The rumbles of a world war are heard from very far off. Like the smell down the street they do not yet seem to threaten the sheltered lives of the Archbalds and Birdsongs.

The terrible story that follows is seen from two points of view, General Archbald's and Jenny Blair's, those of age and youth. The General's long reverie into his own youth, "The Deep Past," is probably the finest piece of prose that Miss Glasgow ever wrote. The picture of a nauseated child being "blooded" by his sporty old grandfather on a fox hunt is for once without sentiment for the great Virginia days. Like Judge Honeywell and Virginius Littlepage, General Archbald has missed the high moments of life and has been married, like all elderly Glasgow gentlemen, to a good woman whom he did not love. He has been a gentleman and done his civic duty because, in the last analysis, nothing else seemed any better or certainly any finer, but he has a much deeper sense of what is wrong with his world than the other two heroes of the trilogy and a mystic sense that in death he may yet find the ecstasy that he has lost without ever possessing. Under the prosperous attorney and the member in good standing of the Episcopal church is a poet. If he were not quite so old, he might have saved his granddaughter.

But nobody is going to do that. Jenny Blair, brought up in innocence by her gallant widowed mother, cannot believe herself capable of doing anything that is not quite nice. She is drawn into an entanglement with Mr. Birdsong because she will not see that adultery is something that could happen to her. She is a little girl, even at eighteen, a bright, innocent, enchanting little girl, and the subtlest thing in this subtle book is that even while we keep seeing the small events of Washington Street from her point of view, we gradually become aware that others are beginning to see her differently, that John Welch, the Birdsongs' ward, suspects what she's up to, that Birdsong is aware that she's tempting him, that even her mother and grandfather begin to sense a change. The warnings proliferate, and the tempo of the book suddenly accelerates until the vision of Jenny Blair as a sharp-toothed little animal, free of all rules and restraints, reaching out to snatch the husband of her desperately ill friend, bursts upon us in its full horror, just before the final tragedy. Eva Birdsong shoots her husband, and his body slumps in the hall amid the carcasses of the ducks that he has killed. It is the ultimate dramatization of the divorce between the Virginian myth and the Virginian fact, the climax of the novel and of Ellen Glasgow's fiction.

John Welch is the best of youth, as Miss Glasgow was coming to see youth, but he is a dry young man, tough and belligerently unsentimental. In assessing Eva Birdsong's chances of surviving her operation he mentions to General Archbald that her kidneys are sound. It is not, of course, agreeable to this gentleman of the old school to hear a lady's vital organs spoken of as plainly as if they were blocks of wood, but he reflects that perhaps such bluntness is the better way, that "wherever there is softness, life is certain to leave its scar." In this he is certainly the spokesman for his creator who felt that all her life she had been constantly soft and constantly wounded, but there is no question of where her sympathies lay. For all her expressed tolerance of Welch and his contemporaries, they lay with the General, and with her sympathies went the conviction that the suffering life was the richer one.

Two more novels were to follow *The Sheltered Life*, but they show an attenuation of powers. *Vein of Iron* (1935) seems a hollow echo of *Barren Ground*. It starts well enough, for it starts in the past where as an older woman Miss Glasgow was increasingly at home, and deals with people whom she had not treated before, the descendants of the Scotch-Irish settlers in the southern part of the Virginia Valley. This was where her father's people had come from, and she was able effectively to evoke in the early chapters the bare, grim Presbyterian elements of the Fincastle family and their village, called, with a labored appropriateness, Ironside. The characters who are hard are very hard, and those who are stoical are very stoical, and even the names of the surrounding geographical features suggest the somber spiritual atmosphere in which these joyless people live: God's Mountain, Thunder Mountain, Shut-in Valley. Mobs of shrieking children cast pebbles at idiots and unmarried mothers alike, though there are few of the latter, as a girl need only point to the man actually, or allegedly, responsible to have him dragged to the altar by her fellow villagers. It seems possible that Miss Glasgow may have written a bit too much of her father's character into Ironside, but the result is very much alive. Such cannot be said of the second part of the novel where the characters move to Queenborough and to the present. Ada Fincastle becomes a serial heroine, a soap-opera queen.

Consider the list of her wrongs. Ralph McBride is wrested from her by an unscrupulous girl friend and returns, a married man, to make her pregnant. Ironside spits at her, and her grandmother dies of the disgrace. Ralph eventually marries her, but war neuroses have made him moody and unfaithful, and in Queenborough, during the depression, they are reduced to desperate want. Ralph, out driving with the girl next door, is nearly paralyzed in an automobile accident. Yet Ada is always superb; her vein of iron sees her through. The reader must take it on faith. One does not see her, as one sees Dorinda in *Barren Ground*, working on her farm, milking cows, supervising the help, purchasing new fields. Even in *Life and Gabriella* one sees what Gabriella does in her shop, so that one has a sense of the therapy which she applies to her sorrow. But Ada relies simply on her inheritance of character.

The book ends on a harsh note of denunciation of the formlessness and aimlessness of life in the 1930's, a theme that is picked up and enlarged upon in Miss Glasgow's final novel, *In This Our Life* (1941), where the amoralism in which she believed Richmond to have been engulfed seems to have affected not only the young but the old and — one almost suspects — the author herself. For how else can one explain Asa Timberlake?

At first blush he seems in the tradition of Honeywell, Littlepage, and Archbald, those elderly, nostalgic gentlemen who have missed the thrills as well as the substance of life, and like them he has his creator's sympathy. "For the sake of a past tradition he had spent nearly thirty years doing things that he hated and not doing things that he liked; and at the end of that long self-discipline, when he was too old to begin over again, he had seen his code of conduct flatten out and shrivel up as utterly as a balloon that is pricked." But *was* it self-discipline? Asa's life has simply gone by default; he is that commonest of American fictional heroes, the husband dominated by a strong-minded hypochondriac wife. But Asa has none of the dignity of his predecessors in the Queenborough trilogy; he is plotting, with the author's apparent approval, a weak man's escape. As soon as his wife shall have inherited the fortune of a rich uncle, he will quietly decamp with the widow of an old friend. Surely he is as bad as the young folk.

Well, not quite, for they are monsters. Roy, the heroine, and Peter have married with the understanding that either may have back her or his liberty on request. Incidentally, there is a similar bargain between the young couple in Mrs. Wharton's equally disapproving novel, *The Glimpses of the Moon*. Roy's sister, Stanley, ditches her fiancé, Craig, in order to take Peter from Roy,

66

and then, having driven Peter to suicide, she returns to rob her sister a second time, of Craig with whom poor Roy has been consoling herself. During all of these goings-on the four characters, like Asa, are saturated with self-pity. One feels that Miss Glasgow's conviction that men are doomed to weakness and that women can rise above their destiny of betrayal only by stoicism has now reached the pitch of an obsession. Yet she works her plot around the gravely offered thesis that love is vital to the young because it is "the only reality left," though it cannot save them because they treat each other "as if they were careless fellow-travellers, to be picked up and dropped, either by accident or by design, on a very brief journey." But that is not necessarily one's own experience of America in 1938 when the action of the novel takes place.

There are, however, moments. There are always moments, even in the least estimable of Ellen Glasgow's books. When Stanley tries to put the blame of her hit-and-run accident on a Negro boy, and the family prepare to back her up, the novel suddenly soars in stature. Here, at last, is a problem that is real and competently handled, the only time, too, in nineteen novels where Miss Glasgow faces, however briefly, what the South has done to its colored people. And Uncle William Fitzroy, the tycoon whose millions have vulgarized him, despite his genteel background, into the likeness of a noisy parvenu, the forerunner of "Big Daddy" in *Cat on a Hot Tin Roof*, seems to bring Tennessee Williams and Ellen Glasgow into brief but entrancing partnership.

Mention should be made of Miss Glasgow's twelve short stories recently assembled in a volume by Richard K. Meeker. It was not a medium that she much liked or in which she enjoyed much success. She was a discursive writer and needed space to appear to her best advantage. Almost half of the stories deal, as might be anticipated, with the struggle of women with men who are not worthy of them, the theme that underlies so much of her "social history" of the South. As Mr. Meeker amusingly sums it up: "Her typical plot sequence runs: girl meets boy; girl is taken advantage of by boy; then girl learns to get along without boy, or girl gets back at boy."

Best of the tales are four ghost stories, all told in the first person, a method adopted in only one of her novels, but a useful one in helping the reader suspend his disbelief. "Dare's Gift" and "Whispering Leaves" are most effective because of their atmosphere of old Virginia mansions which she knew so well how to evoke; but because in her earlier writing she had no interest in keeping things back, because she seemed, on the contrary, to have almost a compulsion to let her reader know what was on her mind at each moment, she had to remain an amateur in the fiction of the supernatural.

In 1954, nine years after Ellen Glasgow's death of heart disease, her literary executors published under the title *The Woman Within* the memoirs that had been confided to their discretion. There were those who were distressed by this posthumous revelation of the author's self-pity and vanity and who claimed that the memoirs gave a wrong impression of a woman who had always seemed in life so gay and bright and full of sympathy for others. But so long as one bears in mind that this is only Ellen Glasgow as Ellen Glasgow saw her, *The Woman Within* is filled with valuable insights.

It also contains some of her best writing. The pages about "Harold S——," the snob and name-dropper, are as good as anything in *The Romantic Comedians*, and the irony is supplied by the memoirist herself who was in love with the man she despised. How could one get a better glimpse of an author at work than in her description of her meeting with Harold: "I observed him for an instant over my cocktail, wondering whether he could be used effectively in a comedy of manners. My curiosity flagged. What on earth could I find to talk about to a person like that?" What indeed? Yet the association that began that night was to last twenty-one years. So we see the novelist looking for a story and finding one — as ironical as any she wrote — happening to herself. Why, she asks herself in despair, was Harold fated to meet every crisis with a spectacular gesture? "Afterwards, when I read in the 'Life Story' of a Balkan Queen, that, as she said farewell to a Southern Colonel, he had fallen on his knees before her and kissed the hem of her skirt, I recognized the last act of chivalry. So Harold had parted from me when he sailed for the Balkans."

The most valuable thing in the memoirs, however, is the picture of a woman's dedication to her art. From the beginning she had wanted to be a writer above everything, and not just a writer, but specifically a novelist. After the publication of her first book she realized that she needed a steadier control over her ideas and material, a philosophy of fiction, a prose style so pure and flexible that it could bend without breaking. From Maupassant she gained a great deal, but not until, by accident, she happened to read *War and Peace* did she know what she needed. "Life must use art; art must use life. . . . One might select realities, but one could not impose on Reality. Not if one were honest in one's interpretation, not if one possessed artistic integrity. For truth to art became in the end simple fidelity to one's own inner vision." She summed up her artistic credo as follows: "I had always wished to escape from the particular into the general, from the provincial into the universal. Never from my earliest blind gropings after truth in art and truth in life had I felt an impulse to write of a single locality or of regional characteristics. From the beginning I had resolved to write of the South, not, in elegy, as a conquered province, but, vitally, as a part of the larger world. Tolstoy made me see clearly what I had realized dimly, that the ordinary is simply the universal observed from the surface, that the direct approach to reality is not without, but within."

It puts one off a bit that Ellen Glasgow struck, again and again, so high a note for herself. As she conceived of her personal sufferings as more intense than anyone else's, so did she conceive of herself as a novelist on a Tolstoian scale. She did not hesitate, in the preface to *Barren Ground*, to nominate it as the one of her books best qualified for immortality, and in her memoirs she described it further, together with the Queenborough trilogy and *Vein of Iron*, as representing "not only the best that was in me, but some of the best work that has been done in American fiction." In her personal philosophy, and despite a sensitive mind that "would always remain an exile on earth," she believed that she had found a code of living that was sufficient for life or for death. And in her later years she loved to play the queen in the New York publishing world, dangling the possibility of her largesse, half in jest, half in earnest, before the different editors who bid for her books. John Farrar relates that when she made her ultimate decision to go to Alfred Harcourt, the latter went down on his knees before her in her hotel suite like Harold S——— before Marie of Romania. But one can see through the boasting and the jesting, with its aspect of essentially southern horseplay, to her never joking resolution and determination to be a great novelist. One can look back at the young Ellen Glasgow like the young Victoria (to evoke another queen), affirming solemnly her will to be good.

The advantages that she brought to her task and ambition were indeed considerable. Out of her wide reading she selected the mightiest and probably the best models to guide her in her recreation of the Virginia scene. She used Hardy as her master in rustic atmosphere, George Eliot as her guide in morality, Maupassant for plot, and Tolstoi for everything. She had the richest source material that any author could wish, consisting simply of a whole state and its whole history, a state, too, that occupies the center of our eastern geography and of our history and that not coincidentally has produced more Presidents than any other. And the social range among Miss Glasgow's characters is far greater than that of most twentieth-century novelists, suggesting that of such Victorians as Trollope, Dickens, Elizabeth Gaskell, and, again, George Eliot.

She not only considered every social group, but she covered wide varieties within each. In the top ranks of the old hierarchy she showed aristocrats in their glory, such as Major Lightfoot, and aristocrats in their decay, such as Beverly Brooke (in *The Ancient Law*). She showed them turning to the new world of business and dominating it, such as General Bolingbroke, and turning to the same world to be dominated and ultimately vulgarized by it, such as William Fitzroy. She showed aristocrats surviving into our own time, such as Judge Honeywell and Virginius Littlepage, having made the necessary adjustments and compromises, respectable, prosperous, but curiously unsatisfied, and she showed aristocrats like Asa Timberlake, who have been beaten into mediocrity and have failed in life without even the consolation and romance of a picturesque decay. Among the women of this world she created such magnificent anachronisms as Mrs. Blake, such noble, docile, and submissive wives as Virginia Pendleton, such apparently submissive but actually dominating mothers as Mrs. Gay, and such a reconstructed success in the North as Gabriella Carr.

In the middle ranks we find the rising businessman, Ben Starr, the risen politician, Gideon Vetch, the corrupt overseer, Bill Fletcher, the poor philosopher, John Fincastle, the "yeoman" farmers, Dorinda Oakley and Nathan Pedlar, the thriving miller, Abel Revercomb, and, among the lower orders, the "poor white" Burr family, the Starrs from whose midst Ben rises, the victims of the Richmond slums whom Stephen Culpeper is made to visit, the village prostitute and her idiot son in *Vein of Iron*, and, of course, all the Negro servants. Despite what has already been said about the limitations of Miss Glasgow's characterization of Negroes, the servants in her novels are absolutely alive and convincing. In at least one instance, that of the maid and companion to Dorinda in *Barren Ground*, the characterization is as successful as of any of the author's other women.

Miss Glasgow had the same range in scenery that she had in human beings, and she could make the transfer without difficulty from the grim mountains and valleys of *Vein of Iron* to the interminable fields of broomsedge in *Barren Ground* and thence to the comfortable mansions of Richmond and to the smaller gentility of Petersburg and Williamsburg. Highly individual in American letters is her ability to pass with equal authority from country to city, from rusticity to sophistication, from the tobacco field to the drawing room, from irony to tragedy.

Yet for all her gifts and advantages she does not stand in the very first rank of American novelists. She was unable sufficiently to pull the tapestry of fiction over her personal grievances and approbations. The latter are always peeping out at the oddest times and in the oddest places. It is strange that a novelist of such cultivation and such fecundity and one who was also such a student of her craft should not have seen her own glaring faults. How is it possible that the woman who could imagine the brilliant repartee of Edmonia Bredalbane, which annihilates every vestige of pretentiousness in Queenborough, should not have torn up the dreary sermon that is called *The Builders*? How could the author of prose which conveys all the beauty and mystery of the desolate countryside in *Barren Ground* have written the tired purple passages in earlier novels which describe the animal charm of handsome men and women in terms that might have been lifted from the very women's magazines that she so violently despised? How, moreover, could she have failed to see that her own bitterness on the subject of men was reflected in her heroines to the point of warping the whole picture of their lives? The mystery of Ellen Glasgow is not so much how she could be so good a writer as how she could on occasion be so bad a one.

Like Edith Wharton, she will be remembered for her women, not her men. The course of her heroes is a curious one. They start, romantically enough, as men of fierce ideals and raging passions, Byronic in their excesses, impatient of injustice and burning to remake the world. Akershem and Burr are men of the people; the lowness of their origin contributes to their strength, their violence, and their sex appeal. They are a bit lurid, but there will come a time in Miss Glasgow's fiction when we would be glad enough to see them again. With Dan Montjoy in *The Battle-Ground* she inaugurated a period of more respectable, conventional heroes. He is followed by Christopher Blake, Ben Starr, and Abel Revercomb, all of them men of considerable strength and power. But in *Virginia* the weak, selfish, deserting male makes his appearance, and he is to stay through to the end of her fiction. Oliver Treadwell, George Fowler, Jason Greylock, George Birdsong, Peter Kingsmill, Martin Welding, Ralph McBride, and Craig Fleming are all faithless to good women who love them and are all faithless more from the weakness of their characters than the force of their passions. What is most appalling in Miss Glasgow's indictment is that the only ground of redemption that she can find in those of them whom she regards as redeemable, i.e. the last three of the list, is a groveling, lachrymose self-pity. Listen to Martin Welding as his father-in-law interrogates him about the unhappiness of his marriage to Mary Victoria:

"Why don't you tell me about it and let me help you?" the older man asked with all the sympathy that he could summon.

The merest flicker of gratitude shone in the sullen misery of Martin's look. "The trouble is that I have come to the end of my rope. I am wondering how much longer I shall be able to stand it."

"Stand what, my boy?"

"Stand the whole thing. Stand life, stand marriage, stand women."

Mr. Littlepage frowned. "But this isn't normal," he said sternly. "This isn't rational."

"Well, what am I to do?"

"You should see a physician."

"I've seen dozens of them since I met Mary Victoria."

"And what do they say?"

"That I'm not normal, I'm not rational."

"Then, it seems to me, you will have to believe it."

"I do believe it, but that doesn't make it easier. I am still that way no matter what I believe."

The men would not matter so much if they were not taken quite so seriously by the women. Lawrence Selden in Edith Wharton's *The House of Mirth* is a passive spectator hero, but Lily Bart suffers little enough from his preference for the sidelines. Miss Glasgow's heroines, on the other hand, are devastated by her worthless men, and it is just here that her fiction is pulled most seriously out of line. Acceptance of Dorinda Oakley and Gabriella Carr as the towers of strength that they must be to accomplish what they do is difficult to reconcile with the long, tortured passages in which they dwell with the lovingness of hypochondriacs upon their grief. One wonders if their kind of women would not have thrown off disappointment and disillusionment with more dispatch and if Miss Glasgow was not attributing her own sensitivity to natures that had, by definition, to possess tougher fibers. In the final novel the question is reduced to absurdity by Roy Timberlake who succeeds in being abandoned by *two* men and suffers equally at the hands of each.

For all her faults, however, it is hard to get away from the fact that without Ellen Glasgow there would be a great gap in our fiction, particularly where it concerns the South. She was determined to reproduce the South as it was, and although we are conscious today of things added and things omitted, we search in vain for any contemporary or predecessor of hers who even approached her accomplishment. Furthermore, it is astonishing to consider how different in style and mood were her three principal works. *Virginia* might not be worthy of Flaubert, but one suspects that Zola would not have disowned it, nor would Hardy have been ashamed of *Barren Ground*. And any novelist of manners would have been delighted to have produced *The Romantic Comedians*.

Frederick P. W. McDowell has astutely pointed out that Ellen Glasgow's accomplishments and limitations as a writer are best suggested in her own judgment of another southern writer, Edgar Allan Poe: "Poe is, to a large extent, a distillation of the Southern. The formalism of his tone, the classical element in his poetry and in many of his stories, the drift toward rhetoric, the aloof and elusive intensity, — all these qualities are Southern. And in his more serious faults of overwriting, sentimental exaggeration, and lapses, now and then, into a pompous or florid style, he belongs to his epoch and even more to his South."

When Ellen Glasgow began her career, there was almost no serious literature in the South. The pioneer element in her work today is obscured by the fact that the romantic school of southern fiction against which she reacted not only has disappeared but has hardly left a trace. Similarly, the modern school has gone so far beyond her in exploration of the freakish and the decadent that she seems as mild in comparison as Mary Johnston or Amélie Rives. She herself enlarged the distance between her work and that of the southern novelists who were becoming popular in her later years by deriding them. "One may admit that the Southern

States have more than an equal share of degeneracy and deterioration; but the multitude of half-wits, and whole idiots, and nymphomaniacs, and paranoiacs, and rakehells in general, that populate the modern literary South could flourish nowhere but in the weird pages of melodrama." Yet she herself is the bridge, and the necessary bridge, between the world of Thomas Nelson Page and the world of William Faulkner, Katherine Anne Porter, Eudora Welty, and Tennessee Williams.

She will probably not be remembered as the historian of Virginia that she wished to be. This ambition may have been too great for the fiction that she produced. Only four of her nineteen novels, *Virginia, Barren Ground, The Romantic Comedians*, and *The Sheltered Life,* have won more than a temporary place in American letters. But her picture of the South emerging from defeat and reconstruction with all its old legends intact and all its old energy preserved and managing to adapt itself, almost without admitting it, to the industrial exigencies of a new age — like the Bourbons in that it had forgotten nothing, but unlike them in that it had learned a lot — is one that has passed into our sense of American history.

Selected Bibliography

Works of Ellen Glasgow

THERE are two collected editions of Ellen Glasgow's work: the Old Dominion Edition (Garden City, N.Y.: Doubleday, Doran, 1929, 1933) and the Virginia Edition (New York: Scribner's, 1938). Both collected editions include Miss Glasgow's prefaces.

NOVELS AND COLLECTIONS OF SHORT STORIES

The Descendant. New York: Harper, 1897.
Phases of an Inferior Planet. New York: Harper, 1898.
The Voice of the People. New York: Doubleday, Page, 1900.
The Battle-Ground. New York: Doubleday, Page, 1902.
The Deliverance. New York: Doubleday, Page, 1904.
The Wheel of Life. New York: Doubleday, Page, 1906.
The Ancient Law. New York: Doubleday, Page, 1908.
The Romance of a Plain Man. New York: Macmillan, 1909.
The Miller of Old Church. Garden City, N.Y.: Doubleday, Page, 1911.
Virginia. Garden City, N.Y.: Doubleday, Page, 1913.
Life and Gabriella. Garden City, N.Y.: Doubleday, Page, 1916.
The Builders. Garden City, N.Y.: Doubleday, Page, 1919.
One Man in His Time. Garden City, N.Y.: Doubleday, Page, 1922.
The Shadowy Third and Other Stories. Garden City, N.Y.: Doubleday, Page, 1923.
Barren Ground. Garden City, N.Y.: Doubleday, Page, 1925.
The Romantic Comedians. Garden City, N.Y.: Doubleday, Page, 1926.
They Stooped to Folly. Garden City, N.Y.: Doubleday, Doran, 1929.
The Sheltered Life. Garden City, N.Y.: Doubleday, Doran, 1932.
Vein of Iron. New York: Harcourt, Brace, 1935.
In This Our Life. New York: Harcourt, Brace, 1941.
The Collected Stories of Ellen Glasgow, edited by Richard K. Meeker. Baton Rouge: Louisiana State University Press, 1963.

POETRY

The Freeman and Other Poems. New York: Doubleday, Page, 1902.

77

NONFICTION

A Certain Measure. New York: Harcourt, Brace, 1943.
The Woman Within. New York: Harcourt, Brace, 1954.
Letters of Ellen Glasgow, edited by Blair Rouse. New York: Harcourt, Brace, 1958.

Bibliography

Kelly, William W. *An Ellen Glasgow Bibliography.* Charlottesville: University Press of Virginia, 1963.

Critical Studies

Becker, Allen. "Ellen Glasgow and the Southern Literary Tradition," *Modern Fiction Studies,* 5:295–303 (Winter 1959–60).
Brooks, Van Wyck. *The Confident Years.* New York: Dutton, 1952.
Geismar, Maxwell. *Rebels and Ancestors.* Boston: Houghton Mifflin, 1953.
Giles, Barbara. "Character and Fate: The Novels of Ellen Glasgow," *Mainstream,* 9:20–31 (September 1956).
Godbold, E. Stanley, Jr. *Ellen Glasgow and the Woman Within.* Baton Rouge: Louisiana State University Press, 1972.
Godshak, W. L., ed. *Voice of the People.* Edited with an introduction. New Haven: College and University Press, 1972.
Hoffman, Frederick J. *The Modern Novel in America.* Chicago: Regnery, 1951.
Kazin, Alfred. *On Native Grounds.* New York: Reynal and Hitchcock, 1942.
MacDonald, Edgar E. "The Glasgow-Cabell Entente," *American Literature,* 41:76–91 (March 1969).
McDowell, Frederick P. W. *Ellen Glasgow and the Ironic Art of Fiction.* Madison: University of Wisconsin Press, 1960. (The only thorough survey of Ellen Glasgow's work, containing an exhaustive bibliography.)
Monroe, N. Elizabeth. *Fifty Years of the American Novel.* New York: Scribner's, 1951.
Patterson, Daniel W. "Ellen Glasgow's Plan for a Social History of Virginia," *Modern Fiction Studies,* 5:353–60 (Winter 1959–60).
Rasper, J. R. *Without Shelter: The Early Career of Ellen Glasgow.* Baton Rouge: Louisiana State University Press, 1971.
Rouse, Blair. *Ellen Glasgow.* New York: Twayne, 1962.
Rubin, Louis D., Jr. *No Place on Earth: Ellen Glasgow, James Branch Cabell, and Richmond-in-Virginia.* Austin: University of Texas Press, 1959. (Supplement to *Texas Quarterly,* Vol. 2.)
Santas, Joan Foster. *Ellen Glasgow's American Dream.* Charlottesville: University Press of Virginia, 1965.
Steele, Oliver. "Ellen Glasgow, Social History and the 'Virginia Edition,'" *Modern Fiction Studies,* 6:173–76 (Summer 1961).

Willa Cather

IT IS customary to speak of Willa Cather as an "elegist" of the American pioneer tradition. "Elegy" suggests celebration and lament for a lost and irrecoverable past; but the boldest and most beautiful of Willa Cather's fictions are characterized by a sense of the past not as an irrecoverable quality of events, wasted in history, but as persistent human truth repossessed — salvaged, redeemed — by virtue of memory and art.

Her art is a singular one. The prose style is suave, candid, transparent, a style shaped and sophisticated in the great European tradition; her teachers were Homer and Virgil, Tolstoi and Flaubert. But the creative vision that is peculiarly hers is deeply primitive, psychologically archaic in an exact sense. In that primitivism was her great strength, for it allowed the back door of her mind to keep open, as it were, to the rumor and movement of ancestral powers and instinctive agencies.

Closely related to this gift was her sensitivity to the land, its textures, horizons, weathers. "Whenever I crossed the Missouri River coming in to Nebraska," she said, "the very smell of the soil tore me to pieces. . . . I almost decided to settle down on a quarter section of land and let my writing go." Elizabeth Sergeant, her friend and a discerning critic of her work, wrote, "I saw that her intimacy with nature lay at the very root . . . of her power to work at all." She had been brought to Nebraska, from Virginia, when she was nine. This was in 1883, when Nebraska was still frontier territory, almost bare of human landmarks; the settlers lived in sod houses, scarcely distinguishable from the earth, or in caves in the clay bluffs; roads were faint wagon trails in a sea of red grass. The removal from an old, lush, settled country to a virtual wilderness was undoubtedly the determinative event of Willa Cather's life; occurring when the child was entering puberty and most sensitive to change, the uprooting from the green valley of her grandparents' home in Virginia, and the casting out upon a limitless wild prairie, opened her sensibility to primordial images and relationships that were to be the most powerful forces in her art.

After a year of homesteading, Charles Cather moved his family into the little town of Red Cloud, where he opened an office dealing in farm loans and mortgages. They lived in a house much like that of the Kronborgs in *The Song of the Lark*, with seven children crowded in a narrow boxcar arrangement of rooms and a leaky attic where the older ones slept. Willa started going to school here; on the farm, her grandmother had begun teaching her Greek and Latin, and she continued these studies now with an old man who kept a general store down the street. Years later her friend Edith Lewis wrote of that Nebraska girlhood, which she too had known: "I remember how lost in the prairies Red Cloud seemed to me, going back to that country after a number of years; as if the hot wind that so much of the time blew over it went on and left it behind, isolated, forgotten by the rest of the world . . . And I felt again that forlornness, that terrible restlessness that comes over young people born in small towns in the middle of the continent." That aridity and drabness formed another decisive pattern in the girl's emotional nature, a traumatic one that reappears in the stories and novels as a desperate impulse of "escape" from a surrounding and voracious mediocrity. Her own resistances took the form of rebellion against conventionality; she cut her hair short like a boy's, wore boy's clothes, created scandal by setting up a laboratory for zoological experiments, hung around listening to the conversation of the older men of the town.

Her "escape" was slow, uneven, costing years of drudgery. From 1891 to 1895, a period of crop failures and financial depression, she attended the state university at Lincoln, meeting many of her expenses by writing for the Sunday issue of the *State Journal*; at a dollar a column, by writing a tremendous number of columns she was able to scrape through. For the next decade, from her twenty-third to her thirty-third year, she worked at various jobs in Pittsburgh: for five years as a newspaperwoman, at first on the *Home Monthly*, a suffocatingly parochial "family magazine," then on the *Daily Leader*, where she read copy, edited telegraphic news, and wrote dramatic criticism; and five years as a teacher of English and Latin in the Pittsburgh high schools. In 1903 she published a book of poems, *April Twilights*, slight pieces of imitative cadence; and in 1905 her first book of stories, *The Troll Garden*, was published by S. S. McClure — who immediately offered her a post in New York on his then brilliant magazine. Her work on *McClure's Magazine* was highly successful — she rapidly became managing editor — and exhausting; probably the most valuable experience during this period was her brief friendship with the writer Sarah Orne Jewett (Miss Jewett died within the year), whose sensitive criticism seems to have reoriented her writing, away from "literary" models and toward the material and the voice which were genuinely her own. In 1912, the year of the publication of her first novel, *Alexander's Bridge*, she resigned from *McClure's*, and from that time on was able to live the quiet and dedicated life of her craft.

Miss Cather said frequently that the only part of her life which made a lasting impression on her imagination and emotion was what happened before she was twenty. No doubt the remark overcondenses and oversimplifies, but one finds an impressive truth in it when one looks at those early years in the light of her mature work. There was the deprived adolescence in the sterile little midwestern town; there were the traumatic tensions leading to "escape." She was never able to free herself from this negative theme, and under its warping tendency she was led frequently to substitute strained personal emotion and belief for creative intuition. But another, far more subtle, essentially mysterious theme was also an effect of that adolescent deprivation: this was the theme of a "self" at once more generic and more individual than the self allowed to live by the constrictions of American adulthood. It is as if the aridities of her girlhood, and the drudgery that followed, had left her with a haunting sense of a "self" that had been effaced and that tormented her for realization. She was to search for it in elusive ways all her life, and sometimes, in her greatest novels, when she left off searching for it she found it.

Connected with that search was a quest for "ancestors." One thinks of that great faceless prairie, stretching empty to the jumping-off places of the earth, where the nine-year-old child was thrust to find its identity. Where were the beginnings? Where the human continuities, the supporting and enfolding "past," the streets, the houses, the doors, the images of care and contact? Even trees were so rare, and had such a hard fight to grow, that one visited them anxiously as if they were persons. One felt instinctively, in that shoreless emptiness, a special charism in the secretive animals — snakes and badgers — that warned one to be friendly with them; one might need their help. When Willa Cather first visited the ancient cliff-dweller ruins of Arizona, in 1912, she experienced a shock of recognition as intense, troubling, and exalting as that felt by Keats when he first saw the Elgin marbles. Here, in these desolate little cities, "mountain built with peaceful citadel," were the places of the ancestors, their streets and doorways, their hanging gardens of cactus, their inner chambers, the signs of their care and contact in traces of the potter's thumb on shards of clay vessels. She was to write of them again and again, and make many pack trips back to that country. Like the theme of the lost self, this too was a theme of recovery: to recover the ancestors, to redeem them from their forgotten places, to make them speak. A great loneliness — the American loneliness — invests these themes: and something else, the need of a form of integration between the self and the human past, in order that life may be affirmed and celebrated. She was to achieve that celebratory form most fully in the two late great novels, *Death Comes for the Archbishop* and *Shadows on the Rock*.

She started late. Her first book of fiction, the seven stories collected in *The Troll Garden*, was published when she was thirty-two; *Alexander's Bridge*, her first novel, when she was thirty-nine; and *O Pioneers!*, the first of her pastoral novels, where the essential nature of her gift began to realize itself, when she was forty. But behind this late start were the years of discipline in which she had been learning how to handle what she knew, and learning what it was that she knew. A number of the stories in *The Troll Garden* are no more than finger exercises in technique and gropings for subject — in a somewhat tenuous Jamesian vein which she was soon to turn away from. But the *novella*-length tale "Paul's Case" is an accomplished piece of workmanship, showing her long discipleship to Flaubert. It is done with his scrupulosity of detail and something of his shaping, tragic poetry.

Paul is a Pittsburgh high school boy, dandyish, anathema to his teachers because they feel his contempt for them, amounting to physical aversion. He comes to their aggrieved and rancorous sitting on his expulsion from school with a "scandalous red carnation" in his buttonhole. His life with his fellow students is one of lies: he tells them about his acquaintance with soloists in visiting opera companies, suppers with them, sending them flowers; when these lies lose effect, desperately he bids his classmates good-bye, saying he is going to travel to Naples, Venice, Egypt. Paul has no channeled talents; he suggests no particular capabilities at all; he is merely an amorphously longing teen-ager, "different" from others in the exclusiveness of his devotion to glamour in the teeth of the brutal body of fate. His existence is a continuous fracture of spirit, between his home in a lower middle class slum on Cordelia Street ("the cold bathroom with the grimy zinc tub, the cracked mirror, the dripping spiggots") and the theater, where he has an actor friend whom he visits behind the scenes, Carnegie Hall where he ushers, and the street outside the Schenley Hotel where he watches at night, in a debauch of envy and longing, the goings and comings of the theatrical crowd.

One has constantly in the back of one's mind the image of Flaubert's Emma Bovary, for Paul, too, is a creature of *les sens*, isolated in the terrifying hebetude of his environment. And like Emma's, his fate comes running to him with his own features, but more eagerly and swiftly than hers; with his adolescent pre-science, he prepares his fate like a diva. His father and the school principal having taken away his "bone" (forbidden him entrance to his aesthetic haunts) and put him to work as a bank messenger, he quietly absconds with a thousand dollars to New York. There he takes a suite at the Waldorf, buys with "endless reconsidering and great care" a frock coat and dress clothes, visits hatters and a shoe house, Tiffany's for silver and a new scarf pin, sends for flowers and champagne, and in his new silk underwear and red robe contemplates his glittering white bathroom. "The nerve-stuff of all sensations was whirling about him like the snow flakes. He burnt like a faggot in a tempest."

He is run down almost immediately. In the newspapers he sees how they are closing in on him (with promises from his father of total forgiveness), and "all the world had become Cordelia Street." Despite a poisonous champagne hangover, he does not flinch from the logic of his dilemma: he takes a cab to the ferry, and in Newark drives out of town to the Pennsylvania tracks. In his coat are some drooping red carnations, and before lying down on the track, "Paul took one of the blossoms carefully from his coat and scooped a little hole in the snow, where he covered it up."

"Paul's Case" is a brilliant adolescent analogue of the "cases" of Faust and Quixote. He has the Faustian hunger for magical experience transcending the despised soil of his animal milieu; he has Quixote's fanatic heroism in facing to the death, with his poor brave sword of pasteboard and forgery, the assaults of the swinish herd whose appetite is for violation. But most of all — because of his modern and reduced mimetic range — he has Emma Bovary's ineffably romantic sensuality, lusting like a saint for ecstasies that can be embodied only in vulgar artifice — until projected, inevitably, upon death. Within the formal sectors of Willa Cather's fiction, Paul is her earliest model of the young, artistically or merely sensitively gifted person in western America, whose inchoate aspiration is offered no imago by the environment, and no direction in which to develop except a blindly accidental one. The ironic detachment of the story gives it the purity and polish of a small classic.

Two of the shorter pieces in *The Troll Garden*, "A Wagner Matinee" and "The Sculptor's Funeral," take firm grip on the fatality of deprivation which was an inherent part of Miss Cather's native Nebraska material. "A Wagner Matinee" is a bleakly effective *récit*, holding in concentration the terrible spiritual toll taken by frontier life, especially upon women. An old aunt of the narrator, grizzled and deformed, comes to visit her nephew in New York; she had been a music teacher at the Boston Conservatory, and marriage had taken her to a Nebraska homestead fifty miles from a railroad, to live at first in a dugout in a hill-side. He takes her to a concert. At the *Tannhäuser* overture, she clutches his coat sleeve. "Then it was I first realized that for her this broke a silence of thirty years; the inconceivable silence of the plains. . . . There came to me an overwhelming sense of the waste and wear we are so powerless to combat; and I saw again the tall, naked house on the prairie, black and grim as a wooden fortress; the black pond where I had learned to swim, its margin pitted with sun-dried cattle tracks; the rain gullied clay banks about the naked house, the four dwarf ash seedlings where the dishcloths were always hung to dry before the kitchen door."

"The Sculptor's Funeral" suffers from a somewhat ponderous use of the Jamesian-Balzacian reflector, but its observation of the working of the frontier curse, the habit of deprivation — horri-fyingly at home in the Protestant mentality — is ferocious. The dead master-sculptor is taken home to Kansas to be buried. There, over the corpse, the observer sees the mother, the voracious mother with "teeth that could tear," frenzied in her sterility, and all the "raw, biting ugliness" that had been the portion of the artist in youth. He understands now the real tragedy of the man's life — not dissipation, as the town-folk say, but "a blow which had fallen earlier and cut deeper . . . a shame not his, and yet so in-escapably his, to hide in his heart from his very boyhood." A drunken lawyer makes the final accusing tirade, against the town's suspicion and hatred of excellence, by which the most promising of its children have been harried to exile, degradation, or suicide. One remembers that, about a hundred years earlier, Stendhal's Julien Sorel had, in the shadow of the guillotine, made a similar accusation of his provincial fathers.

The story "The Garden Lodge" is composed on the motif of the lost instinctive self that has been compromised or frozen into a ghost by the complicated successes of American adulthood. The

86

story's protagonist is a sophisticated woman who patronizes the arts in her suburban home. Her own childhood background had been a slummy, bohemian one, her father an indigent violinist, her mother acquiescent to his futile idealism, the unpaid bills, the mess. She has rejected all that, aiming to make her life a soberly rational and emotionally economic success. After entertaining as house guest a distinguished pianist, whose music had charmed her, she is haunted by "an imploring little girlish ghost that followed her about, wringing its hands and entreating for an hour of life." During a storm, she spends a night in the studio, fingering the piano and at last falling to sleep on the floor, disturbed in dream by that lost and violated child. "There was a moment between world and world, when neither asleep nor awake, she felt her dream grow thin, melting away from her, felt the warmth under her heart growing cold. Something seemed to slip from the clinging hold of her arms, and she groaned protestingly through her parted lips, following it a little way with fluttering hands. . . . The horror was that it had not come from without, but from within. The dream was no blind chance; it was the expression of something she had kept so close a prisoner that she had never seen it herself; it was the wail from the donjon deeps when the watch slept."

Alexander's Bridge (1912) is a distinguished first novel, but Miss Cather almost immediately repudiated it as "literary" — which had become a bad word for her — with a just recognition of what was contrived in its framework and stylish in its situation. Bartley Alexander is a famous engineer of bridges, married to a Bostonian heiress, leading in the "dead calm" of his middle age a gracious life that he loves, but nervously squirming under the constraints of his success — positions on boards of civic enterprise and committees of public welfare, the obligations of his wife's fortune. On his business trips to Europe he occasionally

seeks, or tells himself he is seeking, the affectionately gay incon-
sequence of a mistress of his student years, Hilda Burgoyne, who
has now become a distinguished actress. But he is intuitive enough
to know that it is not really Hilda whom he seeks, but a more
shadowy companion, "some one vastly dearer to him than she
had ever been — his own young self," a youth who waits for him
at the places he used to meet Hilda, links his arm in his, walks
with him. He projects this entity upon Hilda and entoils her in
its charm, which he makes her think is her own. With this acquiescence, the ghostly companion grows younger and more vigorous
and importunate: "He remembered how, when he was a little boy
and his father called him in the morning, he used to leap from
his bed into the full consciousness of himself. That consciousness
was Life itself. Whatever took its place, action, the power of concentrated thought, were only functions of a mechanism useful to
society; things that could be bought in the market. There was
only one thing that had an absolute value for each individual,
and it was just that original impulse, that internal heat, that
feeling of one's self in one's own breast." Even when he is most
conscious of the satisfactions of his home, his friends, the wife
whom he loves, the "thing" breaks loose out of an unknowable
darkness, "sullen and powerful," thrilling him with a sense of
quickened life and stimulating danger. He sacrifices Hilda to it,
and finally is sacrified to it himself — by the story's contrivance,
he is drowned from one of his own bridges, because of a collapse
in its faulty structure.

The finger-pointing symbolism (Alexander fell because of a
flaw in his character, like the flaw in the bridge) is trite and
specious, falsifying the troubled perception which is the story's
strength and truth. Alexander's situation is that of the woman in
"The Garden Lodge," except that the blocked, imprisoned self
approached her only in a dream, attenuated to a child's shape,

88

and she was able when she awoke to force it back into the "donjon deeps" forever; while Alexander's demonic visitor had broken past the watches of the ego and could not be exorcised, although there was no way to establish it, licitly, within the cultural pattern that had trapped his habits.

It would be possible to sketch a kind of allegory of motives between this situation and what happened to Willa Cather when she wrote her next book, *O Pioneers!* (1913). For with *O Pioneers!* the natural forces of her gift — the unknown, unpredictable "self" — suddenly broke through her carefully trained literary habits. If there is a literary precursor, it is Thomas Hardy, but only in the sense that, like Hardy, she had found her subject in her own tribal country, in its ancient geological recalcitrance and its tragic face of blessing. Here she herself was the pioneer, of whom it might be said, as she says of Alexandra, the Swedish farm girl who is the heroine of the book: "For the first time, perhaps, since that land emerged from the waters of geologic ages, a human face was set toward it with love and yearning." But she brought to this discovery a voice that held and used its earlier disciplines, melodically and resonantly.

She scarcely knew what to do with the material, for the way it had put itself together, as a two-part pastoral, seemed to have no formal rationale, and the longer part — the story of Alexandra — had no backbone of structure at all, was as fluid and featureless as the high, oceanic grassland where Alexandra made her farm: the author could only mourn over the "foolish endeavor" she had somehow got on her hands. Ten years later, when she understood better that dark logic which Keats called "Negative Capability," she wrote of her experience with *O Pioneers!*: "When a writer begins to work with his own material, he realizes that, no matter what his literary excursions may have been, he has been working with it from the beginning — by living it. With this ma-

terial he is another writer. He has less and less power of choice
about the moulding of it. It seems to be there of itself, already
moulded. . . . In working with this material he finds that he
need have little to do with literary devices; he comes to depend
more and more on something else — the thing by which our feet
find the road home on a dark night, accounting of themselves
for roots and stones which we had never noticed by day."

Alexandra Bergson's parents had come from Sweden to take up
land in Nebraska, and their death leaves her, in her early twenties,
the head of a family of three brothers. The patch of land, won by
homestead rights, is the only survival relationship they have. It
is the high, dry, prairie country of the Divide, between two rivers,
the coarse, incalculable, primitively resistant ground of an action
so ancient in character it might have taken place in neolithic
times and in that other austere land between two rivers. "The
record of the plow was . . . like the feeble scratches on stone
left by prehistoric races, so indeterminate that they may, after all,
be only the markings of glaciers, and not a record of human striv-
ings." In winter "it is like an iron country . . . One could easily
believe that in that dead landscape the germs of life and fruitful-
ness were extinct forever." Alexandra faces the exigence of that
destiny in the almost unconscious spirit of a person driven by
uranian and chthonic gods, and makes her heroic peace with
them. "Her personal life, her own realization of herself, was almost a subconscious existence; like an underground river that
came to the surface only here and there, at intervals months
apart, and then sank again to flow on under her own fields."

She has a recurrent dream, usually on Sunday mornings when
she is able to lie abed late — a dream as archaic as the whole
action of her story. The subject of the dream is an authentic god
straight out of the unconscious, one of those vegetation and
weather gods by whose urgencies she is compelled and whose

energies sustain her. "Sometimes, as she lay thus luxuriously idle, her eyes closed, she used to have an illusion of being lifted up bodily and carried lightly by some one very strong. It was a man, certainly, who carried her, but he was like no man she knew; he was much larger and stronger and swifter, and he carried her as easily as if she were a sheaf of wheat. She never saw him, but, with eyes closed, she could feel that he was yellow like the sunlight, and there was the smell of ripe cornfields about him. She could feel him approach, bend over her and lift her, and then she could feel herself being carried swiftly off across the fields. . . . As she grew older, this fancy more often came to her when she was tired than when she was fresh and strong. . . . Then, just before she went to sleep, she had the old sensation of being lifted and carried by a strong being who took from her all her bodily weariness." Like Adonis, Attis, and Thammuz, this Eros of the corn and sunlight is a life principle, extending infinitely beyond the human subject, but appearing in the beneficent image of a guardian god to the subject strong enough and obedient enough to attend it.

In a sense, that divine being is the unconscious itself, assuming the image of a strength greater than the personal. Because of the primitive authenticity of the image, it seems right to see reflected here, also, something of the instinctive process by which the book came to be written, as well as those others of Willa Cather's works whose structure obeys laws more obscure and fundamental than literary precepts or even than her own ideas of her purposes: it is the "something else — the thing by which our feet find the road home on a dark night" — a power like that which carried Alexandra in her dream, "larger and stronger and swifter" than conscious intent. The two parts of the Nebraska pastoral — Alexandra's part and that called "The White Mulberry Tree" — are wrought into one form by an instinct as sure as the cycle of seasons, a cycle which itself seems to be the natural commanding form of the novel. The story of Alexandra engages the whole work in the rhythms of the land, powerful tidal urgencies of weather and seasons and their erosions of human life, while the episode of "The White Mulberry Tree" — the love story of Alexandra's young brother Emil and the Bohemian girl Marie Shabata — flashes across those deeper rhythms like a swift springtime, lyrical, brilliant, painful. The episode is saturated with light, bronze and gold on the wide warm fields of grain that smell like baking bread, and gold and green under the leaves of the orchard where Emil and Marie meet their sudden doom, murdered as they lie in first embrace; so that the light ripening the land seems the one great reality, and the blood of the two young lives poured dark into the earth a sacrifice to it.

The Song of the Lark (1915) is a ponderously bulky novel that suffers from autobiographic compulsion. Ostensibly it is modeled on the career of the Swedish opera singer Olive Fremstad. However, Willa Cather's friend Elizabeth Sergeant wrote that she "was deeply — by her own account — identified with her character [Thea Kronborg], who had many of her traits and had undergone many of her own experiences." The setting is changed to Moonstone, Colorado, a small town in the desert west of Denver. Thea, a gifted child in a suffocatingly crowded and brutally inept family, takes her first music lessons from a pathetic, drunken old German; for proper lessons in Chicago she is financed by a brakeman on the Denver train, who is in love with her and who is shortly killed in an accident; from Chicago she goes on to supreme success in New York, where her promoter is a wealthy young dandy, also in love with her. The end of Thea's story explores both the splendors and penalties of success, the bleak asceticism which the artist pays for the presumptions of his gift. The naturalistic, circumstantial form to which the subject lent itself carried its usual vulnerability to "thesis" writing, a weakness inherent also in Miss Cather's attraction to the subject of the artist's struggle. The result is invented plot situations, sagging proportions, made-up dialogue, and a prose that often goes lax. In her preface to a later edition, she wrote that the book should have ended before the successful phase of Thea's career: "What I cared about, and still care about, was the girl's escape; the play of blind chance, the way in which commonplace occurrences fell together to liberate her from commonness." But this too is a thesis, indicating the way in which traumatic personal memory — of her own "escape" — turned into obsessive idea.

"Life began for me," she said, "when I ceased to admire and began to remember." But there is more than one kind of remembering. There is personal memory bound up with the chronology of one's own life and with ego-tensions and resistances. There is what Proust called "bodily memory," which, because it is physical and sensory, may be at once personal and more than personal, for the impulses of the senses register common qualities of experience, timeless as sun and earth, breath and flesh. And there is what the Greeks call *anamnesis*, memory of "important" things, matters whose significance is part of one's heritage — a kind of *commemoration* since it involves other and profounder memories than one's own, buried perhaps as deep as instinct and aroused mysteriously as instinct. There is still a great deal in *The Song of the Lark* that is of the older orders of memory, more broadly based than that of the ego, more essential and more original — in that sense of the word which implies "origins." Toward the end of *O Pioneers!* when Alexandra is almost broken by young Emil's death, she goes to his grave in the night during a storm, and is found there in the morning, drenched, icy, and nearly unconscious, by Crazy Ivar, an old man who lives in a clay bank like a coyote and who can talk with animals and heal them. He and

Alexandra have always understood each other. She tells him: "After you once get cold clear through, the feeling of the rain on you is sweet. . . . It carries you back into the dark, before you were born; you can't see things, but they come to you, somehow, and you know them and aren't afraid of them. Maybe it's like that with the dead. If they feel anything at all, it's the old things, before they were born . . ." In *The Song of the Lark*, Thea, an adolescent only beginning to break through the ugliness and mediocrity surrounding her, hears in a symphony a voice immensely ancient and yet sounding within herself: "a soul new and yet old, that had dreamed something despairing, something glorious, in the dark before it was born; a soul obsessed by what it did not know, under the cloud of a past it could not recall."

Thea tries to hold that "soul" under her cloak, as if it were a child or another self that must be protected in tenderness and darkness lest it be snatched from her before it could grow: "There was some power abroad in the world bent upon taking away from her that feeling with which she had come out of the concert hall. Everything seemed to sweep down on her to tear it out from under her cape. If one had that, the world became one's enemy; people, buildings, wagons, cars, rushed at one to crush it under, to make one let go of it." Like Alexandra's, Thea Kronborg's nature had been formed close to the land, and toughened and simplified in that matrix. She is able to harbor the instinctive self, with its ancient gifts like those a child receives in fairy tales from dwarfs and witches constrained to bless him, because she recognizes both its transcendence and the personal disciplines needed to redeem it from "the cloud of a past it could not recall," to give it feature, to bring it to birth by her own labor.

The voice heard in the symphony is associated with the western desert of her childhood. The desert had moved mysteriously with apparitions older than history, mirages of silver lakes where one

94

saw reflected the images of cattle magnified to a preposterous height and looking like mammoths, "prehistoric beasts standing solitary in the waters that for many thousands of years actually washed over that desert: the mirage itself may be the ghost of that long-vanished sea." Further south were the ruined dwellings of "the Ancient People." Here, in miniature cities honeycombed into clefts of the canyons, were human features of a past extending "back into the dark," a racial history speaking of immemorial experience with a voice of silence: steep trails worn deep into the rock by the Ancient People's generations carrying water up the canyon wall to their hanging gardens, signs of their mysteries, their food, their fire. "Food, fire, water, and something else — even here, in this crack in the world, so far back in the night of the past! Down here at the beginning, that painful thing was already stirring; the seed of sorrow, and of so much delight. . . . A vanished race; but along the trails, in the stream, under the spreading cactus, there still glittered in the sun the bits of their frail clay vessels, fragments of their desire." The discovery of the cliff-dwellings is for Thea Kronborg — as it was for her author — a materialized revelation of something unknown and yet remembered, something ancestral and legendary yet recognizable as an image responding from within the self, an *anamnesis* borne directly to the senses by external forms. Her own gift as a singer seems to her the same impulse that made those forms, given to her in order to salvage their meaning.

In Miss Cather's next book, *My Ántonia* (1918), there occurs a majestic, mysterious image that suggests, in another way, the timeless aspect of the subject matter which seems most naturally her own. Jim Burden (the narrator of the story) and some "hired girls" from the little Nebraska town of Black Hawk have spent a lazy afternoon by the river, ending with a picnic supper. "Presently we saw a curious thing: There were no clouds, the sun was going down in a limpid, gold-washed sky. Just as the lower edge of the red disk rested on the high fields against the horizon, a great black figure suddenly appeared on the face of the sun. We sprang to our feet, straining our eyes toward it. In a moment we realized what it was. On some upland farm, a plough had been left standing in the field. The sun was sinking just behind it. Magnified across the distance by the horizontal light, it stood out against the sun, was exactly contained within the circle of the disk; the handles, the tongue, the share — black against the molten red. There it was, heroic in size, a picture writing on the sun. Even while we whispered about it, our vision disappeared; the ball dropped and dropped until the red tip went beneath the earth. The fields below us were dark, the sky was growing pale, and that forgotten plough had sunk back to its own littleness somewhere on the prairie." The image could have been carved, as a sacred life-symbol, on the stones of a lost temple of Yucatan, or in a tomb of the Valley of Kings. The plow itself, forgotten on that upland farm, could have been left there by some farmer of Chaldea.

The story is as much Jim Burden's as it is Ántonia's. The two children share the initiatory experiences of the wild land to which their parents have brought them. Jim's family, like Willa Cather's, are from Virginia; Ántonia Shimerda's family are Bohemians who have come to take up homestead rights in the new country. Jim's family live in a house, Ántonia's in a cave in a clay bank, the children sleeping in holes tunneled into the gumbo mud. Around them is "nothing but land: not a country at all, but the material out of which countries are made." It is like the sea, featureless and barren, but running with obscure, unaccountable movement as of the rushing of theromorphic gods: "I felt that the grass was the country, as the water is the sea. The red of the grass made all the great prairie the colour . . . of certain seaweeds when they

96

are first washed up. And there was so much motion in it; the whole country seemed, somehow, to be running . . . as if the shaggy grass were a sort of loose hide, and underneath it herds of wild buffalo were galloping, galloping . . ." The ends of the earth are very near. "The light air about me told me that the world ended here": one had only to walk straight on through the red grass to the edge of the world where there would be only sun and sky left.

Out of homely American detail are composed certain friezelike entablatures that have the character of ancient ritual and sculpture. There is the suicide and funeral of Mr. Shimerda, Ántonia's father, a gifted musician who could, finally, not bear the animal life to which the first generation of pioneers was subjected. For his suicide he dressed himself fastidiously in the fine clothes of the concert hall, went out to the cow barn, and shot himself. It was dead winter, and his corpse had got frozen to the ground before it was discovered. It was left there safely till the day of the funeral, when the hired men from the Burden farm "went ahead on horseback to cut the body loose from the pool of blood in which it was frozen fast to the ground." The Shimerdas were Roman Catholic, an anomaly in that predominantly Protestant neighborhood of farmers, and as a suicide he could not be buried in Catholic ground, so his grave was made at a crossroads in the age-old superstition clinging to the suicide. But no roads ever crossed over his grave. "The road from the north curved a little to the east just there, and the road from the west swung out a little to the south; so that the grave, with its tall red grass that was never mowed, was like a little island." And Jim Burden says, "I loved the dim superstition, the propitiatory intent, that had put the grave there; and still more I loved the spirit that could not carry out the sentence — the error from the surveyed lines, the clemency of the soft earth roads along which the home-coming wagons rattled after sunset."

97

There are the hired men on the farm, Jake and Otto, who, with the "sag of their tired shoulders against the whitewashed wall," form a mute memorial as dignified and tender in outline as a Greek stele — nomadic figures who bear with them the ancient pathos of mysterious coming and mysterious departure, "without warning . . . on the westbound train one morning, in their Sunday clothes, with their oilcloth valises — and I never saw them again." And there are the hired girls, girls who like Ántonia came from the farming community to take domestic work in the town of Black Hawk; robust, exuberant, and held in contempt by the townspeople, these girls appear like a sunlit band of caryatids, or like the succession of peasant girls who loved generously and suffered tragically in old ballads, or like the gay interlinked chain of girls in Proust's *À l'ombre des jeunes filles en fleurs.* "When I closed my eyes," Jim Burden says, "I could hear them all laughing — the Danish laundry girls and the three Bohemian Marys. . . . It came over me, as it had never done before, the relation between girls like those and the poetry of Virgil. If there were no girls like them in the world, there would be no poetry. I understood that clearly, for the first time."

Jim Burden, who goes away to the city and returns to the Nebraska farmland only after long intervals, is able to register that Chekhovian "suffering of change" which enters Willa Cather's work during this period. On his last return both he and Ántonia are middle-aged, Jim a weary intellectual nomad, Ántonia married to a Bohemian farmer with a brood of children about her, gay in her orchards and her kitchen. With scarcely a tooth in her head, save for some broken brown snags, she is still able to leave "images in the mind that did not fade — that grew stronger with time . . . She lent herself to immemorial human attitudes which we recognize by instinct as universal and true." The suffering of change, the sense of irreparable loss in time, is one polarity of the

work; the other polarity is the timelessness of those images associated with Ántonia, with the grave of the suicide at the crossroads, with the mute fortitude of the hired men and the pastoral
poetry of the hired girls, and most of all with the earth itself,
carrying in mysterious stroke, like the plow hieroglyphed on the
sun, signs of an original and ultimate relationship between man
and cosmos.

In 1920 Miss Cather collected a number of her earlier short
pieces under the title *Youth and the Bright Medusa*; four of
them were reprinted from *The Troll Garden*, and the others,
which had appeared in *McClure's Magazine*, have merely the
quality of competence. She spent four years writing the next
novel, *One of Ours* (1922), and it is the least attractive of her
books. One would like to see it quietly buried without remark;
but the reasons for its dreariness are instructive. The form of the
book is the naturalistic, circumstantial form of *The Song of the
Lark*, with the same temptation to "thesis," but grayer circumstances and almost insufferably relaxed style. The story is the
fictionized account of a young cousin of hers who was killed at
Cantigny in 1918. Claude Wheeler is a Nebraska farm boy, of
somewhat finer fiber than others, painfully thwarted in sensibility because of the meagerness of his education and the bleakness of his small-town environment: there ought, he feels, to be
"something splendid" about life. His dull miseries are followed
until escape comes through the war; in a strange and disturbing
justification of army life and war, Claude finds in France the
aesthetic order of which he had dreamed in ignorance, and dies
heroically without disillusionment. Miss Cather received the
Pulitzer Prize for this novel, and it seemed to justify her own
feeling about the book; Elizabeth Sergeant says, "She liked this
prize and never ceased to say, in print and out of print, that
Claude was her favorite of all her heroes." And Miss Sergeant

adds astutely, "Was it because he was almost a piece of herself, left behind in Red Cloud?"

In an interview with a reporter, she gave the most wrongheaded of reasons for her feeling that *One of Ours* was an achievement: she said, "I came to know that boy better than I know myself. I have cut out all picture-making because that boy does not see pictures. It was hard to cease to do the thing that I do best, but we all have to pay a price for everything we accomplish and because I was willing to pay so much to write about this boy I felt that I had a right to do so." Her willingness to write in a dull manner because the boy's life was dull, her rationalization of the dullness as a personal sacrifice to her intimate knowledge of her subject — for the cousin who became Claude Wheeler was, after all, as she said, "her own flesh and blood" — these are embarrassing comments on the pitfalls of a temperament that would never wholly know itself; they are the negative aspect of an endowment that remained in large degree unconscious. The ethic of human fidelity runs all through her life as through her work; she never confused the importance of her writing with the importance of even the most obscure human relationships; and it is the same characteristic of fidelity that led her to the mistake of *One of Ours*: "that boy" should not die unknown, the significance of his life should not go unrecorded. But the fidelities of flesh and blood are not the fidelities of art.

A Lost Lady (1923) is a short novel constructed on an altogether different principle, that of the "novel *démeublé*" (to use her own term), the novel disburdened of the lumber of circumstantial detail and stripped to functional episodes. The book has been widely praised as a "small masterpiece." Undoubtedly it owes its appeal to the chief character, Marian Forrester, but the magical quality of that portrait is assured by a fastidious economy of narrative means. Mrs. Forrester appears largely as reflected through the sensibility of young Niel Herbert, in a series of sharply focused vignettes that catch her brilliance and also the disturbing shadow of something illicit in her nature that troubles the bright illusion in the boy's mind. She is first seen as the slender, light-footed lady who runs down from the kitchen of the big house on the hill, to bring hot, freshly baked bread to some small boys who are hunting in the Forrester woods. The charming, gratuitous gesture is typical of her relationship with life, for she has the gift of giving; and the small boys, in their mute and clumsy way, thrill with adoration, as do Captain Forrester's famous and important guests who stop over in the little town of Sweet Water, Nebraska, mainly because of the spell cast by Marian Forrester — the spell of a nameless creature-grace, a secret ardor of the senses: "she had always the power of suggesting things much lovelier than herself, as the perfume of a single flower may call up the whole sweetness of spring"; her eyes, "when they laughed for a moment into one's own, seemed to promise a wild delight that he has not found in life." Her gift is a reckless one, dependent on spendthrift opportunities, and her opportunities are circumscribed. On a winter day, one of the boys from the village, crouched behind a log in the woods, sees Mrs. Forrester and Frank Ellinger, a frequent guest from Denver, get out of their sleigh and go off among the trees, carrying fur robes; it is a long time before they return, and they have forgotten to get the pine boughs which had been their excuse for coming. Ellinger goes back to get the boughs, while Mrs. Forrester waits in the sleigh, close to the hidden boy: "When the strokes of the hatchet rang out from the ravine, he could see her eyelids flutter . . . soft shivers went through her body." When Captain Forrester is impoverished by a bank failure, and soon afterwards suffers a stroke, her opportunities are much narrower, for fewer guests stop off at the big house in Sweet Water; then he dies, and her isolation becomes frantic. One day by accident Niel Herbert catches sight of her through an open door, standing at the kitchen table in an old wrapper, rolling out dough (she is still the maker and giver of bread), and behind her, with his hands on her breasts, is Ivy Peters, an underbred and brutal young man of the town (if he were a character in a Faulkner novel, his name would have been Snopes), who has been buying up the Forrester land. In vignettes such as these, one sees the fatality of Marian Forrester's nature and the slow corrosion overtaking it. Or is it only the corruption of an image in Niel Herbert's mind? He cannot understand her when she says, "I feel such a power to live in me, Niel." And he cannot forgive her because "she preferred life on any terms."

The brilliant, ambiguous portrait to some extent conceals or outweighs a weakness in the book's conception. *A Lost Lady* has consistently been read as a study in degeneration, not only of a character but more especially of a set of values associated with the pioneer generation of Captain Forrester; and evidently Willa Cather thought of the book this way too, for she uses the reflective intelligence of Niel Herbert to appraise and condemn the loss of values. When this happens, the prose immediately becomes cliché, the thought specious, diffuse, and sentimental: "The Old West had been settled by dreamers, great-hearted adventurers who were unpractical to the point of magnificence; a courteous brotherhood, strong in attack but weak in defence, who could conquer but could not hold. Now all the vast territory they had won was to be at the mercy of men like Ivy Peters, who had never dared anything, never risked anything. They would drink up the mirage, dispel the morning freshness, root out the great brooding spirit of freedom, the generous, easy life of the great land-holders. The space, the colour, the princely carelessness of the pioneer they would destroy and cut up into profitable bits, as the match factory splinters the primeval forest." One has only to compare a passage such as this with almost any passage from the great pastorals to feel here the hollow echoes of a prose beating out a thesis and — whether the sentiment itself be true or not — sounding false. Willa Cather's art is an art of the sensuous and concrete, a high art of feeling; the spirit of the "idea" is always deadly to it. Through Niel Herbert one feels that "suffering of change" that one feels through Jim Burden in *My Antonia,* and this is truthful and real — but it is something very different from the idea of the decline of the West that comes dangerously near to spoiling the book.

In *The Professor's House* (1925) two major themes reappear and converge: the theme of the disbarred creative energy of the natural self and the theme of recovery of the "ancestors." The book is constructed like a triptych. The first panel describes Professor St. Peter's family — the complicated relationships that now, in his middle age, he realizes are wholly negative, a formidable system of checks on the power to live. The center panel, "Tom Outland's Story," is curiously dissociated in time and quality from the rest: it tells of the discovery of the cliff-dweller ruins, many years earlier, by one of St. Peter's students (later killed in the war), and of the few months of one intense summer when the boy had lived alone on the Blue Mesa in kinship with the lost Ancient People. The third panel is the professor's private adventure: he comes very near death in the crisis of rediscovery of his earlier self, and not unwillingly; for nothing much can be made of the rough and immature shape in which the forgotten self appears — there is no room for it in the busy, negative circumstances of St. Peter's maturity.

His two married daughters loathe each other, the two sons-in-law are at swords' points, his wife (who had been deeply jealous of Tom Outland's relationship with St. Peter) carries on a curiously sinister flirtation with a son-in-law. In this desiccated atmosphere of impotent emotions, glossed by handsome social clatter, the professor maintains integrity only by reticence and courtesy, often envying Euripides' withdrawal in his old age to a cave by the sea, away from women.

The family goes abroad for the summer, and the professor, left alone in the house, begins work on Tom Outland's notes and diary, to prepare them for publication. Criticism of *The Professor's House* has usually dealt with the bold intrusion of the Tom Outland material into the middle of the novel as a "technical mistake." However, it is only with this middle section that the prose rises out of sophisticated competence and begins to move with that warmth and sensuousness that are characteristic of Willa Cather's writing when it comes from the deeper sources of her feeling.

Young Tom Outland, herding cattle to make a stake for college, had been hunting for steers that had run wild in the canyons of the Blue Mesa, when he came on the cliff-dweller ruins. "I wish I could tell you what I saw there," he writes, "just *as* I saw it, on that first morning, through a veil of lightly falling snow. Far up above me, a thousand feet or so, set in a great cavern in the face of the cliff, I saw a little city of stone, asleep. It was as still as sculpture — and something like that . . . pale little houses of stone nestling close to one another, perched on top of each other, with flat roofs, narrow windows, straight walls, and in the middle of the group, a round tower. . . . A fringe of cedars grew along the edge of the cavern, like a garden. They were the only living things. Such silence and stillness and repose — immortal repose. That village sat looking down into the canyon with the calmness of eternity." It was not only the discovery of the ancient people that gave that summer its intensity in Tom Outland's life; living alone on the high mesa, he experienced the freshness of a land that seemed newly emerged from creation. "And the air, my God, what air! — Soft, tingling, gold, hot with an edge of chill on it, full of the smell of piñons — it was like breathing the sun, breathing the colour of the sky. . . . Up there alone, a close neighbour to the sun, I seemed to get the solar energy in some direct way. And at night, when I watched it drop down behind the edge of the plain below me, I used to feel that I couldn't have borne another hour of that consuming light, that I was full to the brim, and needed dark and sleep."

This sense of organic involvement in the tidal rhythms of the earth, this baptismal freshness of all origins, become related, in the professor's mind, with the creative period of his own youth. He had expected, in fantasy, Tom Outland's ghost to come back again through the garden door to visit with him, "as he had so often done in dreams." But another boy comes, "the boy the Professor had long ago left behind him in Kansas," the original, unregenerate St. Peter. He yields to this "twin," as he calls him, entire possession, as if yielding to an illicit and slightly alarming addiction; and in the arms of his obsession forgets to turn off an old and defective gas heater. He is rescued from asphyxiation by the ancient housekeeper, Augusta, coming to dust the attic where he works. The person of Augusta is beautifully considered: "Augusta was like the taste of bitter herbs; she was the bloomless side of life that he had always run away from, — yet when he had to face it, he found that it wasn't altogether repugnant. . . . She talked about death as she spoke of a hard winter or a rainy March, or any of the sadnesses of nature." She functions, in this delicate and profound psychic drama, as the "mother," older than all knowledge, bitter and at last saving; with her help, in the attic full of old dressmaker's mummies, St. Peter is able to relinquish the young "twin" whose subtle face had suddenly become that of death.

On its fine surfaces, the book confronts the dereliction of middle age with the high, poetic promise of youth, and its dramatic concern is the psychological crisis of renunciation (Willa Cather wrote in Robert Frost's copy that the story was about "letting go with the heart"). True, evidently, as that reading is, there is something wrong under these surfaces. The theme of the lapsed self remains not much beyond the point where it had stood in *Alexander's Bridge*; like Bartley Alexander, trapped in the complicated arrangements he has made for living, St. Peter is able to recover the natural self only as a projection — first upon the youthful ghost of Tom Outland, and then upon the time-bound and uncouth figure of his own boyhood. As with Alexander, the falsification exacts its penalty. But if, by renunciation, the professor escapes death, it is not exactly "life" that he returns to, but the intricate corruption, the emotional and spiritual dearth of his ordinary existence. And despite the youthful exaltation of discovery in "Tom Outland's Story," there is a pervading "deathiness" here also: the immortal repose of the "little city of stone, asleep . . . still as sculpture" is the repose of death.

> And, little town, thy streets for evermore
> Will silent be; and not a soul to tell
> Why thou art desolate, can e'er return.

The psychological problems suggested by the two recovery themes are of very great subtlety and difficulty; and in Willa Cather's insistent, unsatisfied returns to them, one recognizes the "problem-solving" function that the artist's work serves for himself — the experimental, hypothetical character of each piece of work as it attempts another provisional answer or resolution. Though the two themes converge in *The Professor's House* (that is, simply by being juxtaposed, with their relationship left to inference), they are not yet congruent; nor are they yet able to deal with their materials as of the substance of life; the ancestors are dead, and the self has only enough life in it to assent to its own death.

Willa Cather was fifty-two now, about the same age as the professor, and her energies seem to be concentrated more and more deliberately on these themes. It was not until *Death Comes for the Archbishop*, two years later, that the places of the ancestors became populated with the living, in the experience of a self to whom nothing was lost or outgrown, that could comprehend all its states of consciousness as things within reach of the hand.

Meanwhile she wrote *My Mortal Enemy* (1926). It is a curious little book, artistically very attractive, a "novel *démeublé*" like *A Lost Lady*; that it concerns a malicious — though magnetic — character does not altogether account for the slight feeling of puzzled dissatisfaction with which one turns from it. Myra Henshawe is Irish, and this is perhaps the salient fact about her, one which the author understands very well (her own people were Scotch-Irish). She is seen first in her worldly sumptuousness and glamour, as an adept hostess in New York of the early part of the century, warm, mobile, intense, superb in her effects — the impression is drawn with Tolstoian deftness. Behind her, subtly increasing her glamour, is the whispered story of her girlhood elopement with a young German "free-thinker," and her disinheritance by the wealthy, picturesque Irish uncle who had brought her up as an orphan. Signs of malevolence in her charm appear obliquely — the unaccountable Irish malevolence turned against those she loves. After years, Myra is seen again under reduced and somewhat seedy circumstances, living in a rundown apartment-hotel on the West Coast, old and ill, tended with devotion by her engagingly civilized husband, who has always the courtesy to be polite to the devils that run her; she still has the grace of innate magnificence, is still superb in her effects — on her dying bed, she murmurs to the loved husband watching over her, "Why must I die like this, alone with my mortal enemy?"

The malignant sentence is not the last of her stagery. The

uncle who had brought her up and disinherited her (he gave his wealth to a convent) had had a proud funeral. He did not go to the Church but the Church came to him; bishop and clergy met the coffin and "bore it up to the high altar on a river of colour and incense and organ-tone." Myra makes her own spectacular arrangements; sensing death, she gathers up her blankets in the night, takes a taxi to a bare headland on the Pacific where an old twisted cedar leans from the sea, and dies there at dawn. She had imagined that death at dawn: "That is always such a forgiving time. When that first cold, bright streak comes over the water, it's as if all our sins were pardoned; as if the sky leaned over the earth and kissed it and gave it absolution."

Aside from the essential interest of the character, the significance of the book lies in its structural movement toward the metamorphosis occurring in middle age, the invasion of ancestry into personality (a phenomenon with which Proust too was concerned — as in Swann's aging into the Jewish patriarchal type, and in Saint-Loup's increasing resemblance to the medieval Guermantes image). As Myra Henshawe ages, she is invaded more and more by the ungovernable powers of inheritance, which she identifies with her uncle. "We were very proud of each other," she says, "and if he'd lived till now, I'd go back to him and ask his pardon . . . Yes, and because as we grow old we become more and more the stuff our forbears put into us. I can feel his savagery strengthen in me. We think we are so individual and so misunderstood when we are young; but the nature our strain of blood carries is inside there, waiting, like our skeleton." Myra dies overwhelmed by the ancestors — that strange Irish agglomerate of the dark primitive with what is most magical in Christianity and with what is most censorious, turning to the revenge of those magic snakes which St. Patrick drove out of Ireland to lodge in the souls of his converts. The themes of the ancestors and the instinctive self come together here in one person, in a barbaric pattern of destructiveness. But the book leaves one with the unsatisfied sense of something unseated and unreferred, something belonging to a larger context than Myra Henshawe's Irishness, something whose resolution here is perhaps too facile, a kind of ethnic cliché.

After a short prologue, *Death Comes for the Archbishop* (1927) starts in the manner of a legend's "once upon a time": "One afternoon in the autumn of 1851 a solitary horseman, followed by a pack-mule, was pushing through an arid stretch of country somewhere in central New Mexico." The conduct of the book is legendary — with that quality of the most enduring legends that endure because they represent primal human experience, the excesses and elaborative accretions rubbed off by long handling, so that what remains is the rounded core, hand-smoothed to a satiny luster; while the people in the book, the "strong people of the old deep days of life," not only have each their legends but have become their own legends. The prose has the bland, voiced quality of oral telling — not apparently an accident, for Elizabeth Sergeant records that each day, after writing, Willa Cather went alone to a stony place in the woods and read her work aloud to test its sounds and rhythms.

Most of the episodes evoke the virtue of place, textures of earth and weather that are the basis of all sense of reality, and the relationships of human generations silently handing down their wisdom of place. Hence a sacramental character invests not only the experiences of the archbishop, Jean Latour, because of his religious mission, but also the land itself and the habits of the people living there. On that journey in 1851, after traveling three days thirsty in a desert of brick-colored sand hills, the young bishop comes upon a cruciform juniper tree and kneels there to pray to the Mother for water for his animals and himself; and shortly thereafter he comes upon a place called Hidden Water, where a spring has for unknown ages fed human settlement, and recognizes here something familiar from his own anciently settled country, Auvergne: "This spot had been a refuge for humanity long before these Mexicans had come upon it. It was older than history, like those well-heads in his own country where the Roman settlers had set up the image of a river goddess, and later the Christian priests had planted a cross." Across the "life-giving stream" a boy leads a flock of goats to pasture, the angoras leaping the stream in arrows of dazzling whiteness in the sunlight; the people beat out their grain on an earthen threshing-floor and winnow it in the wind "like the Children of Israel." One is in the presence of a way of life like that suggested in the twenty-third Psalm: "He maketh me to lie down in green pastures: he leadeth me beside the still waters. He restoreth my soul."

In Nebraska, the early homesteaders had experienced the emptiness of that wild land as a curse taken into their nerves to be passed on to their children as congenital deprivation (one remembers the gaunt house and the cattle-tracked clay bluffs, the dishcloths hung out to dry and the turkeys picking up refuse about the kitchen door), a curse accommodated by the Protestant taboo on the instinctual. The evocation in this book of the more remote American "ancestors," the southwestern Indians, redresses the balance of instinct, particularly in relation to the land. Moving through the desert with Eusabio, his Navajo guide, the archbishop comes to recognize the vital relationship between land and people: "Travelling with Eusabio was like travelling with the landscape made human." As the white man's way was assertion of himself against the land, "it was the Indian's way to pass through a country without disturbing anything; to pass and leave no trace, like fish through the water, or birds through the air. It was the Indian manner to vanish into the landscape, not to stand out against it. The Hopi villages that were set upon rock mesas, were made to look like the rocks on which they sat, were imperceptible at a distance. The Navajo hogans, among the sand and willows, were made of sand and willows." Two Zuñi runners pass them, saluting by gestures of the open palm but not stopping: "They coursed over the sand with the fleetness of young antelope, their bodies disappearing and reappearing among the sand dunes, like the shadows that eagles cast in their strong, unhurried flight."

In the Nebraska of Willa Cather's generation, human landmarks were scarce and the landmarks that were raised were like the town of Red Cloud where she grew up, hesitant and ugly and traditionless, perpetuating an obstinate sterility. The pueblos where Jean Latour goes on his pilgrimages have Homeric names and associations: "Santo Domingo, breeder of horses; Isleta, whitened with gypsum; Laguna, of wide pastures; and finally, cloud-set Ácoma." The people of the pueblo of Taos appear on their houses a little before sunset, and it is as if American life were seen in a new dimension, new but very old, connected perhaps with the source-lands of civilization in the Middle East, perhaps with Arabia: there were "two large communal houses, shaped like pyramids, gold-coloured in the afternoon light, with the purple mountain lying just behind them. Gold-coloured men in white burnouses came out on the stairlike flights of roofs, and stood still as statues, apparently watching the changing light on the mountain. There was a religious silence over the place; no sound at all but the bleating of goats coming home through clouds of golden dust."

As the Ancient People of the continent are brought alive again in their pueblos — the streets of the ancestors in the heart no more desolate — the land too, and the air, tell of creation and an original relationship. At the rock of Ácoma, steep and scaled by an old path trodden over thousands of years by water-carriers,

111

the archbishop is overtaken by sudden storm, and stops at the top of the mesa to look out over the great plain glittering with rain sheets, the distant mountains bright in sunlight, and "thought that the first Creation morning might have looked like this, when the dry land was first drawn up out of the deep." The aging bishop, tired by journeying and tempted by thoughts of his homeland in France, chooses to die in exile in New Mexico because of the light, dry, aromatic air that had become habitual to the lungs and spiritually necessary, an air that "one could breathe . . . only on the bright edges of the world, on the great grass plains or the sage-brush desert," blowing in through the windows "with the fragrance of hot sun and sage-brush and sweet clover; a wind that made one's body feel light and one's heart cry 'To-day, to-day,' like a child's."

There is no problem of the natural self here, for the self has been living all its potentialities, embodied in an individual and unique mission, in conversation with inheritance and with the heritable. Dying, the archbishop "sat in the middle of his own consciousness; none of his former states of mind were lost or out-grown. They were all within reach of his hand, and all comprehensible." His last conscious image is one of his youth, of the *diligence* for Paris rumbling down a mountain gorge, to take him on his first step toward the new world; but this image is very different from the demons of youth that possessed Bartley Alexander and Professor St. Peter, insidiously negating the developed personality: the image here is that of a young traveler, setting out again in peril and devotion.

Between this book and *Shadows on the Rock* (1931), Willa Cather's father died, a death from which she suffered severe shock, and she had tended her mother through a long paralytic illness; from the personal point of view, there can be no question of the immediate emotional provenience of the central relationship in

112

Shadows on the Rock, that between father and child (Euclide Auclair, apothecary of Quebec, and his small daughter Cécile) — the essential image of human continuity. But the "child" had appeared frequently before, as a psychological symbol, in Willa Cather's writings — the "divine child" of myth and of dreams, making its clamor at the limen of consciousness, requiring entrance. Now the child, the initial and potential self, is the main character.

Again the story starts in the manner of a legend's "once upon a time": "One afternoon late in October of the year 1697, Euclide Auclair, the philosopher apothecary of Quebec, stood on the top of Cap Diamant gazing down the broad, empty river far beneath him." That haunted gaze down the river, where the last ships for France have disappeared before winter isolates the Rock, is a continuous minor motif in the book; for these people are in exile — as, indeed, all the people of Willa Cather's great pastorals are in exile, thrust forth on a wild new earth, cut off from the continuities of the past. But this rock of Quebec — like the desert pueblos of New Mexico — has gathered its own legends out of the raw and dangerous wilderness, and for the child Cécile these impregnate all the steep streets, "ancestors" alive in her love and will and tangible as the air she breathes. As the autumn fog drifts brown from the river, vapors changing density and color to amethyst and red lavender, "It was like walking in a dream. One could not see the people one passed, or the river, or one's own house. Not even the winter snows gave one such a feeling of being cut off from everything and living in a world of twilight and miracles. . . . On such solemn days [All Souls' Day, particularly solemn in Quebec because it is the day of the ancestors of these exiles] all the stories of the rock came to life for Cécile; the shades of the early martyrs and great missionaries drew close about her. All the miracles that had happened there . . . came out of the fog; every spire, every ledge and pinnacle, took on the splendour of legend."

But the sense of the past — of those continuities which are most saving and fruitful — is not confined to "shadows" on the rock: surrounded by wilderness and constantly called upon for responses to primitive situations, the living characters of the book move in simple, agelessly human patterns of figures in legend. Old Bishop Laval goes to the church to ring the bell for five o'clock Mass: "In winter the old man usually carried a little basin as well as his lantern. It was his custom to take the bowl of holy water from the font in the evening, carry it into his kitchen, and put it on the back of the stove, where enough warmth would linger through the night to keep it from freezing." The child Cécile does not always waken at the first bell, ringing in the coldest hour of the night, "but when she did, she felt a peculiar sense of security, as if there must be powerful protection for Kebec in such steadfastness, and the new day, which was yet darkness, was beginning as it should. The punctual bell and the stern old Bishop who rang it began an orderly procession of activities and held life together on the rock, though the winds lashed it and the billows of snow drove over it."

There is another child in the book, little Jacques, whose mother is the town prostitute, and in this doubling of the symbol, the "child" appears redemptorally and sacramentally. The old bishop has come on a winter night from the house of a sick woman; no one else is abroad in that cruel cold. He turns his lantern on the stone steps of the episcopal residence (occupied by the young, graceful, splendid, and presumptuous bishop who has replaced him), and finds there a child crouching, crying and almost frozen. He takes him home to his small poor rooms in the Seminary, makes a fire in the fireplace to heat water for a bath, and warms milk on the hearth with a little cognac. "One strange thing

Jacques could remember afterwards. He was sitting on the edge of a narrow bed, wrapped in a blanket, in the light of a blazing fire. He had just been washed in warm water; the basin was still on the floor. Beside it knelt a very large old man with big eyes and a great drooping nose and a little black cap on his head, and he was rubbing Jacques's feet and legs very softly with a towel. . . . What he remembered particularly was that this old man, after he had dried him like this, bent down and took his foot in his hand and kissed it; first the one foot, then the other." The bishop is told by his servant that the child is the son of the woman called La Grenouille, and the old man nods thoughtfully, "Ah! That, too, may have a meaning." He sits through the night with his swollen legs on a stool, covered in his cloak and sunk in meditation — he has given the child his bed. "This was not an accident, he felt. Why had he found, on the steps of that costly episcopal residence built in scorn of him and his devotion to poverty, a male child, half-clad and crying in the merciless cold? Why had this reminder of his Infant Saviour been just there, under that house which he never passed without bitterness?"

Before she died in 1947, at the age of seventy-three, Willa Cather published four more books, a book of tales, a book of essays, and two novels; and after her death another book of stories appeared and another book of essays. We are told that from 1932 on, she showed signs of deep fatigue. The prose of the two last novels shows weariness. *Lucy Gayhart* (1935) is another semi-autobiographical account of the gifted young person growing up in a little midwestern town; despite its relaxed style, it contains certain moments and insights of great sensitivity. *Sapphira and the Slave Girl* (1940) is Willa Cather's personal quest for her Virginia ancestors — she went back to her early home there to find the materials for the book — but the impulse was perhaps too self-conscious, and the novel has little interest beyond the historical.

The stories in *The Old Beauty and Others* (1948) seem only the somewhat querulous writing of old age.

But the three stories in *Obscure Destinies* (1932) are the finest short pieces she ever wrote. "Neighbour Rosicky," a story set in Nebraska, is about an old Bohemian farmer who dies of heart trouble. There is in this tale that primitive religious or magical sense of relationship with the earth that one finds in Willa Cather's great pastoral novels. Old Rosicky, sent home by the town doctor with a warning, stops by the graveyard where a light fall of snow is settling on the red grass: "It was a nice graveyard, Rosicky reflected . . . . A man could lie down in the long grass and see the complete arch of the sky over him, hear the wagons go by; in summer the mowing-machine rattled right up to the wire fence. And it was so near home. Over there across the corn-stalks his own roof and windmill looked so good to him that he promised himself to mind the Doctor and take care of himself. . . . He wasn't anxious to leave [that place]. And it was a comfort to think that he would never have to go farther than the edge of his own hayfield." The drama of the story is in old Rosicky's relationship with a daughter-in-law, a young girl from town who resents the isolation of farm life and is snobbish in her shabby town-glamour. She is alone with him when he has a severe heart attack, and she holds his hand, a hand not like that of other farmers, but gypsy-like, "nimble and lively and sure, in the way that animals are. . . . It seemed to her that she had never learned so much about life from anything as from old Rosicky's hand. It brought her to herself; it communicated some direct and untranslatable message."

These stories in *Obscure Destinies* face the child with the old and ancestral, gathering up in gentle concreteness the themes of a lifetime. "Old Mrs. Harris" principally concerns a grandmother brought to the Midwest from Virginia, and used as a willing slave by her daughter Victoria. The "immemorial image" here is of the servant girl, Mandy, washing old Mrs. Harris' feet — a conversion of the image in *Shadows on the Rock*, of the old man washing the child's feet. "That had to be done in the kitchen; Victoria didn't like anybody slopping about. Mrs. Harris put an old checked shawl around her shoulders and followed Mandy. Beside the kitchen stove Mandy had a little wooden tub full of warm water. She knelt down and untied Mrs. Harris's garter strings and took off her flat cloth slippers and stockings. 'Oh, Miz' Harris, your feet an' legs is swelled turrible tonight!' 'I expect they air, Mandy. They feel like it.' 'Pore soul!' murmured Mandy. . . . The kitchen was quiet and full of shadow, with only the light from an old lantern. Neither spoke. Mrs. Harris dozed from comfort, and Mandy herself was half asleep as she performed one of the oldest rites of compassion."

In the story "Two Friends" the central image is of a child — the child Willa Cather must have been — listening to two elderly men talking in moonlight on the street of a country town. There was "a row of frail wooden buildings, due to be pulled down any day; tilted, crazy, with outside stairs going up to rickety second-storey porches that sagged in the middle. . . . These abandoned buildings, an eyesore by day, melted together into a curious pile in the moonlight, became an immaterial structure of velvet-white and glossy blackness. . . . The road, just in front of the sidewalk where I sat and played jacks, would be ankle-deep in dust, and seemed to drink up the moonlight like folds of velvet. It drank up sound, too; muffled the wagon-wheels and hoof-beats; lay soft and meek like the last residuum of material things, — the soft bottom resting-place. Nothing in the world, not snow mountains or blue seas, is so beautiful in moonlight as the soft dry summer roads in a farming country, roads where the white dust falls back from the slow wagon-wheel." The two men talking seem more than themselves because of their long shadows cast by moonlight, persons representing cosmic relationships like those calculated by Pythagoras: "When they used to sit in their old places on the sidewalk, two black figures with patches of shadow below, they seemed like two bodies held steady by some law of balance, an unconscious relation like that between the earth and the moon." When the two friends quarrel and abandon each other, it is to the young girl as if a truth had been senselessly wasted.

Willa Cather's stature as a novelist and storyteller will probably always withstand those obscurations which happen to a major writer almost with the regularity of the displacement of one generation by another; for her best work reaches into human truths immeasurably older than the historical American past from which she drew her factual materials, truths that provide the essential forms of experience and that therefore cannot become "past" truths, either obsolescent or elegiac — although they are of the primitive kind that may affront our self-ignorance and stir our resistances. For the same reason, the dense world of the five senses which she creates in her best novels and stories is one that cannot be interpreted by an abstraction (a "world-view" of some kind); her work rests on an intuitive or instinctive wisdom, conveying "a direct and untranslatable message" like old Rosicky's gypsy hand, or like the image of the black plow picture-written on the molten sun. What she did was very difficult, for she had to give up conventional literary methods, in which she was accomplished, and go blindly into herself for essential truth. Yet it was through that giving up and blindness that she was able to speak in a way that often reveals to the reader something extraordinarily valuable that seems to have been in his mind always.

Selected Bibliography

Works of Willa Cather

The Troll Garden. New York: McClure, Phillips, 1905.
Alexander's Bridge. Boston: Houghton Mifflin, 1912.
O Pioneers! Boston: Houghton Mifflin, 1913.
The Song of the Lark. Boston: Houghton Mifflin, 1915.
My Antonia. Boston: Houghton Mifflin, 1918.
Youth and the Bright Medusa. New York: Knopf, 1920.
One of Ours. New York: Knopf, 1922.
A Lost Lady. New York: Knopf, 1923.
The Professor's House. New York: Knopf, 1925.
My Mortal Enemy. New York: Knopf, 1926.
Death Comes for the Archbishop. New York: Knopf, 1927.
Shadows on the Rock. New York: Knopf, 1931.
Obscure Destinies. New York: Knopf, 1932.
Lucy Gayhart. New York: Knopf, 1935.
Not under Forty. New York: Knopf, 1936.
Sapphira and the Slave Girl. New York: Knopf, 1940.
The Old Beauty and Others. New York: Knopf, 1948.
Willa Cather on Writing. New York: Knopf, 1949.

Critical and Biographical Studies

Bennett, Mildred R. *The World of Willa Cather.* Lincoln: University of Nebraska Press, 1961.
Brown, E. K., and Leon Edel. *Willa Cather: A Critical Biography.* New York: Knopf, 1953.
Curtin, W. D., ed. *The World and the Parish: Willa Cather's Articles and Reviews, 1893–1902.* 2 vols. Lincoln: University of Nebraska Press, 1970.

NOTE: Perhaps it would be good to note that during the past five years or so almost all of Willa Cather's novels and short stories have been nicely reissued by Knopf in their Vintage paperback series. Now most everything is available, including the late stories. This should all be easily obtainable information — out of the Vintage catalogue or Paperbound Books in Print.

Daiches, David. *Willa Cather: A Critical Introduction*. New York: Collier, 1962.

Faulkner, Virginia, and Mildred Bennett, eds. *Willa Cather's Collected Short Fiction 1892–1912*. Lincoln: University of Nebraska Press, 1965. Revised edition, 1970.

Geismar, Maxwell. *The Last of the Provincials: The American Novel, 1915–1925*. Boston: Houghton Mifflin, 1947.

Gelfant, Blanche. "The Forgotten Reaping Hook: Sex in *My Antonia*," *American Literature*, 43:60–82 (March 1971).

Giannone, Richard. *Music in Willa Cather's Fiction*. Lincoln: University of Nebraska Press, 1968.

Kates, George N. "Willa Cather's Unfinished Avignon Story," in Willa Cather, *Five Stories*. New York: Random House, 1956.

Kazin, Alfred. "Elegy and Satire: Willa Cather and Ellen Glasgow," in *On Native Grounds*. New York: Harcourt, Brace, 1942.

Lewis, Edith. *Willa Cather Living*. New York: Knopf, 1953.

McFarland, Dorothy Tuck. *Willa Cather*. New York: Ungar, 1972.

Martin, Terence. "The Drama of Memory in *My Antonia*," *PMLA*, 74:304–11 (March 1969).

Randall, John H. *The Landscape and the Looking Glass: Willa Cather's Search for Value*. Boston: Houghton Mifflin, 1960.

Schroeter, James, ed. *Willa Cather and Her Critics*. Ithaca: Cornell University Press, 1966. (This is a most valuable collection of essays on Cather written over the years by reviewers, scholars, and historians.)

Sergeant, Elizabeth Shepley. *Willa Cather: A Memoir*. Philadelphia: Lippincott, 1953.

Slote, Bernice, and Virginia Faulkner. *The Art of Willa Cather*. Willa Cather International Seminar, University of Nebraska, 1973. Lincoln: University of Nebraska Press, 1974. (An interesting collection of discussions and papers given at the Willa Cather Centennial.)

Slote, Bernice. *The Kingdom of Art: Willa Cather's First Principles and Critical Statements, 1893–1896*. Selected and edited with two essays and a commentary. Lincoln: University of Nebraska Press, 1966.

Slote, Bernice. *Uncle Valentine and Other Stories: Willa Cather's Uncollected Short Fiction, 1915–1929*. Edited with an introduction. Lincoln: University of Nebraska Press, 1973.

Slote, Bernice. "Willa Cather," in *Sixteen Modern American Authors*, edited by J. R. Bryer. New York: Norton, 1973.

Slote, Bernice. "Willa Cather as a Regional Writer," *Kansas Quarterly*, 2:7–15 (Spring 1970).

Stewart, D. H. "Cather's Mortal Comedy," *Queen's Quarterly*, 73:244–59 (Summer 1966).

Stouck, David. *Willa Cather's Imagination.* Lincoln: University of Nebraska Press, 1973.

Trilling, Lionel. "Willa Cather," in *After the Genteel Tradition: American Writers since 1910,* edited by Malcolm Cowley. New York: Norton, 1937.

Woodress, James. *Willa Cather: Her Life and Art.* New York: Pegasus, 1970.

Katherine Anne Porter

KATHERINE ANNE PORTER was born May 15, 1890, at Indian Creek, Texas. She was educated in convent schools in Louisiana and has lived in New York, Mexico, Paris, and for short periods elsewhere in the United States and in Europe. Her first published volume was a limited edition of a few stories published under the title *Flowering Judas* in 1930. In 1935 this book was expanded and republished. A second volume, *Pale Horse, Pale Rider*, containing three long stories, appeared in 1939. *The Leaning Tower and Other Stories* was published in 1944. A collection of essays and magazine articles, *The Days Before*, appeared in 1952. Ten years later, after a period of relative silence, the novel that had been announced twenty years earlier came out under the title *Ship of Fools*, and it gave Miss Porter her first big commercial and popular success.

Katherine Anne Porter's output has not been great, considering the years that she has been writing; but there is probably no other writer of fiction in America who has maintained so consistently high a level. Her subjects are drawn from her own background in the South, life in Mexico, in the urban East, in Europe, and, in one case at least, in the Rocky Mountains. Miss Porter's method, as she herself has confessed, is to write "from memory," even in certain instances to employ her past self as principal character. When a remembered incident strikes her as having significance, she makes a note; when details accumulate, she adds more notes. At some point in the process, all the details seem to merge into a pattern. With her notes about her, but seldom used, she writes the story. Most of her notes begin simply: "Remember!"

122

How such moments occur we can deduce from a passage in her short story "The Grave." Here the principal character is a woman named Miranda (Katherine Anne Porter's name for the character based on her own experience), who is recalling certain events from childhood. "One day she was picking her path among the puddles and crushed refuse of a market street in a strange city of a strange country, when without warning, plain and clear in its true colors as if she looked through a frame upon a scene that had not stirred nor changed since the moment it happened, the episode of that far-off day leaped from its burial place before her mind's eye." What "leaped," of course, was not merely the episode, but the total composition, as suggested by the phrase "from its burial place," for the story is about the discovery of treasure (knowledge) by two children digging about in the abandoned grave of an old burial ground.

Born and educated in the South, reared as a Roman Catholic, Miss Porter retains Catholic and southern habits of mind. Her awareness, as she says of Miranda, is a "powerful social sense" that detects special and subtle meanings in experience and translates them into fiction. If we think of Miranda's background as being roughly parallel to Miss Porter's, we can say that Katherine Anne Porter's family had moved, within the lifetime of her grandmother, from Kentucky into Louisiana, and from there to Texas. As with most southern families, it had retained a strong sense of family unity as well as an awareness of its place in the framework of southern history and southern society. The grandfather, although he had died before the family left Kentucky, and even though the move itself was necessitated by his imprudence, moved with the family each time they were uprooted, for his grave ". . . had been twice disturbed in his long repose by the constancy and possessiveness of his widow. She removed his bones first to Louisiana and then to Texas as if she had set out to find her own burial place, knowing well she would never return to the places she had left."

The family was Scotch-Presbyterian, inheriting a rugged stubbornness as its national legacy, a determined set of moral values from its religion. When the grandmother talked about "all the important appearances of life, and especially about the rearing of the young," she "relied with perfect acquiescence on the dogma that children were conceived in sin and brought forth in iniquity." Miranda, her brother, and her sister, we are told, "loved their Grandmother; she was the only reality to them in a world that seemed otherwise without fixed authority or refuge . . . just the same they felt that Grandmother was a tyrant, and they wished to be free of her." Miranda's rebellion took the form of running away from the convent and eloping, and something of this sort occurred in the life of Katherine Anne Porter.

As a non-practicing Catholic and a liberal southerner, Miss Porter has found the principal themes in her fiction in the tensions provided between fixed social and moral positions and the necessities of movement and alteration. Within a broad framework, she has dealt subtly with the distinctions between orthodox Christianity and revolution, between Roman and Protestant attitudes, between desire and responsibility, between reality and the dream. In brief, she has utilized the divine vision, but she has qualified it by focusing sharply upon "the human condition"; she has rejected irresponsible decision, as she has indecision. Her fiction portrays a small but inclusive, grotesque but convincing, world, rendered as at times absurd, always pathetic, but rendered, finally, with compassion.

Katherine Anne Porter's first published story was "María Concepción," completed in the summer of 1922 and published in *Century* magazine in December of that year. Her next story, "He," appeared in *New Masses* in 1927, followed by "Magic" in *transi-*

tion and "Rope" in the *Second American Caravan* in 1928. "The Jilting of Granny Weatherall" appeared in *transition* in 1929 and "Flowering Judas" was printed in *Hound and Horn* in the spring of 1930. These stories were collected in a volume titled *Flowering Judas and Other Stories* and printed in a limited edition of 600 copies later in 1930.

This small volume contained some of Miss Porter's best work, and the response to it was immediate. In the second, and regular, edition in 1935, four new stories were added: "Theft," "That Tree," "The Cracked Looking-Glass," and "Hacienda."

The contents of this first volume remain characteristic of Katherine Anne Porter's subject matter and themes. Her use of her Mexican experiences is obvious in such stories as "María Concepción," "Flowering Judas," "That Tree," and "Hacienda." Her southern background supplied the material for "Magic," "He," and "The Jilting of Granny Weatherall." Her Catholic upbringing is reflected in "Flowering Judas," in "The Cracked Looking-Glass," and, less obviously, in "That Tree." Her use of an urban background, less frequent than the rural, appears in "Theft."

Christian morality in a world where traditional values are threatened is at the heart of all these stories; and they are, ultimately, complex fables in which the tensions between the old order and the new provide a dramatic framework for the events. In "María Concepción," we have a story of competition between wife and mistress, set in the simple surroundings of a primitive Mexican village. Here moral choice is made, not alone by the principal characters, but by the whole community, for they condone the killing of the mistress by the wife, not because they approve of bloodshed, but because they believe that, in a contest between simple sexual pleasure and the marriage bed, marriage and the family must win out. In "Hacienda," many social levels of modern Mexico are represented, ranging from the Indians who manufacture don Genaro's pulque and the simple peasants of the village to the Russian film troupe and the American impressario from Hollywood. What is rendered, finally, is a complicated waste-land inhabited by a new order that has rejected the old values, but has discovered no common basis for the new. The result is a small comedy of no-manners, set in a land that still reflects, though dimly, its former mannered vitality.

"The Jilting of Granny Weatherall" tells the story of the death of its aged and crotchety heroine, whose passing is portrayed as a second betrayal at the altar. Granny had been betrayed by one bridegroom early in life, and the betrayal had rankled; now she is betrayed by the holy bridegroom, whose coming she has pathet-ically awaited on her deathbed. The other side of the coin is depicted in "The Cracked Looking-Glass," where the marriage of a young woman to an older man is revealed as the incomplete image reflected by a broken mirror, the sensibilities warped and tangled by unfulfillment. "That Tree" is the story of an American writer in Mexico whose midwestern bride destroys his integrity as a poet, deserts him, then returns only after he has succeeded as a hack. It is a study in shallow love accomplished through super-ficial success.

The problem of the modern wasteland, as displayed in these stories, is the pathetic inability of man to live according to his dreams. This pathos appears in its most specific and controlled form in the title story, "Flowering Judas." In this work, modern experience is presented, not so much as a fragmentation of man-ners and belief but rather as an ironic tension between two power-ful competing forces: Christian faith and revolutionary hope. Caught between these two is the heroine, Laura, an American girl of southern Catholic background, who lends her support to the Mexican Marxist forces of revolution.

Laura's predicament is that she cannot free herself from her early religious training and beliefs, so cannot give herself wholly to the revolutionary cause. This condition places her in a kind of limbo, like the old man in T. S. Eliot's "Gerontion" (from which poem Miss Porter found her title, perhaps even her theme), who complains that he has lost his "sight, smell, hearing, taste and touch." Likewise, Laura loses the use of her senses. Although a beautiful woman, she clothes herself like a nun and can respond to none of the would-be lovers who woo her. She rejects Braggioni, the revolutionary general; she outwits the young army captain who takes her riding; she unknowingly teases a young man from the Typographers Union by throwing him a rose (the symbol of love) when she can feel nothing for him. She even fails to react to the children whom she teaches when they bring her flowers and scribble on the blackboard "We lov ar ticher." Her principal contribution to the cause is to carry narcotics to the prisoners in jail, so that they may sleep away their imprisonment.

The story is one of Laura's inability to love. She cannot love erotically as a woman, humanely as a dedicated revolutionary, or divinely as a communicant in the church. Without love, the story says, the world is a wasteland; but Miss Porter goes on to examine and develop the consequences of this condition. Her central imagery is taken from the concept of Christian atonement, but with overtones of the pagan ritual that preceded the sacrament, derived certainly from Eliot's poem that contains the title of the story:

> In the juvescence of the year
> Came Christ the tiger
> In depraved May, dogwood and chestnut, flowering judas
> To be eaten, to be divided, to be drunk
> Among whispers.

"Christ the tiger" refers to the pagan ritual in which the blood

of a slain tiger is drunk in order to engender in the participants
the courage of the tiger heart. The Christian ritual is symbolic
rather than direct: the symbolic blood of Christ is drunk in remembrance of atonement; that is, to recall the agony and sym-
bolically to engender the virtues of Christ in the participants. In
the Christian sacrament, faith in, and love of, Christ alters the
substance of bread and wine into the spiritual flesh and blood of
Christ. Without faith-love the act becomes cannibalistic, for there
is no such alteration, as there was not in the pagan sacrament. By
a subtle alteration (or misreading) of Eliot's line, Miss Porter has
Laura eat, not the blood of Christ the tiger, but the blossoms of
the flowering Judas, the symbol of Christ's betrayer; so that Laura's
betrayal of Christ, of Braggioni, and of Eugenio (the prisoner who
dies of an overdose of her drugs) becomes a betrayal of man, a
cannibalistic, not a saving, gesture, as Eugenio reminds her when
he appears to her in her guilty dream that ends the story.

In "Flowering Judas," with all its accumulated symbols and
background mythology, Katherine Anne Porter achieved more
than a mere definition of modern man's condition, she embodied
an attitude that demonstrated the necessity for the application
of the ancient verities of faith and love as a fructifying element
in any human existence, whether of the old order or the new.

Miss Porter's second volume of stories, *Pale Horse, Pale Rider:
Three Short Novels*, which appeared in 1939, is composed of three
long short stories (not short novels, as the title suggested): "Old
Mortality," "Noon Wine," and the title story, "Pale Horse, Pale
Rider." In two of these stories, "Old Mortality" and "Pale Horse,
Pale Rider," the events for the first time concern the character
named Miranda. In the third, "Noon Wine," the narrator appears
to be Miranda (or the author herself) in a remembered incident
from childhood.

These facts are of little importance so far as a reading or an evaluation of the works is concerned, but they may be of considerable interest to anyone curious about the manner in which Miss Porter composes her stories. She has called her method writing from memory. Once, in describing how she had come to write the story "Old Mortality," her tongue slipped and instead of saying "Miranda's father said . . ." she made the remark *"My father said . . ."* On the other hand, Laura of "Flowering Judas," although she appears to resemble Miranda in the Catholic background, the experience in Mexico, the interest in social causes, the relation to Mexican children's art, was modeled on an American friend of Miss Porter's, a schoolteacher in Mexico during the author's residence there. She was not, of course, merely a portrait of that girl; she was, Miss Porter supposed, a combination of a good many people, just as was the character Braggioni in the same story. On the other hand, the events of "Pale Horse, Pale Rider" were many of them actual events that took place when Miss Porter was working as a reporter on the *Rocky Mountain News* in Denver during World War I.

One of the important things to notice about Miss Porter's characters is that the central figures all exhibit qualities that have some point of similarity with her own experience. If they are Irish or Mexican, they are also Roman Catholic, or they are political liberals. They are usually southern. This may account for the relatively small amount that Miss Porter has written, but it also could account for the consistently high level that her work represents. When necessary she displays a range of perception of ordinary manners and mannerisms that is almost uncanny; but usually such qualities as are rendered are attached to persons well within the limits of her own experience.

The long short story "Noon Wine" is a case in point. The events of this story center upon a Mr. Thompson, a West Texas farmer, and upon his guilt — the psychological effects of his unpremeditated killing of a visitor to his farm. The whole atmosphere of the Thompson place, as rendered by Miss Porter, seems to suggest that such an event must actually have occurred in the years between 1896 and 1905, even if not precisely as it is related in the story. It is clear that the author knew very well the kind of people Mr. and Mrs. Thompson were, even if she did not know exactly these same persons. Mr. Helton, another victim in the story, who is a Swede and who came from North Dakota, is an interesting and successful character, occupying his proper place in the story, but his role is not made so prominent as that of the Thompsons, and thus does not bear so heavy a weight of probability. We can imagine that the story began from a memory either of the event or of the character of Mr. Thompson, or both, in the mind of the author, who was probably about eleven or twelve years of age at the time of the murder and suicide. It could have begun from the events alone, and the characters could have been supplied from other memories; but however it happened, the character at the center of the story is of a type that Miss Porter could have known well, while the less familiar Mr. Helton got into the story only because he was necessary to the events.

The important point here is that such memory as we are talking about in discussing Miss Porter's work is not "mere memory," not only a memory of something that occurred, but something that happened within the long history of personal, family, and regional events; finally, within an even longer history. In referring to a friendship between Miranda's grandmother and a Negro maid in a later story, Miss Porter writes: "The friendship between the two old women had begun in early childhood, and was based on what seemed even to them almost mythical events." Miss Porter treats her memories also as "mythical events."

When we speak of myth, we are, of course, referring to a form of tribal memory, a preserving of events of the past as a means of justifying and explaining the views of the present. Every society adapts "myth" to its own purposes, either myths that it has transported from elsewhere and uses as a means of organizing its memories, or myths that it has created from its own past. Herman Melville has spoken of "historic memory," implying that it is at least one quality of the artist's general "prescience."

There can be no better phrase to describe Miss Porter's special sensibility than to call it "historic memory." Such memory, though it does, as Melville explained, "go far backward through long defiles of doom," begins with the specific present: the young girl finding a carved dove in an abandoned grave and trading it for a gold ring, another remembering the image of a dead aunt preserved in a family photograph as the family memory and contrasting it with the living present, the memory of illness and death during the influenza epidemic, the memories of Mexican revolutionaries, of moving picture companies on location, of Mexican women and West Texas farmers stirred to violence by passion. Partly these memories are controlled by a Catholic sensibility that seeks out the ceremony and order in the events, partly by a southern habit of thought that metamorphoses reality into "romance," not the romance of inferior southern authors, who see the events as picturesque and quaint manifestations of a peculiar social order, but something nearer the "romance" that Nathaniel Hawthorne sought in his New England novels, a romance that links man of the present with his ideals, the long legendary concepts of man in a continued and continuing past.

The rendering and utilization of myth is, in Katherine Anne Porter's stories, both subject matter and method. Neither as a southerner nor as a Catholic is she orthodox (that is, she does not mistake the myth for the reality); for her it becomes only another kind of reality. The important thing in a short story such as "The Jilting of Granny Weatherall" is not merely that a proud and stubborn old lady dies, unable to forget the jilting of a long-lost lover, but that the story reflects a particular, but not uncommon, attitude toward death. What is significant in a story such as "Flowering Judas" is not that Laura fails to escape the conflict between a conservative upbringing and the desire to assist in liberal political causes, but that such a conflict is at the bottom of the whole idea of man's Christian redemption; that there is something Christlike about such a dilemma.

Perhaps the most complete instance of a short story that utilizes a specifically southern background and memory for the creation of this larger, more generalized "truth" is "Old Mortality," where Miss Porter's subject matter is southern attitudes as expressed through family history, and where the theme is concerned with the nature of reality — particularly with self-definition. The story is told from the point of view of Miranda between the ages of eight and eighteen, and its details agree with all the other Miranda stories insofar as they relate events in a family that had moved from Kentucky to Louisiana and from there to Texas. At the center of the story are the memories of a girl, Amy, about whose long courtship and brief marriage to "Uncle Gabriel" the aura of romance has accumulated. We meet her first in a photograph in the family parlor, "a spirited-looking young woman, with dark curly hair cropped and parted on the side, a short oval face with straight eyebrows, and a large curved mouth." The family legend represents her as a vivacious, daring, and extremely beautiful girl, against whom the beauty and grace of later members of the family are forever to be judged. It tells of her using her cruel beauty to tantalize Uncle Gabriel until he despaired of ever winning her, of her precipitating events at a ball that caused a family scandal and disgrace. It tells of her sad suffering from an incurable illness, of her sudden and romantic marriage to Gabriel, and of her early death.

But the legend, which is more than just a romantic memory of Aunt Amy, is also a reflection of the family's attitude toward all events of the past — memories which Miranda can't share and an attitude that she cannot adopt because of discrepancies that she senses between such stories as related by the family and the actual facts that she perceives in the people and events that surround her in the everyday life of the present. In the photograph of Amy, for instance, "The clothes were not even romantic looking, but merely most terribly out of fashion"; in the talk about the slimness of the women in the family, Miranda is reminded of Great-Aunt Keziah, in Kentucky, whose husband, Great-Uncle John Jacob, "had refused to allow her to ride his good horses after she had achieved two hundred and twenty pounds"; in watching her grandmother crying over her accumulation of ornaments of the past, Miranda sees only "dowdy little wreaths and necklaces, some of them made of pearly shells; such moth-eaten bunches of pink ostrich feathers for the hair; such clumsy big breast pins and bracelets of gold and colored enamel; such silly-looking combs, standing up on tall teeth capped with seed pearls and French paste." Yet despite these disappointing incongruities, the child Miranda struggled to believe there was "a life beyond a life in this world, as well as in the next"; such episodes as members of the family remembered confirmed "the nobility of human feeling, the divinity of man's vision of the unseen, the importance of life and death, the depths of the human heart, the romantic value of tragedy."

Another view is suggested in the second section of the story, when Miranda and her sister have become schoolgirls in a New Orleans convent. During vacation on their grandmother's farm, they had read books detailing accounts of how "beautiful but unlucky maidens, who for mysterious reasons had been trapped by nuns and priests in dire collusion . . . 'immured' in convents, where they were forced to take the veil — an appalling rite during which the victims shrieked dreadfully — and condemned forever after to most uncomfortable and disorderly existences. They seemed to divide their time between lying chained in dark cells and assisting other nuns to bury throttled infants under stones in moldering rat-infested dungeons." In Miranda's actual experience at the convent, no one even hinted that she should become a nun. "On the contrary Miranda felt that the discouraging attitude of Sister Claude and Sister Austin and Sister Ursula towards her expressed ambition to be a nun barely veiled a deeply critical knowledge of her spiritual deficiencies."

The most disheartening disillusion during this period came, however, when Miranda actually met the legendary Uncle Gabriel for the first time. His race horse was running in New Orleans and her father had taken her to bet a dollar on it, despite the fact that odds against the horse were a hundred to one. " 'Can that be our Uncle Gabriel?' " Miranda asked herself. " 'Is that Aunt Amy's handsome romantic beau? Is that the man who wrote the poem about our Aunt Amy?' " Uncle Gabriel, as she met him, "was a shabby fat man with bloodshot blue eyes, sad beaten eyes, and a big melancholy laugh, like a groan." His· language was coarse, and he was a drunkard. Even though his horse won the race and brought Miranda a hundred unexpected dollars — an event that had the making of a legend in itself — Miranda saw that victory had been purchased, not as a result of beauty, but at the price of agony; for the mare when seen close up "was bleeding at the nose," and "Her eyes were wild and her knees were trembling."

In legend, the past was beautiful or tragic. In art, it might be horrible and dangerous. In the present of Miranda's experience, it was ugly or merely commonplace. In the first section of "Old Mortality," we get the view of the past as seen through the eyes of the elders with their memories, not as it actually was, but as they wanted it to be. In section two, we get the view of it through the eyes of Miranda herself, who judges it merely as it is reflected in her present. By section three, Miranda is eighteen. She has eloped and married, but she is still struggling to understand her own relationship to the past. To her, her elopement seemed in the romantic tradition of Aunt Amy and Uncle Gabriel, although we soon learn that the marriage is, in fact, a failure. We meet her on the train coming home for the funeral of Uncle Gabriel. His body has been returned to lie beside Amy's, as though in a final attempt to justify the legend, even though he has married again, and (it is hinted) there are better and more real reasons for him to be buried beside his second wife, who had shared the greater part of his wandering, homeless, and meaningless existence. On the train, Miranda runs into Cousin Eva, also returning for the funeral, whose own life had been burdened by a constant comparison with the legend of Amy. While Amy was beautiful, thoughtless, impulsive, and daring, Cousin Eva had been homely, studious, and dedicated to high purposes. Amy had died and been preserved in the romantic legend; Eva had lived to develop a character and a reputation as a fighter for women's rights. In a sense, Cousin Eva's good works, too, were part of her own legend of homeliness and dedication. At bottom, Miranda finds her a bitter, prematurely aged woman; but it is Cousin Eva who provides her with a third view of the legend of Aunt Amy. She hints that it was nothing but sublimated sex that caused the young girls of Amy's day to behave as they did. " 'Those parties and dances were their market, a girl couldn't afford to miss out, there were always rivals waiting to cut the ground from under her. . . . It was just sex,' she said in despair; 'their minds dwelt on nothing else. They didn't call it that, it was all smothered under pretty names, but that's all it was, sex.' "

The older generation, then, had two ways of looking at the past:

the romantic way of Miranda's father and of other members of the family, and the "enlightened" way of Cousin Eva. Each way was different, and each was wrong. But the old did have something in common; they had their memories. Thus, when the train arrived at the station, it was Cousin Eva and Miranda's father who sat together in the back seat of the automobile and talked about old times; it was Miranda who was excluded from these memories, and who sat beside the driver in the front. Yet Miranda feels that she has a memory now and the beginning of her own legend — the legend of her elopement. Strangely enough, neither Cousin Eva nor her father will accept it. When reminded by Miranda of it, Cousin Eva says: "Shameful, shameful. . . . If you had been my child I should have brought you home and spanked you." Her father resented it. When he met her at the train, he showed it in his coldness.

"He had not forgiven her, she knew that. When would he? She could not guess, but she felt it would come of itself, without words and without acknowledgment on either side, for by the time it arrived neither of them would need to remember what had caused their division, nor why it had seemed so important. Surely old people cannot hold their grudges forever because the young want to live, too, she thought, in her arrogance, her pride. I will make my own mistakes, not yours; I cannot depend upon you beyond a certain point, why depend at all? There was something more beyond, but this was a first step to take, and she took it, walking in silence beside her elders who were no longer Cousin Eva and Father, since they had forgotten her presence, but had become Eva and Harry, who knew each other well, who were comfortable with each other, being contemporaries on equal terms, who occupied by right their place in this world, at the time of life to which they had arrived by paths familiar to them both. They need not play their roles of daughter, of son, to aged persons who did not understand them; nor of father and elderly female cousin to young persons whom they did not understand. They were precisely themselves; their eyes cleared, their voices relaxed into perfect naturalness, they need not weigh their words or calculate the effect of their manner. 'It is I who have no place,' thought Miranda. 'Where are my people and my own time?' "

Miranda is not merely a southern child, in southern history, reflected through the sensibility of a southern author, even though she is, partly at least, all these things. She is any child, anywhere, seeking definition of herself through her past and present. Katherine Anne Porter's southern history, whether legendary or actual, provides the concrete experience through which "historic memory" may function. Thus when she wrote the concluding sentence of "Old Mortality," she was expressing, not the dilemma of Miranda alone, but the dilemma of all who seek understanding. "At least I can know the truth about what happens to me," Miranda thinks, "making a promise to herself, in her hopefulness, her ignorance."

"Old Mortality" is an initiation story, a familiar type among the forms of fiction. Yet the initiation story itself falls into two kinds: one in which the character himself undergoes the initiation and grows into knowledge; another in which the character has only partial awareness of what his experience means, but through which the reader is brought to knowledge. "Old Mortality" is of the first kind. Miss Porter's other Miranda story in this volume, "Pale Horse, Pale Rider," is of the second.

"Pale Horse, Pale Rider" is set in the concluding days of World War I. Miranda is now twenty-four years of age and is working as a reporter on a western newspaper. She falls in love with Adam Barclay, a second lieutenant from Texas who has completed his training and is awaiting orders for shipment overseas. Events of the story concern their attempts to preserve sanity in the nightmare hysteria of war: the pressure to buy "Liberty Bonds," the enforced attentions of society ladies upon hospitalized soldiers, the confusion of identities amid the constant movement and uniformed dress, and, finally, the influenza epidemic that struck senselessly and without warning. Miranda contracts influenza. She recovers, but Adam has been infected by her, and when she wakes from delirium, she learns that he has died.

The parallel between Miss Porter's story and the Adam and Eve legend (the initial initiation) is interesting and meaningful. It recalls the author's use of Christian atonement to define and clarify the events of "Flowering Judas." As Eve was tempted to knowledge, and through her temptation brought about Adam's fall, so Miranda, who sees through the incompleteness and the pretense of the war orators, wishes to face the facts of life and death in wartime; but in so doing she brings about the death of her lover.

The use of the legend raises the story to a level above its specific time and place, so that it is really a story about how a person faces death (knowledge) anytime, anywhere. A second legend fortifies and enriches the first; it is Miranda's childhood fable of the Pale Horseman, the not wholly fearful rider who calls to escort her into the land of death, but to whom she says, "I'm not going with you this time." Death (evil) is a tempter, and one is more cleverly armed to resist him when one has knowledge (truth). Adam, who is presented as more innocent than Miranda (". . . there was no resentment or revolt in him. Pure, she thought, all the way through, flawless, complete, as the sacrificial lamb must be"), appears unaware of danger, though he is facing the most direct threat of death in war. Miranda's delirium in her illness is really a descent into a world of her own evil, a world that is represented during full consciousness by all the hypocrisies and cruelties of war and wartime. When she recovers, it is to discover that Adam, the personification of health and life, had ridden away with the

138

pale rider. But Miranda's descent is also a descent into knowledge (one of Miss Porter's later stories is titled "The Downward Path to Wisdom"); death and evil were facts to be faced and recognized for what they were, not hidden behind war slogans or the smooth phrases of the patriotic orators. Adam was gone, and he could not be summoned back, either by magic or by an act of will. All that was left was time ("the dead cold light of tomorrow"). The war, too, was a descent, and so the theme broadens and picks up all the specific ugly incidents connected with wartime hysteria. Adam's death was, of course, the final descent, and this fact suggests that love, which was the means by which Miranda is saved, was also a first step toward death.

"She said, 'I love you,' and stood up trembling, trying by the mere act of her will to bring him to sight before her. If I could call you up from the grave I would, she said, if I could see your ghost I would say, I.believe. . . . 'I believe,' she said aloud. 'Oh, let me see you once more.' The room was silent, empty, the shade was gone from it, struck away by the sudden violence of her rising and speaking aloud. She came to herself as if out of sleep. Oh, no, that is not the way, I must never do that, she warned herself."

Miranda's awareness of the finality of death is heightened by the irony of the fact that Adam met death, not on the battlefield, but through her, at a training camp on the very eve of the armistice.

The three stories of *Pale Horse, Pale Rider* appeared in print originally in 1937 and 1938. "Noon Wine" was published in *Story* in June 1937; "Old Mortality" and "Pale Horse, Pale Rider" both appeared in the *Southern Review*, in the spring and summer issues of 1938.

In Katherine Anne Porter's third collection, *The Leaning Tower and Other Stories*, which came out in 1944, there are six related stories dealing with Miranda and the background of Miranda's family, two unrelated stories, and the long title story, "The Leaning Tower," recounting the experiences of a young American in Berlin in the days just preceding World War II.

During the period between the appearance of *Pale Horse, Pale Rider* and that of *The Leaning Tower*, Katherine Anne Porter's literary reputation developed slowly and in a way unusual in American letters. Little was known about her personally, and legends accumulated. It was known that she was a beautiful woman and that she had been associated in some way with the film colony in Mexico, and it was rumored that she had been one of the early silent film heroines, perhaps a Mack Sennett bathing beauty. It was said that she moved often from place to place and that she carried with her a huge trunkful of unfinished material that she would not allow to be published because she was not convinced of its value. She was said to have engaged in a love affair with a Mexican revolutionary. She was thought to be ill with some fatal disease. Word did get around that she was working on a long novel and that she had projected a biography of Cotton Mather.

Most of these rumors were at best half-truths, as we now know, but they were circulated without malice, almost with affection, by young writers in search of a public image for an author whom they admired and whom each felt he had discovered for himself. Miss Porter had first gone to Mexico, she has told us, with her father. In 1931 she sailed from Mexico to Europe as the recipient of a Guggenheim fellowship. She was married to an American government official. During the middle thirties she lived in Baton Rouge, Louisiana, where her second husband was business manager of the *Southern Review*, and in New York and Connecticut, where she experienced near-poverty. In 1937 the Book-of-the-Month Club gave her a special award of $2500, "in consideration of her previous achievement and her promise for the future." She did not become a known personality on the national literary scene until after World War II, when she emerged as a favorite lecturer at writers' conferences and a visiting lecturer at several American universities. Of her career, she once said, "I went to Europe in 1931 an unknown and returned to find myself a celebrity."

The Leaning Tower and Other Stories is a more uneven collection than the two previous books. Six of the nine stories had previous publication in magazines, beginning in 1935 with the appearance of "The Circus" in the *Southern Review* and "The Grave" in the *Virginia Quarterly Review*. In 1936, "The Old Order" appeared in the *Southern Review* and was reprinted in the *Best American Short Stories* for that year. "A Day's Work" was printed in the *Nation* in 1940. "The Leaning Tower" appeared in the *Southern Review* in 1941.

Each of the related stories in *The Leaning Tower* gains something from the others, as this group of stories shapes into a kind of mythical corpus of the family. Some are slighter than others, little more than character sketches, justifying their presence more by what they contribute to the general legend than by what they themselves represent as stories. At their best, as in "The Grave" and "The Old Order," they rank among Miss Porter's most successful works. The two shorter stories not dealing with Miranda's background, "The Downward Path to Wisdom" and "A Day's Work," display the author at her near best; while the long story that closes the volume and supplies its title, "The Leaning Tower," comes the nearest to failure of anything that Katherine Anne Porter has published.

"The Source" is one of the slighter pieces, dealing as it does with the grandmother's annual visit to the farm in her late years, recounting little more than how she put the Negro quarters into shape again and how she took her customary ride on her old horse, the last of a long line she had owned; but it does evoke an excellent image of the willful and courageous old lady that we are to meet again in other stories of this group. The story is told from the point of view of the three grandchildren whom she had taken in after the death of their mother (Maria, Paul, and Miranda), undoubtedly with Miranda as recorder, although this is not insisted upon. We are told that "They loved their Grandmother; she was the only reality to them in a world that seemed otherwise without fixed authority or refuge, since their mother had died so early that only the eldest girl remembered her vaguely: just the same they felt that Grandmother was a tyrant, and they wished to be free of her." It is the ambivalence of the children toward the old lady that justifies calling so slight a piece a story at all. Miranda and her sister and brother come to recognize the difficulty of making a simple judgment, either of persons such as their grandmother or of the things these people do. This recognition is one stage of the complex initiation that Miranda undergoes in all of the stories in which she figures.

The second story, "The Witness," is similarly the sketch of a single character, again told from the children's point of view. It is an account of Uncle Jimbilly, the former slave, who carved miniature tombstones from blocks of wood to be placed over the graves of the children's pets. Uncle Jimbilly is firm in his simple, almost primitive, morality. From him the children hear exorbitant threats of punishment awaiting them for some accidental misdeed, listen to extravagant accounts of tortures practiced upon heathen unbelievers; but they come to know, by the very exaggeration of his accounts and threats, that Uncle Jimbilly's aim is not so much to evoke terror in them as it is to gain expression for his own subordinated emotions. Again the reader feels that he is looking in upon another colorful stage of childhood recognition.

"The Last Leaf" is the story of Aunt Nannie, wife of Uncle

Jimbilly, to whom she had been married "with truly royal policy, with an eye to the blood and family stability," in the days of slavery. Aunt Nannie had been the personal servant and lifelong companion of the children's grandmother. Now having survived the grandmother and resigned to her own end, old Nannie had asked for and been granted the use of a small cottage on the family place. The story ends with an incident between Nannie and Uncle Jimbilly, when the old man, from whom she had been separated for many years, attempts to move in with her. " 'I don' aim to pass my las' days waitin on no man,' " Nannie tells him; " 'I've served my time, I've done my do, and dat's all.' "

It is in "The Old Order" that we learn about Nannie's relationship to the grandmother. Here we are given the most complete background of Miranda's family available in any of the stories. The grandmother was, we are told, the great-granddaughter of "Kentucky's most famous pioneer" (Daniel Boone). She is the daughter "of a notably heroic captain in the War of 1812." Born Sophia Jane Gay in 1827, the grandmother had been given Nannie as a companion when her father bought her and her parents at the slavemarket in New Orleans while the grandmother was still a child. Nannie and Sophia Jane grew up together, and both were married the same year. Each had many children. Nannie served as wet nurse for Sophia Jane's first four children; then, when Nannie fell ill at the time of the fourth, Sophia Jane nursed the Negro baby along with her own. Grandmother had married a Macdonald, a second cousin, and in him she came later to see "all the faults she had most abhorred in her elder brother: lack of aim, failure to act at crises, a philosophic detachment from practical affairs, a tendency to set projects on foot and then leave them to perish or to be finished by someone else; and a profound conviction that everyone around him should be happy to wait upon him hand and foot." He died in middle age, leaving her with a family of nine living children that she moved from Kentucky to Louisiana, then to Texas. He left her "with all the responsibilities of a man but with none of the privileges."

Sophia Jane had three married sons in Texas at the time of her death, although one of her daughters-in-law had died at the birth of her third child (Miranda), and the grandmother had taken the children in as her own. She died at the home of another daughter-in-law, "after a day spent in helping the Mexican gardener . . . put the garden to rights," just after saying to her son and daughter-in-law how well she felt "in the bracing mountain air."

The authority of this story lies in the unnamed narrator, who is, we can be sure, Miranda, speaking again for the three surviving children of Sophia Jane's son Harry. Through it the author explores the family background, centering about the lifelong relationship between Sophia Jane and Aunt Nannie, the white mistress and the black slave, servant, and companion. It is in the importance given these events by the authority of the teller that the story gains its significance. As suggested earlier, the events in Miranda's (Katherine Anne Porter's) memories take on a mythical character that is part of the emotional education of the surviving grandchildren.

Another story, "The Circus," is the first story in this volume told clearly from Miranda's point of view, and it adds details to the background of family events depicted in "The Old Order," yet has the sharp focus of a story in which events are centered about a single character. These events take place during a time of family reunion, when Miranda, still very young, is allowed to accompany the family to a circus. Her grandmother, father, brother and sister, cousins and aunts are all present when Miranda becomes frightened at the sight of a clown performing on a high-wire and has to be taken home by a Negro servant. Meanwhile, she has felt intimations of evil in the eyes of the roughly dressed

144

little boys peering up from the dust beneath the women's skirts; she has measured appearance and reality in the close-up glimpse she got of a dwarf-clown, whom she had not thought could be human, let alone adult; she experiences remorse and compassion in the realization that she has spoiled the day for Dicey, the Negro servant. She tries banishing the terror by transforming it in her mind into childhood visions of romance; but when sleep comes, the terror, the terribly "real" image, returns, and she must turn again to the sympathetic and resigned patience of Dicey.

The most successful of these stories, apart from their place in the general mythical background, is the second Miranda story, "The Grave." It rivals in its completeness such earlier stories as "Flowering Judas," "Old Mortality," and "Pale Horse, Pale Rider." As in "The Circus," Miranda is a child, several years older, and the events are portrayed from the point of view of an adult narrator who is the grown Miranda. It is a story of sexual initiation but one in which the term "sex" has the widest possible implications. In it Miranda, "with her powerful social sense, which was like a fine set of antennae radiating from every pore of her skin," discovers her own feminine nature in the unearthing of a gold ring from the abandoned grave where her grandfather had once been buried. The grave, as title and as symbol, has multiple significance. Abandoned, it recalls the movement and the fluctuating fortunes of the family. As one of the several resting places of her grandparent, it reminds her of the whole family myth. When her brother Paul shoots a rabbit, and it is discovered that the animal contained a family of unborn young buried inside its body, this discovery conveyed to Miranda the puzzling and ambiguous nature of death and birth. There are three graves in the story. First, there is the actual grave, then there is the grave of the dead mother rabbit's body, and, finally, there is the grave of the mind, the repository of knowledge and memory, "heaped over by accumulated thousands of impressions," until the moment "when without warning, plain and clear in its true colors . . . [the childhood scene] leaped from its burial place" in the knowing mind of the mature Miranda.

"The Grave," which is the last of the Miranda stories in this volume, suggests the movement from innocence to knowledge, from the innocence of the dove (which is one of the objects found in the grave), to the gold ring (which is Miranda's sign for the luxury of her own femininity), to the dead mother rabbit (the mystery of birth and death). In the awareness of decay and death comes the important knowledge of the mature self, felt but not understood, recognized in its completeness only later when recalled by a similar sensual awareness.

"The Downard Path to Wisdom" (which does not appear to be related to the Miranda series, although there is the occurrence of the name Stephen, who was one of Miranda's uncles) is a more cruel, less subtle, initiation, this time of a young boy caught in the terrifying events of family discord. The child's "wisdom" becomes finally a protective awareness that he hates everyone with whom he has come into contact: his parents, his grandmother, his uncle, the servant, and even the little girl who had aroused in him the first stirring of masculine ego.

"A Day's Work" is a story of adults, set in an Irish-Catholic background similar to that of Miss Porter's earlier "The Cracked Looking-Glass." In this story, the author displays the same aversion to Catholic puritanism that she had earlier shown to midwestern Protestant puritanism in her story "That Tree." It is a "depression story," a pathetic tale of a man's attempt to preserve his male dignity in the face of the loss of his job and all prospects for the future and in the presence of a vindictive wife who hides her moral ugliness behind a public mask of pious self-righteousness. It is a story of human failure, complex in its suggestion of causes, humorous in many of its incidents, caustic in its criticism of aspects of society and human character, tough in its denial of hope; yet compassionate in its over-all tone and aim.

In one way or another, all these short stories in *The Leaning Tower* represent Katherine Anne Porter at her usual high level of competence. However, in the title story, "The Leaning Tower," her sensitivity appears to have failed her. The story is remarkable primarily for its difference from the stories that had come before. Where the central symbolism of "Flowering Judas" and "The Grave" had been functionally and unobtrusively integrated with the events, the symbol of the tawdry replica of the Leaning Tower of Pisa that appears in this work seems almost willfully applied. Where the righteous anger of Miranda against the vulgar pressures of the war had permeated the telling of "Pale Horse, Pale Rider," a similar emotion in "The Leaning Tower" is dissipated by its focus upon objects incapable of containing it. Where the characters of "Noon Wine" emerged through the rendering of specific detail into the warmth of true humanity, the characters in this story remain wooden figures, almost caricatures. Where the events of Miranda's coming of age in "Old Mortality" were suffused with the glow of girlish memory and illuminated by the background family myth, the incidents in Berlin in the early thirties that take place in "The Leaning Tower" are presented through the inadequate mind of a young American visitor whose memories, if they may be called that, come indirectly and second-hand.

There is, perhaps, an explanation for the failure of this story. It was written in the period just preceding our entry into World War II, years filled with such events as the Spanish Civil War, the German invasion of Poland, and the fall of France, yet the story is set almost ten years earlier, in the Germany barely preceding the rise of Hitler; thus, the author was writing under the impulse of emotions aroused by events at the time of composition, which must have clouded (if not falsified) memories of the original events. Even so, such intense awareness as we are accustomed to in Katherine Anne Porter might have succeeded in transcending these limitations had she not chosen to tell the story through the eyes of a young man, attributing to him insights that seem more appropriate to a Miranda than to the person he was intended to be. His character remains in doubt; therefore, he becomes a doubtful authority for the other characters and events that are rendered through him. Even the fact that he comes from western Texas, which would appear to ally him with the background myth of Miranda and her family, does little to convince us of his worthiness for the difficult role the author has assigned him.

The story itself is a simple one. Charles Upton, having heard in his childhood of the wonders of Berlin from one of his friends, has come from America to Germany in the winter of 1931 to study art. Moving from a dreary hotel into a rooming house run by a middle-aged Viennese woman, Charles becomes acquainted with the woman's three other lodgers: Hans von Gehring, a Heidelberg student who is in Berlin to have an infected dueling scar treated; Tadeusz Mey, a Polish pianist; and Otto Bussen, a peasant-born student of mathematics from the University of Berlin. A good deal of the story is made up of talk among the four roomers, much of it about various nationalities and classes in their different backgrounds. It all ends in a New Year's Eve drinking party at a small restaurant run by two friends of Otto, where the mixture of politics, sex, *Gemütlichkeit*, and mutual distrust appears intended to render the dislocated world of Germany in the 1930's and to foreshadow the violent events to come. Unlike other Katherine Anne Porter stories, the talk is not good enough, the incidents too spare to carry such implications, and so the story falls back upon its title image, the small replica of the Tower of Pisa that Charles

148

awkwardly knocks off its pedestal on his first visit to the pension. The ornament is returned the night of the party, imperfectly mended, to serve as symbol for the futile attempts of man to hold onto memories and dreams, perhaps, in its mending, symbolic of the fate of German society between the two wars. But the symbol is imperfectly integrated with the events; it remains a symbol, shedding its own single light, taking on no added dimensions from the action or the characters in the story.

Following the publication of *The Leaning Tower* in 1944, eighteen years were to elapse before the appearance of any more fiction by Katherine Anne Porter in book form. In 1962, her long-awaited novel (excerpts from which had appeared in magazines over the years) was published under the title *Ship of Fools*. It had an immediate critical success, which was not unusual; what was unusual was its tremendous commercial success, gaining for its author not only the financial security that had eluded her for forty years, but removing from her the onus of being known primarily as "a writer's writer."

The setting of *Ship of Fools* is a German vessel sailing from Veracruz, Mexico, to Bremerhaven, Germany, in 1931, thus paralleling the author's first voyage to Europe after winning a Guggenheim Foundation fellowship. Miss Porter's first title was to have been *The Promised Land.* It was then changed to *No Safe Harbour* and was identified as such in the excerpts that began appearing in periodicals in 1944 and continued almost to the date of publication. Its final title, Miss Porter tells us in a prefatory note, was taken from a moral allegory by Sebastian Brant, *Das Narrenschiff,* published in Latin as *Stultifera Navis* in 1494. Miss Porter's *Ship of Fools* is also an allegory. It might be called "a moral allegory for our time," or, perhaps more accurately reflecting the present concerns, "an existentialist fable." The ship is called *Vera* (truth), and the most general contrast represented in its passengers and crew (who are the characters of the novel) is a familiar one from the author's short fiction: a juxtaposition of passionate, indolent, irresponsible Latins with the cold, calculating, and self-righteous Nordics. These extremes not only represent a majority of the passengers and crew, but also suggest the beginning of the voyage in Mexico and its ending in Germany. Adding the necessary complexity are the characters that fall between these extremes: an Indian nursemaid, four Americans, a family of Swiss, a Mexican political agitator, a Basque, a Swede, and six Cuban medical students on their way to France. As a voyage, events may be likened to Dante's progress in *The Divine Comedy*, not in any specific way, but in the sense that Katherine Anne Porter, in this novel, is concerned with arriving at a sense of felicity for our time in much the way that Dante was for his. *Ship of Fools* is a comedy for today in the same high sense that Dante used the term in the fourteenth century.

The word "fool," as used by Miss Porter in her title, contains a double irony. In one sense she is using it as Brant must have used it, as "God's fool," suggesting man's foolishness as compared to God's wisdom. Similarly, the foolishness of the acts committed aboard ship resemble the absurdities of human action as portrayed by modern existentialism. Whether one takes the traditional Christian view of man as fool or the modern atheistic view of man as absurd, one comes from either with a feeling that truth is being expressed, only the framework has been altered. In each case man is viewed as a pathetic creature, struggling in one instance to overcome his limitations and approach God's province, in the other to organize the actions of his life around an impossible dream. In each case, he is more to be pitied than condemned.

Appropriate to this ideological point of view, Miss Porter has chosen in *Ship of Fools* to see the action from the position of an omniscient narrator (something unusual, and considered particu-

larly risky, in our time). The authorial eye is located mostly away
from and above the characters, effaced in the modern manner, but
capable upon occasion of moving into their very minds to provide
insights into their often warped, sometimes tender, occasionally
right ways of thinking. Necessary to this view is a strong sense of
authorial responsibility, and Miss Porter gains this, one feels, by
the extreme honesty and objectivity of her vision. She has, as she
has been reported to have said to a friend, not "loaded the dice"
against her characters. "I would not take sides," she said. "I was
on everybody's side."

It might be objected that to be "on everybody's side" is to be
on no side, but the attitude behind such a statement illuminates
what has been constant in Katherine Anne Porter's work: a sense
of understanding based on a firm belief in the imperfectibility of
man, but an understanding held with compassion. Understanding
without compassion might have led to bitterness, cynicism, even
arrogance; compassion without understanding could easily have
led to sentimentality.

The action of *Ship of Fools* is made up of three sections: Part I,
Embarkation; Part II, High Sea; Part III, The Harbors. Each is
prefaced with an epigram. The first is a quotation from Baude-
laire: "*Quand partons-nous vers le bonheur?*" (When do you sail
for happiness?); the second is from a song by Brahms: "*Kein Haus,
Keine Heimat*" (No House, No Home); the third is from Saint
Paul: "For here have we no continuing city . . ." Glenway Wescott has warned the reader not to put too much emphasis upon
Miss Porter's allegorical intentions. To disregard them, however,
would be more serious, particularly the implications of the section
headings: man persists in setting sail for happiness, only to find
himself, after all, houseless and homeless, to become aware at last
that his city is doomed. It is significant that Miss Porter gives only
the first clause of Paul's advice to the Hebrews. The complete

verse reads: "For here have we no continuing city, but we seek one to come." To have quoted the verse entire would have been to acknowledge the hopes and consolation of orthodox Christianity. Miss Porter's consolation is of another sort, not un-Christian, but certainly secular. Like Miranda in "Pale Horse, Pale Rider," she is unable to invoke the mystery: "Oh, no, that is not the way, I must never do that, she warned herself." As with Miranda, the reality lies only in "the dazed silence that follows the ceasing of the heavy guns; noiseless houses with the shades drawn, empty streets, the dead cold light of tomorrow." Yet the recurring hope ("Now there would be time for everything"), the recurring struggle.

Ship of Fools is a story of forlorn hope and recurring struggle. In Part I we become acquainted with the various characters, recognize their relations to each other, necessary or personal, as groups and nationalities; we come to sense their very real and pathetic isolation. In Part II, which has more than half the book's pages, the major events occur; and this might be called The Wasteland Section (*Kein Haus, Keine Heimat*), containing as it does the torment of the passengers in steerage, the struggle for detachment or for involvement of the passengers and ship's officers above, their regimented hates and their pathetic attempts to love. In Part III, as the ship nears its destination, the effects of the preceding events begin to tell. A bacchanalian fiesta put on by a group of Spanish dancers in honor of the captain brings out all the hidden fears, guilts, and repressions of the participants, followed by the usual remorse and readjustment in relationships.

We see the passengers of the ship *Vera* first as they assemble for boarding in the Mexican port town of Veracruz. We see them through the eyes of the townspeople, who, the author tells us, "live as initiates in local custom"; we see them from the point of view of the author, against a background of "alternate violence and lethargy"; they remain at a distance, a cosmopolitan group fleeing Mexico, or being deported, or merely departing on some private errand; we watch them undergo the many little inconveniences of leaving a foreign port, see them "emerging from the mildewed dimness of the customs sheds, blinking their eyes against the blinding sunlight," all having "the look of invalids crawling into hospital on their last legs."

The cast of characters is necessarily large. Among the passengers and crew in the upper class, the Germans appear in greatest number. They include Frau Rittersdorf, whose husband died in the war and who keeps a journal; Frau Otto Schmitt, recently widowed, accompanying her husband's remains back to the fatherland; Herr Siegfried Rieber, publisher of a ladies' garment trade magazine; Fräulein Lizzi Spöckenkieker, who is said to own three ladies' dress shops; Herr Karl Glocken, a hunchback; Herr Wilhelm Freytag, who works for an oil company, is married to a Jewess, and is returning to Germany to fetch his wife and her mother back to Mexico; Herr Julius Löwenthal, a Jewish manufacturer and salesman of Catholic religious articles; and the following groups: Herr Professor Hutten, his wife, and their bulldog Bébé; Herr Karl Baumgartner, his wife, and son Hans; Herr Wilibald Graf, a dying man in a wheelchair, who is accompanied by his nephew and attendant, Johann.

The second largest group are the Spaniards and Mexicans. The Spaniards include a singing and dancing group, made up of four men and four women, along with the two children, twins, of one of the couples; and La Condesa, who is called a "déclassée noblewoman who has lived many years in Cuba," but is now being deported as a political undesirable to Tenerife. The Mexicans include the wife of an attaché to the Mexican embassy in Paris, her infant child, and an Indian nurse; two Catholic priests; and a bride and groom going on a honeymoon to Spain.

Other nationals included are four Americans: William **Denny,**
a young Texas engineer; Mary Treadwell, a forty-five-year-old
divorcée; and an unmarried couple, David Scott and Jenny **Brown,**
traveling together to Europe. There is a Swiss family, Herr Hein-
rich Lutz, his wife, and their adolescent daughter. There is a
Swede, Arne Hansen. There is a group of six medical students
from Cuba. The occupants of the steerage are almost nine hundred
Spanish workmen being deported from Cuba after the failure of
the Cuban sugar crop.

It is difficult to say who are the principal characters in the events
of the novel. Obviously Miss Porter has attempted to give each
his share in the action. Among the ship's personnel, the doctor
and the captain appear most prominent. Captain Thiele is the
embodiment of Teutonic authority, firm, unyielding, formal, and
wrongheaded. Dr. Schumann represents, within the German *Kul-
tur*, almost exactly the opposite. He is warm and compassionate,
although somewhat impersonal; he is a devout Bavarian Catholic
with a heart condition that might cause death at any moment,
suffering too from guilt at his inability to do more than supply
drugs for the patient for whom he would do most, La Condesa.
Among the passengers, relations are established between Arne
Hansen, trapped in his masculine, but sterile, lust, and Amparo,
the Spanish dancer-prostitute; between Jenny Brown, the American companion of David Scott, and Wilhelm Freytag, who has a
Jewish wife in Germany; between Johann, the nephew of Wilibald Graf, and Concha, another of the Spanish women, who effects Johann's sexual initiation, not without tenderness, but for
a price; between William Denny, a carbuncular young American,
and Pastora, a third Spanish dancer, who provide a study in awk-
wardness and frustration; and, finally, there is the highly comic
affair between Siegfried Rieber and Lizzi Spöckenkieker that ends
in estrangement after weeks of teasing and attempted conquest.

The one character among the voyagers who chooses isolation, as protection against personal pain and disgust, is Julius Löwenthal, the Jew. The single relationship that is evoked but rendered with slight detail is that of the Mexican newlyweds, who appear in their momentary bliss as entirely sufficient unto themselves.

The steerage passengers are seen generally only as a group, viewed from above by the first-class passengers; but from them do emerge two figures of significance to the novel. One is a Basque, known only as Echegaray, who carves wooden figures with a pen-knife and who is drowned when he jumps overboard to save the Huttens' bulldog, cast into the sea by the Spanish twins. The other is an unnamed political agitator who makes fun of the re-ligious observances among the steerage passengers and is struck over the head with a wrench by one of them after he had laughed during the services for Echegaray.

The significance of these two figures, like the significance of the Mexican honeymooners, lies in the very vagueness with which the author presents them, almost without name, with only the brief and fatal accident to define the one, with only his political position and his wound to define the other. Both are, in a sense, savior figures, reminiscent of Miss Porter's use of such figures in "Flowering Judas," but presented with less insistence in the novel than in the short story. Also, an additional level of significance is added in the case of the Basque, who, if he is a crucified Christ in his plunge into the sea and dies ironically in an attempt to save an aged and repulsive bulldog, is also a "creator," whose artistry is presented as more genuine than that of the American couple in the upper class who call themselves artists. The agitator, as mod-ern savior, is allied to La Condesa (the political exile), who, like Eugenio of "Flowering Judas," can gain peace only in the sleepy world of drugs administered by Dr. Schumann. The ship's doctor, like Laura, serves the cause of betrayal, and so is inhibited from meaningful action.

The similarity of these themes in the novel and in the short story suggests that the themes of *Ship of Fools* may not be too different from themes present in the earlier works and that the principal differences lie in the necessary richness of the longer work and in the technical excellence that integrates and unifies so diverse a body of material. We can see in the puritanical Protestantism of the German society on the ship a resemblance to the attitude of Miriam, the midwestern schoolteacher wife of the artist-turned-journalist of "That Tree," where self-righteous self-assurance appears to triumph over the more leisurely, apparently indolent, ambitions of the poet. We can see in the cheerful amorality of the Spanish dancers a resemblance to María Rosa and Juan Villegas in "María Concepción." There is a hint of María Concepción herself in the brief appearance of the Indian nurse for Señora de Ortega's infant on board the ship. The vacillations and misunderstandings of Jenny Brown and David Scott are reminiscent of the husband-wife relationship in "Rope." Ric and Rac, the Spanish twins of the novel, have no counterparts in the short stories, but they do, nevertheless, represent what Miranda reported as her grandmother's conviction in "The Old Order," that children were born in evil, thus were to a degree the embodiment of it in its most simple and direct form.

Incidents of special importance in the novel include the banishing of Herr Freytag from the captain's table because it is learned that he has married a Jew, the throwing overboard of Frau Hutten's bulldog (which resulted in the death and burial of Echegaray), the riot in the steerage that followed the funeral of the drowned Basque, the posting on the bulletin board of "truth notes" concerning the various passengers by the Cuban students, the meetings of Dr. Schumann and La Condesa, and, finally, the various events preceding, during, and following the fiesta put on in honor of the captain by the Spanish dancing troupe. These would include the stopover at Santa Cruz, where the Spaniards steal the tawdry prizes to be given away at the party; the fight between Herr Rieber and Arne Hansen; the recognition of special qualities of character by Frau Rittersdorf and Mary Treadwell; the quarrel and reconciliation of the Baumgartners; the rebellion of Johann against Herr Graf that leads to his going to Concha; the humiliating beating of William Denny; and the ironic confrontation between the proper Prussian captain and the easygoing members of the Spanish dancing group.

There is little "story," in the conventional sense, in *Ship of Fools*. Perhaps the nearest thing to it is the affair between Jenny Brown and David Scott, because the fluctuations of love and hate, or even like and dislike, are acted out during the voyage, and their relationship had a prior origin in Mexico and presumably will have a future in Europe. There is a sense, however, in which each character represents a little "story" of his own, and each thread of plot is intertwined with others to form the over-all pattern of the book. We come to know each character briefly at a moment that constitutes for most of them a particular crisis or alteration of attitude. But the individual stories are not resolved; rather, what serves for resolution resides in the remarkable ability of the author to make the total composition come alive, both in its rendering of the individual characters and in its evoking a kind of over-all theme, or meaning. Yet it is less a "meaning," in the sense of reducible paraphrase, than it is an attitude subtly conveyed.

Perhaps the nearest Katherine Anne Porter comes to expressing what the story is about is when she has Mary Treadwell interpret the effusive show of manners between Herr and Frau Baumgartner at the end of the voyage (significantly Miss Porter put the major portion of the passage in italics): "What they were saying to each other was only, *Love me, love me in spite of all! Whether or not I love you, whether I am fit to love, whether you are able to love, even if there is no such thing as love, love me!*" Where had the trouble come from? Mrs. Treadwell considers her own case: ". . . what had it been but the childish refusal to admit and accept on some term or other the difference between what one hoped was true and what one discovers to be the mere laws of the human condition?" *The mere laws of the human condition!* This is skepticism, and if we need a name to distinguish Miss Porter's special attitude, perhaps "skepticism" will do. The only truth available to man lies in "the human condition."

It is the human condition that is represented aboard the *Vera*. But that condition varies from country to country and race to race; it differs even in individuals. The one thing we can know is that the dream, whether it be of race superiority or of the perfect relation between man and woman, will never be achieved. Man becomes "foolish," in that quasi-religious sense, when he pursues it; but pursue it he will, because that, too, is part of "the human condition." The novel says it better than this, because the skill of the author proved equal to the larger and more complicated intentions that the book itself embodies.

The critical reception of *Ship of Fools* when it first appeared was almost unanimously enthusiastic. What dissent occurred concerned itself with three features of the novel: the rendering of the characters, the pessimism of the theme, and what some critics considered an absence of suspense. Stanley Kauffmann, a reviewer for the *New Republic*, wrote: "The characters are well perceived and described, but we know all that Miss Porter can say about them after the third or fourth of their episodes." Granville Hicks, writing for the *Saturday Review*, said: "There is in [the novel], so far as I can see, no sense of human possibility. Although we have known her people uncommonly well, we watch unconcerned as, in the curiously muted ending, they drift away from us." The *New Yorker* review by Howard Moss complained that *Ship of Fools* was "devoid of one of the excitements of realistic fiction. The reader is never given that special satisfaction of the drama of design, in which the strings having come unwound, are ultimately tied together in a knot. Miss Porter scorns patness and falseness, but by the very choice of her method, she also lets go of suspense."

It is difficult to answer the charge of dullness or of inadequate character portrayal except by counter-assertion. One can point to the novel's tremendous popular success, but Theodore Solotaroff, writing in *Commentary*, dismisses this explanation by calling the novel the long awaited work of a beloved figure — the "Eleanor Roosevelt" of letters. In a curiously vituperative article, he characterizes *Ship of Fools* as "massive, unexciting, and saturnine." Such charges are reminiscent of the response made to another American work a century earlier, when one critic called *Moby Dick* ". . . trash, belonging to the worst school of Bedlam literature." Many considered Melville's novel dull, its action clogged by extraneous matter.

There is, however, a key to Miss Porter's method — a key that has long since opened and preserved the treasures of Herman Melville's masterpiece. This method is pointed out most clearly by Eric Auerbach in his critical volume *Mimesis*. Auerbach discusses a puzzling quality of epic narrative, what he calls the retarding principle and what Goethe characterized as "the retarding element appropriate to Homeric epic." Such retardation consisted in the breaking off of a dramatic incident in order to shift and explore the background character of the event. It was, Auerbach maintains, "In dire opposition to the element of suspense." Miss Porter utilizes this retarding principle in the construction of her comic-epic, much as it was used by Dante in *The Divine Comedy*, for the purposes of deepening and enriching her narrative; and these are the qualities that impressed most critics of the novel.

The charge that *Ship of Fools* shows little "sense of human possibility" reminds us of early charges made against another significant American work, *The Waste Land* of T. S. Eliot. As does Eliot in his poem, Miss Porter portrays much of modern life as sterile and impotent, but she also suggests, as does Eliot, the fructifying possibilities of love. She is less extreme than Jean-Paul Sartre in her rendering of what is disgusting and absurd in human life, nearer to Albert Camus in her attitude of detached observation; superior, perhaps, to either in the over-all sense of compassion that finally pervades her work.

In addition to *Ship of Fools* and her three volumes of short fiction, Katherine Anne Porter has written magazine articles, book reviews, introductions to books by other authors, and she has engaged in various symposia on the problems of the writer and the craft of writing. A collection of such writing appeared in 1952, titled *The Days Before*. In it she lists her nonfiction under three headings: critical writings, personal and particular pieces, and articles dealing with Mexico.

As a literary critic, Miss Porter appears more allied to the European method of the personal essay than to any of the current American fashions, perhaps because of the sense of private awareness that she conveys. Yet her discussions of authors as various as Thomas Hardy, Willa Cather, and Katherine Mansfield consist of more than personal insight. Her own standards for writing come forth clearly in her reply to questions asked her in a symposium in 1939. She had been asked whether Henry James or Walt Whitman had the most relevancy "to the present and future of American writing." She replied: "Henry James and Walt Whitman are relevant to the past and present of American literature or of any other literature"; but, she went on, "For myself I choose James, holding as I do with the conscious, disciplined artist, the serious expert against the expansive, indiscriminately 'cosmic' sort."

Katherine Anne Porter is a major figure in what has become a literary revival in American letters in the twentieth century. If the first American Renaissance (so named by F. O. Matthiessen) occurred in the mid-nineteenth century with the writings of Emerson, Thoreau, Whitman, Hawthorne, Melville, James, and Twain, the second would include such contemporaries of Miss Porter as Theodore Dreiser, Ezra Pound, T. S. Eliot, Sherwood Anderson, Robert Frost, Wallace Stevens, William Carlos Williams, Hart Crane, Ernest Hemingway, F. Scott Fitzgerald, William Faulkner, and John Steinbeck.

Strictly speaking, the first "renaissance" was less a rebirth than it was a birth — a coming of age in American letters; it was not a movement in literature, but, rather, an upsurge of creative power. The same might be said of what was truly a "renaissance" in the twentieth century. In neither case did the achieving writers represent a common concept either of American attitudes or of an American craft. There is a sense in which Hawthorne and Melville may be seen as motivated, at least in part, by a spirit of rebellion against certain contemporary attitudes, notably those of the so-called transcendentalists. Similarly, there is a sense in which such authors as Thoreau and Whitman (in some respects Twain) may be seen as a literary continuation of Emersonian transcendentalism.

In Miss Porter's generation, the dichotomy remained. Sherwood Anderson, Ernest Hemingway, and John Steinbeck, among the prose writers, continue a tradition that would appear to have been first given shape in Emerson, carried on with some alteration in the writings of Mark Twain and Stephen Crane. On the other hand, F. Scott Fitzgerald and (to a lesser extent) William Faulkner and Katherine Anne Porter derive from Hawthorne, Melville, and James. What this means is that in our literary traditions a split between two somewhat contrary attitudes still prevails and that Katherine Anne Porter's preference, as she herself makes clear with the necessary qualifications, remains with what we might call the "ameliorists" — those writers who would not make so severe a break with the traditions and ideas of Europe as was implicit in the writings of Emerson, Whitman, and Twain.

Speaking generally upon what is a complex subject, we might also say that such southern contemporaries of Miss Porter as William Faulkner, Allen Tate, John Crowe Ransom, Caroline Gordon, and Robert Penn Warren fall into this classification, and Katherine Anne Porter remains one with her region. In some respects she is even more pure in her devotion to craft, more austere in her opposition to what might be called "leveling" or "popularizing" tendencies than any other American writer since Henry James.

James has obviously been Miss Porter's model as craftsman, but she speaks often of her early attraction to a very different kind of writer, Laurence Sterne, in whose eighteenth-century manner she had steeped herself. Among women writers, she admired Katherine Mansfield and disliked Gertrude Stein. What she admired in Mansfield was "a certain grim, quiet ruthlessness of judgment, an unsparing and sometimes cruel eye, a natural malicious wit, and intelligent humor"; what she disliked in Gertrude Stein was the absence of moral, intellectual, and aesthetic judgment. It is true, perhaps, that what Katherine Anne Porter liked best in others were qualities nearest to her own, but such preferences were based less on personal prejudice than they were on the same tough, intellectual honesty that governed her own writing.

Katherine Anne Porter at the age of seventy-two announced

that she had three more books to write. With the completion of *Ship of Fools*, additional short stories by Miss Porter began to appear in American magazines. One of these, "St. Augustine and the Bullfights," has been called by Glenway Wescott a masterpiece; while another, "Holiday," won the O. Henry Awards first prize for 1962. Perhaps her next book will be another collection of short stories, hopefully with a further filling out of the Miranda series. It could be another novel, although this appears unlikely. With financial security assured for the first time in her long career, Miss Porter returned to Europe, ostensibly to complete her long-announced book on Cotton Mather.

Selected Bibliography

Principal Works of Katherine Anne Porter

Flowering Judas and Other Stories. New York: Harcourt, Brace, 1930 (limited edition).
Katherine Anne Porter's French Song Book. Paris: Harrison, 1933.
Hacienda. New York: Harrison, 1934.
Flowering Judas and Other Stories. New York: Harcourt, Brace, 1935.
Noon Wine. Detroit: Schuman's, 1937.
Pale Horse, Pale Rider: Three Short Novels. New York: Harcourt, Brace, 1939.
The Leaning Tower and Other Stories. New York: Harcourt, Brace, 1944.
The Days Before. New York: Harcourt, Brace, 1952.
Ship of Fools. Boston: Little, Brown, 1962.

Bibliographies

Schwartz, Edward. *Katherine Anne Porter: A Critical Bibliography* (with an introduction by Robert Penn Warren). New York: New York Public Library, 1953.
Sylvester, William A. "Selected and Critical Bibliography of the Uncollected Works of Katherine Anne Porter," *Bulletin of Bibliography*, 19:36 (January 1947).

Critical Studies

Allen, Charles G. "Katherine Anne Porter: Psychology as Art," *Southwest Review*, 41:223–30 (Summer 1956).
Block, Maxine, ed. *Current Biography*. New York: H. W. Wilson, 1940. (Portrait.)
Current-Garcia, E., and W. R. Patrick. "The Short Story in America," *American Short Stories*. New York: Scott, Foresman, 1952. Pp. xliii, lxi.
Hartley, Lodowick. "Katherine Anne Porter," *Sewanee Review*, 48:206–16 (April 1940).
Hartley, Lodowick and George Core, eds. *Katherine Anne Porter: A Critical Symposium*. Athens: University of Georgia Press, 1969.
Hendrick, George. *Katherine Anne Porter*. New York: Twayne Publishers, 1965.

Herbst, Josephine. "Miss Porter and Miss Stein," *Partisan Review*, 15:568–72 (May 1948).

Johnson, J. W. "Another Look at Katherine Anne Porter," *Virginia Quarterly Review*, 36:598–613 (Fall 1960).

Kaplan, Charles. "True Witness: Katherine Anne Porter," *Colorado Quarterly*, 7:319–27 (Winter 1959).

Marshall, Margaret. "Writers in the Wilderness: Katherine Anne Porter," *Nation*, 150:473–75 (April 13, 1940).

Mooney, Harry John, Jr. *The Fiction and Criticism of Katherine Anne Porter.* Pittsburgh: University of Pittsburgh Press, 1957.

Nance, William L. *Katherine Anne Porter and the Art of Rejection.* Chapel Hill: University of North Carolina Press, 1964.

Poss, S. A. "Variations on a Theme in Four Stories of Katherine Anne Porter," *Twentieth Century Literature*, 4:21–29 (April–July 1958).

Schorer, Mark. "Biographia Literaria," *New Republic*, 127:18–19 (November 10, 1952).

Schwartz, Edward. "The Way of Dissent: Katherine Anne Porter's Critical Position," *Western Humanities Review*, 8:119–30 (Spring 1954).

Voss. Arthur. *The American Short Story.* Norman: University of Oklahoma Press, 1973.

Warren, Robert Penn. "Katherine Anne Porter (Irony with a Center)," *Kenyon Review*, 4:29–42 (Winter 1942).

———. "Uncorrupted Consciousness: The Stories of Katherine Anne Porter," *Yale Review*, 55:280–90 (Winter 1966).

Wescott, Glenway. "Katherine Anne Porter: The Making of a Novel," *Atlantic*, 209:43–49 (April 1962).

West, Ray B., Jr. "Katherine Anne Porter: Symbol and Theme in 'Flowering Judas,'" *Accent*, 7:182–87 (Spring 1947).

———. "Katherine Anne Porter and 'Historic Memory,'" *Hopkins Review*, 6:16–27 (Fall 1952).

———. *The Short Story in America.* Chicago: Regnery, 1952. Pp. 72–76.

Wilson, Edmund. "Katherine Anne Porter," *New Yorker*, 20:72–75 (September 30, 1944).

Young, Vernon A. "The Art of Katherine Anne Porter," *New Mexico Quarterly*, 15:326–41 (Autumn 1945).

J. A. BRYANT, JR.

Eudora Welty

Eudora Welty was born in 1909 in Jackson, Mississippi. She went to school there; and there, after making excursions to Wisconsin (for an A.B. degree) and to New York (for courses in advertising at Columbia), she returned to live and do her work. Some people in the South might not think of her as being entirely southern. Her father came from Ohio, never a part of the South; and her mother was a native of West Virginia, which is only geographically southern. Once when she was just beginning to be known, she complained playfully to a young reporter that the only thing that had made her suffer as a child was the stigma of having a Yankee for a father. She was probably recognizing that the reporter was himself no southerner and would be amused to hear a person from Mississippi say something like that, but she was probably also describing a sting that once had been real. Now by repeated choice Eudora Welty has confirmed the mode of life that accident of birth bestowed; and if choice of residence has anything to do with what one is, she is, by virtue of a place chosen many times, as southern as Mississippi soil itself.

Her conspicuous attachment to a region does not, however, mean that she accepts the label "regionalist." "Place," she has written in her essay "Place in Fiction" (1956), "is one of the lesser angels that watch over the racing hand of fiction." It is an angel like character, plot, and the rest, but a small angel, subservient to feeling, who wears the crown, "soars highest of them all and rightly relegates place into the shade." The importance of place is that an author's feelings tend to be associated with it; thus place serves naturally as a repository for feelings that must even-

166

tually inhabit the novel taking shape in his head. Respect for place, moreover, makes an author pay attention to detail, makes him work harder to portray things with clarity, and finally prepares him to see through things as well. Of Faulkner's "Spotted Horses" Miss Welty has written: ". . . in all that shining fidelity to place lies the heart and secret of this tale's comic glory." In such faithfulness lies at least part, certainly, of the secret of her own wonderfully effective stories. Yet Eudora Welty's master is always fiction itself, never Mississippi.

For a full account of Eudora Welty's life down to 1962 the reader may consult Ruth M. Vande Kieft's book-length essay. Even a brief sketch, however, should mention that she spent two years as a student at Mississippi State College for Women (Columbus) before going north to take her degree and that her early interests were painting and photography. Miss Welty's career as a writer began formally in June of 1936 with the publication of "Death of a Traveling Salesman" in a little magazine called *Manuscript*, edited by John Rood. Since then her stories have appeared in a variety of magazines, from the *Southern Review* to the *New Yorker*. They have been anthologized, commented upon, translated into numerous languages including Burmese and Japanese, and collected in four volumes, *A Curtain of Green* (1941), *The Wide Net* (1943), *The Golden Apples* (1949), and *The Bride of the Innisfallen* (1955). She has also published, in addition to several uncollected pieces, three novels, *The Robber Bridegroom* (1942), *Delta Wedding* (1946), and *The Ponder Heart* (1954), a small collection of critical essays, *Three Papers on Fiction* (1962), and a children's story, *The Shoe Bird* (1964). Many honors have come to her, among them two first prizes in the O. Henry Memorial Contest, a Guggenheim Fellowship, election to the National Institute of Arts and Letters, the William Dean Howells Medal of the Academy of Arts and Letters, appointment as Honorary Consultant of the Library of Congress, and several honorary degrees. She has taught or lectured at many institutions in this country and at Cambridge University in England.

From the first her stories attracted the attention of discriminating readers. Among her earliest admirers was Ford Madox Ford, who tried diligently during the last year of his life to find a publisher for her collected stories. Her most effective champions, however, were the people associated with the *Southern Review* in nearby Baton Rouge: Albert Erskine, who had discovered her for the *Review*; Robert Penn Warren, who became one of her first real critics; and Katherine Anne Porter, who encouraged her and wrote an introduction to the volume when it finally appeared. The wide range of the stories in *A Curtain of Green* strongly suggested that the author had been conducting a series of experiments in fiction. The setting for most of the stories was small-town or rural Mississippi, but the characters included murderers, psychotics, suicides, deaf-mutes, the mentally retarded, the senile, and a host of people whom southern gentility used to refer to as "common." There were enough such characters, in fact, to prompt metropolitan reviewers to use terms like "Gothic," "grotesque," and "caricature" and to make superficial comparisons with Faulkner and Poe. As Miss Porter has observed, however, Eudora Welty's caricatures are "but individuals exactly and clearly presented." If some characters in her stories are unsavory, they are nevertheless real; and like other forms of truth, they properly evoke a mixed response.

One of the stories, "A Memory," both illustrates and produces that response. The narrator is a young girl, sensitive and naively austere, who tells how her daydreams on a city beach were interrupted by the appearance of a disquieting group of bathers — a man, two women, and two boys, "brown and roughened, but not foreigners." The sight of these well-meaning but ugly people cavorting on a public beach erases from the girl's mind all thoughts of the boy she loves, the subject of her morning reverie; and the disorder the people leave behind makes her feel keenly both the beauty and the insubstantiality of most youthful dreams. Anyone who has visited such a beach will recognize these bathers and possibly deplore them, but the story does not ask us either to laugh or to condemn. It does not ask us to side with the girl. Neither does it try to persuade us that the girl has achieved a real understanding of her experience or even that we ourselves have. As the memory of the young boy rushes back, compounded now with the morning's unpleasantness, she weeps inexplicably for "the small worn white pavilion" that uselessly ornaments the discredited beach. We too see it, feel with the girl, and are inexplicably disturbed.

The postmistress at China Grove, Mississippi, in "Why I Live at the P.O." is as disturbed as the girl in "A Memory" and as vulgar as the rednecked bathers there; she is also funny. Miss Porter has called her "a terrifying case of dementia praecox," but this diagnosis is probably an exaggeration. As her monologue progresses (such names as Stella-Rondo, Shirley-T., and Papa-Daddy are enough to indicate the tone of it), we look back at a recent disruptive sequence of events in the family circle which has so outraged her sense of fair play that she has gathered up everything she can lay claim to and carried the lot down to the post office, her post office ("the next to smallest P.O. in the entire state of Mississippi"), where for five days she has reigned unchallenged and happy, or so she says. If there is anything terrifying about all this, it is not the questionable psychosis or even the speaker's alienation, but the exposure of human pettiness, unwittingly burlesqued in the language and gestures of an ethically insensitive narrator. Undoubtedly the postmistress of China Grove has been grievously abused and by people quite as insensitive as she is, but one feels no inclination either to support her quarrel or to side with her excommunicated victims.

A similar hesitation perplexes us at the end of "Lily Daw and the Three Ladies," in which a young mentally retarded girl frustrates the good intentions of three female pillars of society by making a marriage just as they are about to send her to the Ellisville Institute for the Feeble-Minded of Mississippi. The story does not suggest whether we are to rejoice at Lily's triumph, which will surely be brief, or at the discomfiture of the three absurd ladies. Nor does "Petrified Man," a longer story, reveal its secret. No reader is likely to sympathize with Leota, the beauty operator whose narrative dominates it, or with Mrs. Fletcher, the customer who provides a willing ear, or with Mrs. Pike, who accepts Leota's friendship, imposes upon her hospitality, and uses her copy of *Startling G-Man Tales* to identify the petrified man in a visiting carnival as a rapist wanted for assaulting four women in California. The rapist provides no outlet for our feelings, and all the others are as distasteful as they are funny so that we find little relish in any laughter that the story may provide. Again we have been presented with a spectacle of petty barbarism that we feel is authentic and suspect may be universal. It can best be characterized as a trap for those who would cast stones.

Robert Penn Warren has remarked on the theme of isolation that appears in most of these early stories. Lily Daw, for example, is isolated by her childlike mind from the adult community she is determined to join; and all the unpleasant people in "Why I Live at the P.O." are isolated from one another as well as from the rest of Mississippi. Then there are the pair of newlywed deaf-mutes in "The Key," the old couple who struggle against the frost in "The Whistle," Old Mister Marblehall with his two lonely lives, the young people in "Flowers for Marjorie," the frightening pair of old women in "A Visit of Charity," and the heroic isolation of Phoenix Jackson in "A Worn Path." Most memorable of all perhaps are the two traveling salesmen. First, there is Tom Harris of "The Hitch-Hikers," in whose car, stopped at a small Delta town, one hitchhiker has fatally wounded another. In the fate of these three lonely people, in the town's inadequate response to the event that they bring to it, and in Harris' unexpected encounter with a lonely stranger, we come — and maybe Harris does also — to a sharper awareness of universal human loneliness and of the universal urge to find some kind of relief for it. Then there is the dying salesman R. J. Bowman, stumbling along the moonlit hill road in the back country, terrified by the explosions of a heart gone berserk but needlessly embarrassed by something no one else hears or cares about. The one clear example of psychotic isolation in *A Curtain of Green* is Clytie, a demented young woman of a decadent family who in her story runs about town staring into faces until at last she finds in the surface of a barrel of rain water the face she has been looking for and plunges beneath that surface to her death.

Now and then, however, one of these lonely characters will challenge his isolation in some way, usually by resorting to an act of poetry. Even for simpleminded Lily Daw the means of escape is to imagine a wedding and a normal life until something of both are suddenly and fantastically within her grasp; and for Ruby Fisher in "A Piece of News" it is the more nearly normal but still childlike capacity for daydreaming that makes her seize upon the chance appearance of a name like hers in a scrap of newspaper from another state and build from that a delicious fantasy in which she plays the role of a glamorous backwoods Camille. For Powerhouse, a Negro jazz pianist reminiscent of the late Fats Waller, it is the off-duty activity of the improvisational genius that moves his fingers in public performances.

Condemned by his race and his circumstances to play as long as he lives the monotonous role of court jester to a middle-class population, Powerhouse is reduced to creating his own private world of variety and excitement. He has a telegram, he declares, which says "Your wife is dead" and is signed "Uranus Knockwood." This improbable fiction provides creative release for Powerhouse and most of his musicians as they drink beer in a Negro restaurant during the break for intermission. When an unimaginative member of the group suggests that Powerhouse step over to the pay telephone and find out the "truth," he seethes inwardly, "That is one crazy drummer that's going to get his neck broken some day."

By contrast, for the loneliness of young Steve in "Keela, the Outcast Indian Maiden" no solution, imaginative or otherwise, is practicable. Steve's sense of isolation results from guilt acquired when, as a barker in a carnival, he drummed up trade for a small clubfooted Negro man who was dressed up as an Indian woman and forced several times a day to eat a live chicken. Fortunately the show was raided and the Negro sent home to Cane Springs, Mississippi; but the young man, though legally exonerated, has ever since led an Ancient-Mariner-like existence, wandering from place to place, confessing. We see him at his moment of ultimate confrontation; having come at last to Cane Springs, he has found a restaurant operator, named Max, who can take him to the clubfooted Negro's home, and there he hopes to receive forgiveness. What he finds instead is a grinning little man, virtually mindless and without sense of injury and thus incapable of forgiving anything. Steve's real tragedy, however, is his inability to recognize that the restaurant operator has been moved by the incident and would offer sympathy. His conclusion is a despairing, "I got to catch a ride some place." We feel that this character will probably take his isolation with him.

A very different kind of story but one that anticipates in theme Miss Welty's second collection is the title story, "A Curtain of Green." This tells of a young widow, Mrs. Larkin, whose husband has died the summer before when a great chinaberry tree by the driveway suddenly tilted forward, "dark and slow like a cloud," upon his car and crushed him to death. Mrs. Larkin's response to nature's blow has been to challenge the ambiguous curtain of green that stands between man's pretense at maintaining order and whatever it is that continually creates man's world and controls its destiny. Instead of commanding a naughty nature to return to its place or at least to make a show of respecting its betters, Mrs. Larkin chooses to subvert her enemy by participating in its luxuriant wildness (particularly evident in a place like Mississippi) and discovering its mysterious purpose, whatever that may be. Her neighbors, of course, do not know what to make of her. She plants whole catalogues of things; she plans not at all for neatness and makes no gesture of sharing any bounty that comes to her. At the end of her story, however, the purpose of the nonhuman world remains as mysterious as ever; for Mrs. Larkin succeeds only in finding herself one afternoon identified with the daemon of the chinaberry tree — or at any rate a similar daemon — as inexplicably she stands behind her kneeling Negro helper and threatens him with an upraised hoe. She is prevented from senseless murder by a "human" impulse, or by a moment of faintness, or perhaps by the equally senseless intrusion of a summer rain, which makes her hesitate. Anyhow she lowers her hoe and soon afterwards falls on her back amidst the rank growth and lies there quietly, as a silent nature assumes again its beneficent mask and showers her face with raindrops.

In her second collection, *The Wide Net and Other Stories,* Eudora Welty extended her range somewhat. At one extreme is "First Love," a touching story in which young Joel Mayes, deaf-mute, bootblack, and orphan in the Natchez of 1807, finds his first opportunity to know and communicate love in an encounter with Aaron Burr. During the time preceding Burr's preliminary trial for treason Burr stays at the inn where Joel was deposited as an orphan and where he has since lived as a servant. The boy shares his humble room with Burr, penetrates the older man's reserve, sees his anxieties, observes his last desperate conferences with Blennerhassett, and comforts him in his nightmares. Protected by his own physical infirmities from perceiving too clearly the disturbing things about Burr's personality, Joel notices the man's capacity for greatness and his need for love, which love Joel gives in the only way he can, with the clasp of his hand. The story does not invoke our sympathy for Burr, however; it asks us only to see Burr's part in Joel's awakening to a fuller participation in humanity. At the other end of the range is a "Gothic" tale, "The Purple Hat," in which a fat and aging armed guard at a New Orleans gambling casino tells how over the years he has fed his insatiable curiosity on a mysterious, perennially middle-aged woman with a purple hat. Peering down from his place on the catwalk beneath the dome of the casino, the guard has seen countless young men ensnared by their fascination for the woman's hat and for the mysterious vial with plunger that serves as one of its ornaments. As this unpleasant story nears an end, we realize that the woman is about to ensnare the young alcoholic who has been listening with us to the guard's recital.

These two stories are at the virtuosic limits of Miss Welty's performance in the short story and command our attention much as stories or paintings produced on a dare. Nevertheless, they also exhibit many of the solid virtues that distinguish her other work: her respect for the visual impression, which abides even when she is most concerned to insist on the existence of something beyond the immediately visible; her ability to make language suggest several dimensions of reality simultaneously, by use of allusion, by selection of detail, and by free (and sometimes licentious) use of metaphor; and above all her almost infallible ear for idiomatic diction and rhythm and her unembarrassed use of both.

The other six stories of *The Wide Net* are more naturalistically presented, and each shows humanity in some way addressing itself to the mysteries beyond that curtain of green which Miss Welty's authentic reporting establishes. For example, at the climax of "A Still Moment" Lorenzo Dow, evangelist, Audubon, painter and ornithologist, and Murrell, outlaw of the Natchez Trace, confront a heron in the forest. The three men are one in the intensity of their vision: "It was as if three whirlwinds had drawn together at some center, to find there feeding in peace a snowy heron." Yet it is Audubon who challenges the bird and the natural world that it represents. To paint the bird, he must know it intimately; so fixing the creature as best he can with his memory, he pulls the trigger and kills it. The shot is their signal for dispersal. Lorenzo Dow, bent on saving souls, rides away, thanking Heaven for an escape from the temptation to love nature. Murrell lets the shot stand for the one with which he would have given Lorenzo his death. Audubon, signifying by his concatenation of gestures the mystery and the ruthlessness of art, puts the dead bird in his bag, later to draw and paint and learn again the futility of trying to fathom the even more mysterious loveliness that surrounds him in the Mississippi forest.

Two stories in the book court trouble by what might be called spurious penetrations of the curtain. In one of these, "The Winds," the violence of an equinoctial storm is made to symbolize the transition of a young girl to adolescence and thence to maturity. Miss Welty's technique is misplaced here, for the correspondence is too obvious and worn to be redeemed by any but the most extraordinary of strategies. Even less successful is "Asphodel," in which three maiden ladies celebrate their liberation from a community tyrant and mad woman, Miss Sabina, by picnicking on the abandoned lawn of what once was Miss Sabina's home, now a pasture for goats. There as they spread their banquet and recount the dead woman's story, they suddenly see a naked man standing by the columns of the vanished mansion. "That was Mr. Don McInnis," says one of them, thinking it is Miss Sabina's unfaithful husband, presumably long dead. "It was not," says another. "It was a vine in the wind." "He was bucknaked," says the first. "He was as naked as an old goat. He must be as old as the hills." Clearly we are to think of a reincarnation of Dionysus as the ladies flee in a mixture of anger, indignation, and suppressed pleasure. Unfortunately there is too much telling here and too little presentation; we have had a ghost story, and we are not convinced.

The remaining three stories in the book are among Miss Welty's best, both as demonstrations of technique and as transparent re-creations of the natural world in which we see clearly enough what is before us but also perceive more than meets our eyes. "Livvie" has received more attention than the other two. This is the tale of a young woman who, at the death of her ancient husband, Solomon, transfers her devotion to the brash young fieldhand Cash, who has tried to claim it in advance. The story is thus one of temptations. At the climax the gaudily dressed young buck and his skittish woman end their Easter chase at Solomon's bedside, perhaps with murder in mind, only to discover there that the wise old man is prepared to surrender his authority with dignity and forgiveness and to die virtually of his own free will. Seldom in fiction has January given way to May with such grace and avoidance of pain. Nature wins effortlessly here, and the peach tree is blooming as the young couple burst out of the house into the sunlight. In "At the Landing" nature is less gracious. There the girl of the story, Jenny, also escapes when an aged guardian (this time a grandfather) dies; but Jenny's Dionysus arrives in the form of a river man, "Floyd . . . with his wrist hung with a great long catfish," who rescues her from the river flood, takes her to a secret place on the top of a hill, violates her, feeds her, and leaves her without specifically making her his own. Thus before achieving a second union with her god, Jenny must patiently and shamelessly follow him from one mud flat to another and finally submit to a succession of painful rapes by the primitive river men who casually take her in an abandoned houseboat. This is Jenny's initiation, the price she must pay for a chance at the life she would seek with those who live on the far side of the curtain of green. Yet payment gives Jenny no guarantee of achievement. As the story ends Billy Floyd has not come to claim her, and she continues to wait.

The most successful story in *The Wide Net* is the one from which the book takes its title. The net itself is a seine that young William Wallace Jamieson borrows from Old Doc on the hill when his wife Hazel, pregnant and depressed by a sense of neglect, has left a note saying she is going to drown herself. Hazel, of course, is going to do nothing of the sort, but her threat provides an occasion for a river dragging in which William Wallace, like Mrs. Larkin of the earlier collection, confronts the mysterious curtain of green: "The willow trees leaned overhead under muscadine vines, and their trailing leaves hung like waterfalls in the morning air. The thing that seemed like silence must have been the endless cry of all the crickets and locusts in the world, rising and falling." As the stream fills their net with fish, eels, and even alligators, the initial apprehensiveness for Hazel's life vanishes. They become wanderers, explorers, in a world mysterious, inviting, and endless. Once William Wallace in a perfunctory dive for the body of his wife senses in the watery depth that he has somehow fathomed the cause of her unhappiness, which is simply that strange insatiable longing that characterizes all sentient humanity; but he does not long reflect on the matter. With the others he eats fish, sleeps in the sunshine, thrills to the electric charge of a summer thunderstorm, and eventually returns to town to discover the impracticality of his expedition. Hazel is alive and well, yet no one regrets the effort. "The excursion is the same when you go looking for your sorrow as when you go looking for your joy," says Doc. Hazel is happy with the reassurance that her husband loves her, but William Wallace is happier.

In between these two successful collections of short stories Miss Welty published her first novel, called *The Robber Bridegroom* after one of Grimm's fairy tales. In addition to the general shape of Grimm's story, suggestions and reminiscences of a number of other tales are discoverable there, among them "The Little Goose Girl," "Rumpelstiltskin," "Little Snow White," "The Fisherman and His Wife," "Beauty and the Beast," Charles Perrault's "Cinderella," and the Hellenic myth of Cupid and Psyche. Moreover, a great deal of American folklore and near-folklore gets worked into the narrative, the stories of Davy Crockett and Mike Fink, the atrocities of Big Harpe and Little Harpe, and tall tales about Indians, frontiersmen, and bandits of the Natchez Trace. So much of this sort of thing appears, in fact, that one critic has been moved to credit the author with recovering "the fabulous innocence of our departed frontier."

Such an observation about *The Robber Bridegroom* gets additional justification from the pose Miss Welty assumes in telling her story. It is something like the one assumed by a canny maiden aunt, whose diction, asides, and silly puns are all devices of a naturally gifted teller of tales who knows how to make children giggle, shiver, and sit still. Children in the South are familiar with such performances, and it is to be assumed that children elsewhere know something like them. Almost any passage will illustrate: "Now Rosamond was a great liar, and nobody could believe a word she said. . . . she did not mean to tell anything but the truth, but when she opened her mouth in answer to a question, the lies would simply fall out like diamonds and pearls. Her father had tried scolding her, and threatening to send her away to the Female Academy, and then marching her off without her supper . . . Salome, on the other hand, said she should be given a dose of Dr. Peachtree." Part of our delight in this sort of thing undoubtedly is nostalgic, but that pleasure would pale here if it did not serve as a doorway to something else.

Miss Welty gives us all that Grimm gives and considerably more. The latter tells how a young maiden was bestowed by her father unknowingly upon a murderous bandit and how she eventually succeeded in capturing that bandit by her courage and her wits. This is clearly the basic plot of the novel; but Miss Welty has fattened it on the fruit of the Natchez Trace and allowed it to mature in the light of her own sophisticated reflection, and she does not expect us to take much of it simply at face value. A clue to what she would have us see comes two thirds of the way through the book when Clement Musgrove, father to the girl Rosamond, says of Jamie Lockhart, "If being a bandit were his breadth and scope, I should find him and kill him for sure. . . . But since in addition he loves my daughter, he must be not the one man, but two, and I should be afraid of killing the second. For all things are double, and this should keep us from taking liberties with the outside world, and acting too quickly to finish things off." Sophisticated fairy tales sometimes suggest that things in life may be double (for example, Perrault's "Cinderella"), but even in these tales characters are not given to reflecting on the matter or working out enunciations of principle. Morever, in genuinely primitive stories we do not get beyond the limited "breadth and scope." Grimm's story gave the girl two suitors, a bad one to outwit and a good one to live with happily ever after. Putting the two together, as Miss Welty has done, would have spoiled all the "fabulous innocence" and made a solution impossible.

Each of the three principals in the story is double in some way. For example, Clement Musgrove is both a wanderer and a planter. Rosamond, his daughter, is as beautiful as truth itself, but she is a congenital liar; and Jamie Lockhart, we know, is bandit as well as bridegroom. Clement's ambiguity may be explained as restlessness: he is the man who lost his youth with the death of a first wife and now perfunctorily spins out his days with an efficient shrew. Only in the presence of Rosamond, who preserves the image of her youthful mother, does he find happiness. Soon after the story begins he meets Jamie at an inn and learns of his heroic qualities in an encounter the two have with Mike Fink; thereafter his dream is to find happiness for the young man, who would make a fine heir, in a union with the lovely Rosamond. But the young people are really people and not pawns, and they must make their own arrangements. This means a period of adventuring, testing, exposing, rejecting and accepting, and finally coming to understand and respect that doubleness which is the occasion for conflicts between them and the condition of their continuing interest and happiness in one another.

The ability to perceive and appreciate doubleness is not a common gift; but Clement possesses naturally, as we have seen, a high degree of it. His meditation continues: "All things are divided in half — night and day, the soul and body, and sorrow and joy and youth and age, and sometimes I wonder if even my own wife has not been the one person all the time, and I loved her beauty so well at the beginning that it is only now that the ugliness has struck through to beset me like a madness." He is being too generous here. Salome, his shrewish second wife, is not double at all; neither are the savage Goat, son of a neighboring widow, Mike Fink, the two Harps (to use Miss Welty's spelling), or the marauding Indians. Perhaps that is why such characters in this book strike us as evil instead of merely wicked or naughty as they would in a fairy tale where the rest of the characters are equally one-sided. Still Clement's perceptions are good enough to enable him to single out Jamie, who knew in his heart "that he was a hero and had always been one, only with the power to look both ways and to see a thing from all sides." And it is Jamie's perceptivity that enables him in turn to see Rosamond's saving "duplicity"; for Rosamond's fibbing apparently is another instance of that creative kind of fabrication that enables Ruby Fisher and Powerhouse of *A Curtain of Green* to redeem their unsatisfying lives. Thus poetry of a kind rewards all three: Jamie and Rosamond with a fine mansion, a hundred slaves, and rich merchants to go boating with, and Clement with the knowledge that his children have such things. Miss Welty has him return to the Trace, of his own will, alone: "For he was an innocent of the wilderness, and a planter of Rodney's Landing, and this was his good." We suspect that his was the greatest good, after all.

Eudora Welty's second novel, *Delta Wedding*, appeared in 1945. It was well received on the whole, though certain New York critics chided her for failing to recognize the moral and sociological shortcomings of life in the Mississippi Delta. The story is built around the visit of a little nine-year-old girl, Laura

McRaven, of Jackson, to the country place Shellmound, where her uncle, Battle Fairchild, and his wife, Ellen, preside over a household of eight children and a ninth expected, associated aunts and great-aunts, and numerous Negro servants. The occasion for her visit is the forthcoming marriage of Battle's seventeen-year-old daughter, Dabney, to Troy Flavin, Shellmound's overseer, aged thirty-four. For Battle and Ellen Fairchild the event seems to threaten a first break in the integrity of their immediate family. To young Laura the thought of having a vacation with all her cousins is almost more exciting than the prospect of seeing a wedding, especially since her mother has died earlier in the year and she cannot therefore take her rightful role in it as flower girl. As the story proceeds, however, the substitute comes down with chickenpox, and Laura does indeed participate in the wedding. Afterwards, on a late summer picnic, held in honor of the returning honeymooners, her heart overflows with happiness as her sense of finding acceptance in her mother's family matures within her.

Even so, Laura McRaven is not at the center of *Delta Wedding*, and we do not see Shellmound through her eyes. The author guides our attention freely over the whole collection of people who at this point in time constitute "the Fairchilds." Seldom has a family been portrayed so effectively. We see it and sympathize with it, gladly or perhaps reluctantly, as our predisposition requires; and as our experience permits, we see the universality of it as well. A plantation family in the Mississippi Delta does not differ essentially from large families that have developed elsewhere in other agrarian economies — in the American Middle West, in rural England, in France, or in Russia. The mystery celebrated in *Delta Wedding* is the love that can bind such a family together even after the frontier, sociological or geographic, which has required it to stand together in a particular place has passed on. She might easily have written about some decaying family, for there are many such in Mississippi and in other parts of the South. She has chosen instead to write of a rarer kind.

The principal characters may be divided into two groups, one large and one small. First, there are the blooded Fairchilds headed by Battle, master of Shellmound. These include Battle's four sons, Orrin, Roy, Little Battle, and Ranny; and his four daughters, Shelley, Dabney, India, and Bluet. In addition there are two brothers, George, who lives in Memphis with his wife, Robbie; and Denis, dead in World War I, whose demented widow lives in the town and whose retarded child, Maureen, lives at Shellmound. Two great-aunts, Aunt Mac and Aunt Shannon, live in the house; two maiden sisters, Primrose and Jim Allen, live not far away in a smaller house which really belongs to George. Still another sister, Tempe, has married an alcoholic and lives at Inverness. Laura McRaven is also a blooded Fairchild, but her mother, Annie Laurie Fairchild, decided to marry a young lawyer and move to Jackson. The second group consists of characters who are Fairchilds by association. There are three of these: Ellen, who for all her eight children is still regarded as a Virginian and an outsider; Robbie, who has married George but who at the beginning of the novel has run away from him; and Troy Flavin, a man from the hills of northeastern Mississippi, unaware of the cultural gulf that separates him from his bride-to-be.

It is possible to think of the main action of the novel as the merging of these two groups in the marriage of Troy and Dabney. All the activity that confronts us as we read has to do with preparation for the wedding, the events surrounding it, or the picnic given in the couple's honor as they return from their honeymoon. Troy's intrusion into this established family is cer-

tainly symbolic of the main action even if it is not identifiable
with it; and the family's acceptance of him is symptomatic of the
complex of attitudes that will make possible a resolution of conflicts at the end. But Troy's conflict is no more at the true center
of this novel than Ellen's, which is deeper and more painful.
After spending years in the circle of Fairchilds, Ellen is still
something of an alien. Her role has been to endure things, not to
precipitate them. Hence she will not herself resolve conflicts,
but her reservoir of sympathy and strength will help to ensure
that resolutions last. Like Troy Flavin she contributes to the
action and illuminates it, but she works at the periphery of the
storm.

At dead center is Ellen's brother-in-law George, blooded Fairchild, abandoned by his wife just as he was about to return to
Shellmound for Dabney's wedding. This storm threatens disaster
for the whole clan. The event that precipitated it took place two
weeks before the time of the narrative. All the family except Battle and Ellen had gone on a fishing excursion to a place called
Drowning Lake. Afterwards they were coming home by the short-
est path, the railway track, and had all reached the trestle just
as the local passenger train, popularly called the Yellow Dog,
suddenly threatened to overtake them. No real crisis would have
arisen, however, had not Maureen, dancing on the crossties,
caught her foot and George, ignoring all danger, knelt and worked
patiently to free the child before the train should catch them
both. The engineer saw them in time and stopped the train, and
all the others jumped or fell into the dry creek bed below; but
Robbie was furious that her husband should have elected to stay
with an idiot child and thus run the risk of leaving her a widow.
We do not see Robbie face to face until halfway through the
novel when she decides to return and make a public display of
her vexation. Her reunion with George is the true Delta wedding

of the piece. At the end she is reconciled with the Fairchilds — as much as one can ever be with a whole family — and she and George have decided to leave Memphis, return to the little house near Shellmound, and be Fairchilds for the rest of their lives. Thus the end of the action is the vindication of that family bond — mysterious, compelling, and in the final reckoning good, as Robbie's behavior testifies. The three characters for whom vindication seems most important, however, are George, Laura, and Ellen; and these are the characters who help us most to participate in that sense of family which few readers in a restless age are lucky enough to experience directly.

Delta Wedding, the embodiment of that sense, is too rich to be summed up in a few pages, but one or two details which serve as clarifying symbols should be mentioned. Obviously significant in this way is the little night lamp that Aunts Primrose and Jim Allen give to Dabney as a wedding present. When the candle inside is lighted, the clay-colored chimney reddens and reveals a picture of a city — London, the aunts say — engulfed by flames, which seem frighteningly real as the candle gives them motion. The lamp is supposed to suggest the transformation that can come to people and families when some great spiritual happiness — or perhaps a crisis — warms them from within. The image that enables Laura to grasp the mystery of the Fairchilds is more revealing. All the laughing, kissing relatives make her think of the birdhouse in a zoo that her father has taken her to: ". . . the sparkle of motion was like a rainbow, while it was the very thing that broke your heart, for the birds that flew were caged all the time and could not fly out." Shellmound is the cage which Laura is compelled to try to enter; her need for love will not let her hold back indefinitely, and yet she knows that, once inside, she may not ever again be able to break free. We recall this when we see her double triumph at the end of the novel, signalized by her simultaneous acceptance into the family and her decision to return to her father in Jackson.

Another detail unites Laura and Ellen in a significant way. In the first part of the book we hear Ellen refer to a lost garnet pin that Battle has given her. As the novel proceeds, she continues to look for it, even to the point of sending Shelley, India, and Laura on a visit to Partheny, an old Negro woman who has mindless moments, experiences trances, and may perhaps return the article if she has stolen it or discover its whereabouts in a vision if she has not. The pin is a badge of acceptance which Ellen once needed desperately but which she now seeks for the sake of sentiment. Laura eventually finds the pin in the grass at an old abandoned house, Marmion, rightfully hers but in the years immediately ahead destined to serve as a home for Dabney and Troy. Returning across the Yazoo to Shellmound, however, she is tumbled into the river by her companion Roy, who fishes her out and apologizes. In the scramble she loses the rosy pin. At the end of the novel she has decided not to tell Ellen either of finding the pin or of the unfortunate accident by which it was lost a second time; for she knows deep inside that the pin itself does not particularly matter. Now, lost forever, it is a treasure that secretly belongs to them both and unites them.

In the end what makes this family a living, continuing thing is the capacity of a sufficient number of the people in it to participate with compassion, selflessness, and intensity in the daily lives of all the others, whether linked by blood or by simple affection. As George says at one point, "I don't think it matters what *happens* to a person, or what comes." There is always something going on in a family like this one: people marry, die, run away, play games, join armies, or fight duels. But family living is participation moment by moment in whatever comes or happens; and George's unusual capacity for that is the door by which

Robbie returns and the window by which Laura comes to see. Near the end of the story it also enables him to offer the embrace in which Ellen finds, without loss of her love for Battle, the supreme consolation of friendship and the fulfillment of a life.

The Golden Apples consists of seven separable pieces, all with titles of their own and all previously published. Yet this collection, if it may be called that, stands together as a recognizable whole just as clearly as *Delta Wedding* with its formally inseparable parts. It also makes much of the authentic contemporary setting which distinguished *Delta Wedding*, but it reintroduces that element of the fabulous which had all but dominated *The Robber Bridegroom* seven years earlier. The pattern for this combination had been displayed in "Asphodel," one of the stories in *The Wide Net*; but there the shape of Greek myth had resisted fusion with its Mississippi setting, and an improbable "Gothic" tale resulted. In *The Golden Apples* fusion does occur, and for the space of seven stories a credible Mississippi becomes a mirror with a range stretching geographically east, west, north, and south and temporally from the Mississippi of the 1920's at least as far back as primitive Greece. Also somewhere within this broad sweep is the region of Celtic folklore as preserved in the poems of William Butler Yeats and particularly in "The Song of the Wandering Aengus," which tells of an elusive Ondine and of the quests she inspires for, among other things, the golden apples of the sun. Thus the golden apples of classical mythology, which Atlas stole for Hercules, symbolize also the quest of a Mississippi Irishman, King MacLain, who fished for trout in many streams, dreamed of gold till his life wore out, and passed his restlessness on to others without ever quite realizing what it was he had been looking for. So that we may know, Miss Welty has another of the principal characters, Virgie Rainey, contemplate with melancholy the futility of her own wandering, past and to come. In her mind's eye she sees a picture that once hung on the wall of her music teacher's studio, a picture of Perseus holding the head of the Medusa. Her teacher had explained that it was the same thing as Siegfried and the dragon, but now Virgie knows that there is really no end to what the picture stands for: "Endless the Medusa, and Perseus endless." At the end of the book, as she sits staring into the rain that happens to be falling at that moment, she thinks suddenly that even such a familiar occurrence as rainfall is never confined simply to Mississippi. It is "the rain of fall, maybe on the whole South, for all she knew on the everywhere." And as she continues to stare, she hears through the rain's percussive music "the running of the horse and bear, the stroke of the leopard, the dragon's crusty slither, and the glimmer and the trumpet of the swan," and she senses her participation in the perennial vibrations of earthly life.

The title of the first chapter, "Shower of Gold," specifically invites us to think of the Danaë story. In the monologue of Virgie Rainey's mother, Miss Katie Rainey of Morgana, Mississippi, we learn how King MacLain, a tea and spice salesman long given to unexplained absences (he is the story's Zeus figure), on one brief return home met his albino wife, Snowdie, in the woods and got her with twins. When Zeus visited Danaë in her cell, of course, he begot Perseus; but Snowdie's twins are a Castor and Pollux, destined to disturb their father's peace of mind as Perseus did, though less seriously. This, in fact, is the main business of the amusing story that Katie Rainey tells, how King MacLain returned home on one of his visits and got as far as the front steps only to be put to flight by the spectacle of two little boys masked with Halloween false faces, decorated with scraps from their mother's sewing basket, and roaring on roller skates around the MacLains' wooden porch like a Mississippi tornado.

Like Castor and Pollux the twins eventually go forth to seek gold of their own. One of them, named Lucius Randall but called Ran, goes only a few blocks. He courts and marries Jinny Love Stark, an attractive and sensual but uninspired young woman of a locally prominent family. Jinny Love is soon unfaithful to Ran in her casual, unfeeling way; then he to her, though not unfeelingly. He leaves their home, returns to the house where he grew up (now a boardinghouse), and engages desperately in an affair with a country girl named Maideen Sumrall. That Jinny Love may represent false gold and Maideen the true never occurs to him, even after Maideen has committed suicide. At the end of this story, "The Whole World Knows," he is crying out to his father and to his brother in anguish, "What you went and found, was it better than this?" But Ran is destined only to desire the gold, never actually to see it. In a later story we find him again, adjusted to small-town life, wived once more and more or less comfortably blind.

His brother Eugene fares little better. In "Music from Spain" we find that he has wandered westward, all the way to San Francisco, where he is married to a woman of Latin extraction by whom he has had one golden child. The child has recently died. At breakfast one morning Eugene suddenly reaches across the table, slaps his wife, and walks out of the apartment. For the first hour or so his quest, unexpectedly resumed, is as aimless as it is fantastic; but it achieves some point when quite by chance he rescues from the noonday traffic rush a Spanish guitarist whom he and Emma had heard in a recital the previous evening. Eugene knows no Spanish, and the Spaniard knows no English; but the two eat lunch together, walk up and down the hill streets of San Francisco, and make their way finally to "Land's End," where, misunderstanding one another's gestures, they grapple furiously in a mutual release of tensions. Afterwards as a token of reconciliation Eugene uses his last penny to buy coffee for the Spaniard and then makes his way home again. Back at the apartment he finds nothing changed. Emma has neither understood the slap nor remembered it, all the day's wandering has come to nothing, and the glitter of Eugene's dream has now vanished forever. Later we learn that he returned to Morgana and died there.

The Perseus of *The Golden Apples* is Loch Morrison, whom we first encounter as a small boy in the long story "June Recital." The Morrison home is next door to the now abandoned MacLain house; and Loch, confined to his bed with malaria, is amusing himself by inspecting it through his father's telescope. The telescope enables him to spy upon Virgie Rainey and her sailor friend, whom she entertains on a bare mattress in an upstairs room. Downstairs the lovemaking is counterpointed by the frantic activity of old Miss Eckhart, retired piano teacher, who once lived in the Rainey home and rejoiced in Virgie as the only pupil in Morgana with any talent. Now Virgie has prostituted that talent by playing "professionally" at the local movie theater; and Miss Eckhart with the madness of frustration and senility absurdly tries to set the house on fire. King MacLain, temporarily in town, with two of his friends puts out the fire and saves the building. Virgie escapes, as does the sailor, and the town turns the whole business into gossip.

This story is the crossroads of the book. Virgie Rainey and King MacLain, the two principal wanderers in it, pass here and almost meet, while a third wanderer, younger than either, watches, appropriately from a distance and through a glass. It precedes the dispiriting chapters that deal with the fruitless wandering of Ran and Eugene, MacLain's acknowledged offspring and his legitimate successors; and it prepares the reader for one more story apiece about Loch and Virgie, who wait until the Zeus of Morgana is too old for escapades and then steal his dream away.

Loch Morrison's second story comes close to tragedy, but it

marks his discovery of strength to escape the trap that made King MacLain, for all his canny ways, more like a small-town philanderer than a god. Loch, as Boy Scout and lifesaver, is spending a week at Moon Lake with a group of girl campers, whom he despises. The girls adore him, of course, but he declares his indifference by spending much of the time in his tent and the rest crashing through the treetops like Tarzan of the Apes. His testing comes when Easter, a young girl from the local orphanage and quite possibly another offspring of King MacLain's, makes a bad dive and embeds her head in the soft mud of the lake bottom. Easter's attractive power is similar to Loch's. She is independent and daring, and she has breasts coming. Jinny Love Stark, who later will capture Ran MacLain, taunts her for not having a family or a decent name; but Easter maintains her dignity. She intends to become a singer, she says. Loch's success in rescuing and reviving the girl lifts him over the imperceptible line that separates childish Boy Scout from genuine protector. The arduous process of artificial respiration provokes a variety of responses. Some of the girls are frightened, some are contemptuous, a fellow orphan bids for Easter's winter coat in case she dies, and Jinny Love Stark's mother is appalled by the suggestiveness of the business. Loch, however, shares none of these feelings. Rejecting praise, he simply does his work and then returns to the privacy of his tent, where he briefly resumes his silly chest beating and then abandons gestures to stare thoughtfully into the night. We learn later that he has abandoned Morgana for New York and done well there.

The last story, originally called "The Hummingbirds" but retitled "The Wanderers" for the book, tells how Virgie Rainey, having tried repeatedly to break with Morgana, returns during her mother's last days, watches over the old woman, and buries her when she dies. In describing the funeral Miss Welty has left out nothing proper to such an event: the cakes, ham, and deviled eggs, the profusion of cut flowers, the sitting up with the body, the continual murmur of clichés, the relatives from remote corners of the state, the stray preacher who knew the deceased in her childhood, the meeting of friends, the condoling, the old people arriving, the trip to the cemetery, the farewells, and the loneliness after. In this vast ceremonial occasion most of Morgana and the nearby hamlet of MacLain pass before us. Prominent are those who have attracted our attention before: Miss Snowdie, who now supervises the "laying out" of her friend; King MacLain, weary, senile, too old to gather golden apples; Ran MacLain and Jinny Love, unfeeling as ever but wedded again and reunited with the community; the memory of Eugene (dead) and of Loch (transferred to New York) and of Loch's mother (a suicide) and of Miss Eckhart (also dead), who tried vainly to give them her Beethoven.

Miss Welty's control here shows an advance over that of *Delta Wedding*, where a tendency to diffuseness was sometimes evident in such passages. In this last chapter of *The Golden Apples* she lets everything filter through the consciousness of Virgie Rainey, whose review of the details we see is steadily bringing her to an awareness of her own action, which is the action of the book: that is, her seizure of "kingship" from King MacLain. MacLain's wandering, we learn, has finally been stopped by Miss Snowdie (she used a detective agency), who now makes a home for him, watches his diet, and dictates all his movements. Virgie, younger but aware of youth's brevity, has returned home at least partly out of kindness; she has dutifully outlived the dying and now enjoys the freedom that selflessness and time have conferred upon her. She is also ready for understanding.

The crisis comes during the funeral service proper. While a child in a peach-colored dress is singing "O Love That Will Not

Let Me Go," MacLain sneaks into the hall and tiptoes down to the table where the ham has been set out, there to nibble at forbidden flesh and steal a little marrow bone to suck on. As he returns to the room, he catches Virgie's glance and makes a face at her ". . . like a silent yell. It was a yell at everything—including death, not leaving it out—and he did not mind taking his present animosity out on Virgie Rainey; indeed, he chose her. Then he cracked the little bone in his teeth." Virgie is not fully aware of what is happening at this point, but she knows enough to refute the mindless old lady who keeps repeating, "Child, you just don't know yet what you've lost." She does not bother. Neither does she bother to respond to King MacLain's grimace. She knows both the pain of her wound and the joy of her freedom, and in the richness of that strangely compounded knowledge she senses her kinship with all the MacLains, especially with Mr. King, her spiritual father. Where his sons Ran and Eugene have failed him, she of no blood kin at all has succeeded.

Virgie Rainey visits two graveyards in "The Wanderers," one at Morgana to bury her mother and another seven miles down the road to see again where the MacLains are buried. She makes her pilgrimage to the latter the day after her mother's funeral, after she has decided on the spur of the moment to leave town immediately and thereby shocked and offended some. Once at the village of MacLain, Virgie climbs up on the old stile in front of the courthouse and sits in the rain thinking of the MacLains buried and living and of Miss Eckhart, there by Miss Snowdie's wish, and of Perseus and Beethoven, all wanderers, all hummingbirds. On her perch she reminds us more of Yeats's golden nightingale, reluctantly faithful to time and metamorphosed into something transcending time, cognizant of what is past, passing, and to come. And as she sits there listening to the magical percussion of the rain, she sees as on a screen before her the "hideous and delectable face" Mr. King MacLain has made, smiles, and hears the world beating in her ears.

After *The Golden Apples* no book-length work of Miss Welty's appeared for more than four years. Then in December of 1953 the *New Yorker* published her short novel called *The Ponder Heart*. Separate publication followed in 1954 and a dramatization for Broadway, by Jerome Chodorov and Joseph Fields, in 1956. In this book the narrative voice of *The Robber Bridegroom* found an appropriate visible embodiment in the dominating person of Miss Edna Earle Ponder, spinster and manager of the Beulah Hotel in Clay, Mississippi. Otherwise *The Ponder Heart* seemed more like an expanded short story than a successor to the other novels, and it depended more heavily than the rest of Miss Welty's work on local color for its effectiveness. Miss Ponder's listener is a young girl, old enough to drive a car (which has broken down — the reason for her being at the Beulah) but not too old to be imposed on with a story the length of a long Mississippi summer "evening," or afternoon. We see her only briefly, however, as she sits there on the porch vainly trying to read; and we never learn her name. Throughout the afternoon the only voice we hear directly is the narrator's, unsophisticated, recognizably provincial, and inexhaustible, relieved only by the "transcribed" conversation of others who come and go in her story of Uncle Daniel Ponder and the heart that brought him much joy in life and now near the end much sadness as well.

Uncle Daniel is an amiable old gentleman, mentally retarded, who lives with his niece at the Beulah, where he vainly waits for guests to stop or old friends from the town to drop in for a visit. His life, as Miss Edna Earle tells it, was uneventful until he reached his forties; and then his father, Grandpa Ponder, managed to marry him off to a local widow named Teacake Magee. This marriage soon fell through, however; and Grandpa, by now thoroughly exasperated by his son's habit of giving everything away, had him committed to the asylum in Jackson. The asylum proved to be no solution either, for Daniel was neither mad nor neurotic, just innocent; he quickly escaped and married a poor-white seventeen-year-old named Bonnie Dee Peacock. Grandpa's death soon after made Daniel rich, and the Ponder wealth became a matter of great interest to Bonnie Dee and her family.

For the rest of the novel Edna Earle's voice ripples along with no significant shift in attitude. We continue to get digressions about life in Clay, the importance of knowing one's place and having a family connection, her never-to-be-realized hope of marriage with Mr. Springer, a traveling salesman. The story of Uncle Daniel, however, becomes less consistently amusing. Bonnie Dee runs away, returns, shortly afterwards sends Daniel back to the Beulah, abuses the Ponder credit until stopped, then recalls her husband abruptly early one afternoon and just as abruptly dies before supper during a violent thunderstorm. The Peacocks bury her after what is surely one of the funniest funerals in literature, as Edna Earle reports it; but throughout we are kept ignorant about what really happened during that fateful thunderstorm, and we do not learn until the Peacocks have charged Daniel with murder and brought him to trial. There in the courtroom scene Edna Earle gets around to telling us, though not the court, how Daniel found his young wife terrified at the mounting storm, tickled her playfully to divert her attention to himself, and was still tickling her neck when she died of fright. Daniel himself brings the trial to an end, literally by giving away most of his fortune, drawn out of the bank when an inexperienced teller was on duty. Thus with a profligate gesture of love he alienates most of the citizens of Clay, who take the gift but in the embarrassment of their spiritual poverty cannot give in return.

The loneliness to which the two surviving Ponders thus inadvertently condemn themselves, however, is graced with its own kind of triumph. Apparently by losing her hope of marriage and children and giving her life to the "nitwit" in her house, Edna Earle has discovered her own capability for love and the capability that seems to be within all those who discover the power of the Ponder heart. Her occasional moralizing prepares us for a concluding demonstration of her own charity as Uncle Daniel makes his way down to greet the visitor. "I'd like to warn you again," she says, "he may try to give you something — may think he's got something to give. If he does, do me a favor. Make out like you accept it. Tell him thank you." With this small gesture love blossoms visibly on the porch of the Beulah, and moralizing and narrative are both vindicated.

Miss Welty's third collection of short stories appeared on the tide of public interest that surrounded *The Ponder Heart*; but *The Bride of the Innisfallen*, as it was called, did not become a popular book. Nevertheless, the seven stories there constituted a technical advance over anything she had done up to this time. In three of these she continued her custom of using the contemporary deep South as the scene, in one she used for the first and only time a Civil War setting, and in two others she drew upon her European travels. In the remaining story she moved the reader directly to a mythical island in the Mediterranean and there had the sorceress Circe give her own version of Odysseus' visit. In none did plot, or external activity sequentially and logically ordered, have the importance that it had had in much of her other work. Journalistic critics understandably resented this aspect of the new stories and wrote with some asperity about it, but vindication of her method has come with repeated readings. What the characters in the stories learn is based upon their own observations, collected by them and then evaluated without strict reference to space and time. We, even as careful readers, can never

196

know more data than these poetically gifted characters know; but the author guides us beyond the frame of the story to a level of understanding that with the characters themselves remains principally a level of feeling. In all the stories the path to understanding is self-evident but not marked; the reader must pay strict attention. In only one of them is the main character given no hope of eventually catching up with the reader; and that is Circe's story, which ends with the semi-goddess's cry of frustration at being unable to penetrate the clay-bound mystery that mortals with their "strange felicity" seem to know. The other six stories in *The Bride of the Innisfallen* communicate with varying capability that "strange felicity" peculiar to mortals. Their success is due in large part to the author's respect for the clay of the region, wherever she has happened to be working.

"Ladies in Spring" is a story about a Mississippi spring and a young boy's initiation in it. The most important of the ladies is Miss Hattie Purcell, mistress of the post office at Royals, Mississippi, and rainmaker for that community. The narration focuses on the consciousness of the boy Dewey, as he goes fishing with his father (nicknamed Blackie), passes the postmistress in the woods, catches a six-inch goggle-eye, and sees a mysterious second lady calling to his father from the trees. This lady, we suspect, is Opal Purcell, Miss Hattie's niece, who joins them as they walk home in the pouring rain. Opal says she has been out looking for poke salad, and Dewey gives no sign that he disbelieves her. Back at the post office he remains with Miss Hattie until the rain stops and then goes home to scare his mother with the fish he has caught. Shortly thereafter he idly returns to the river bank, where he sees a small black stray dog and thinks for the moment that it looks like Miss Hattie. Fifteen years later it occurs to him that Opal Purcell was probably the one who called to his father that afternoon from the willow trees.

The beauty of the author's technique in elaborating this bare story is that it scarcely seems to be a technique at all. It is almost as if the season itself had taken young Dewey in hand, sowing data like seeds for the awakening to come later. Take, for example, the wetness that appears everywhere in the story as soon as the drought breaks — in the trees, on the grass, on the flowers that pop out as the water begins to fall, and on the faces of the country people in the little town. Wetness also seems to bring out details of color, particularly blue and pink, as they turn up in the flowers, in the clothes hung out to dry, and in the patchwork quilt that Opal throws over her head to run from one house to another. The movie house is "magnesia-bottle blue," and three red hens wait on its porch. When Opal declares that her excursion in the woods has been innocent, she has wet cheeks and a blue violet hanging in her dress; later these details are transformed in Dewey's observation that the "big sky-blue violets his mother loved were blooming, wet as cheeks." His father's nickname is Blackie, and black is the color of his face when the secrets of his life momentarily weigh heavily upon him; black is also the color of the mysterious little dog that Dewey sees on his return to the scene of the fishing, and the little black dog looks like the mysterious rainmaking postmistress. But all this connectedness is left in the story just as it comes to Dewey, a collection of hints, rich and strange, and scarcely more conclusive in its immediacy than such things can ever be at the moment of perception in real life. To comprehend a story of this kind, one must be willing to live with it a bit, as one lives with Turgenev's *Sportsman's Sketches*, which it resembles.

Another initiation story is "Kin," told by a young woman, Dicey Hastings, who has returned to her former home, a little courthouse town, "several hours by inconvenient train ride from Jackson," for a visit with her Mississippi relatives. Into the delicious and interminable round of talk that can go on among leisurely southern women whose complex blood connections give them topics comes an unexpected letter which prompts Dicey's Aunt Ethel to insist that she and her cousin Kate spend an afternoon at Mingo, home of Uncle Felix and once a favorite objective for Sunday excursions. The two girls accede reluctantly. Uncle Felix is an incredibly ancient widower, barely hanging on to life and enduring his last days under the watchful eye of an unlovely spinster, related on both sides of the house, whom they call Sister Anne. They arrive at the country place to find it overrun with strangers and learn that Sister Anne has turned the parlor over for the day to an itinerant photographer, who is making portraits of all the country folk there and will also make one of Sister Anne, free. Uncle Felix has been moved temporarily to the storeroom. There the girls visit with him and are touched by his pathetic attempts to identify himself and them and make out what place he is in. Dicey recalls painfully the happy moments that Uncle Felix once gave her with his stereoptican, which lies now unused on a barrel there in the storeroom; and she receives a "message" that he gives her written on the flyleaf of a hymnal. It speaks of a Daisy long forgotten and of some midnight meeting long past. The pity that all this moves them to and the shock that Sister Anne's commonness gives them are both parts of the awakening of these young women to the evanescence of their own youth and the inevitability of their mortality.

"The Burning," frequently criticized for being enigmatic, brings its characters to the same points of awareness but does so with finality. The story is not enigmatic about anything that matters. It tells how a band of Sherman's soldiers forced their way into a plantation home near Jackson, raped one of the two ladies they found there, forced these ladies, Miss Myra and Miss Theo, out of the house along with their maid, Delilah, looted the place (with the help of a number of dispossessed Negro slaves), and burned it to the ground. The fire reveals the presence of a fourth person in the establishment, a youth named Phinny, the sequestered bastard of one of the persons in the household, possibly Miss Myra, when he bellows like a bull until the flames consume him. Afterwards the ladies and Delilah wander across the fields until they find a deserted hammock. There with the hammock rope Miss Theo murders Miss Myra and makes a fumbling but ultimately successful attempt to hang herself. Delilah returns to the ruins of the house and gathers up the bones of the unfortunate Phinny. Then she makes her way into oblivion.

The point of the story begins to clarify as references are made to.a large Venetian mirror into which the ladies stare when the soldiers invade their parlor. The mirror, blackened but still usable, lies there among the ruins as Delilah stoops to gather her bones. In it she sees, however, not the ruin about her but something she herself has never seen before, the image of a vanished Venetian civilization, lords and ladies, gorgeous red birds, and monkeys in velvet — all symbolic of the society that until recently flourished at that very spot and also seemed immortal. Frightened at the thought of approaching night with its tangible army of hostile creatures, live birds, bats, and serpents, Delilah gathers up her bones, seizes a Jubilee cup and a black locust stick, and follows the smell of horses, fire, and men until she finds safety from all three at the river's edge. The moment she enters the water to wade across, her old knowledge of when it will rain next, once laughed at by her betters as superstition, rises to the surface of her mind as the only certainty remaining in a now discredited world.

"Going to Naples," "The Bride of the Innisfallen," and "No Room for You, My Love," are alike in that they carry Eudora Welty out of her own private region. That they are all successful indicates that though she writes best about what she knows, she generally knows whatever she sees. The least impressive of the three, "Going to Naples," suffers only by comparison with the company it keeps. The first part of the story takes place on the *Pomona,* a slow ship sailing from New York to Naples in a warm September of a Holy Year. Most of the passengers are Italian-American pilgrims and old people going home to Italy to die. An American spinster provides a slight focus for some of the things we see, but she does not figure significantly in the action. Our attention is directed mainly to the relationship of Mrs. C. Serto and her daughter Gabriella, who is eighteen, marriageable, but still fat and a bit hysterical even for a late adolescent. Mrs. Serto's unspoken objective for the journey is to find a husband for Gabriella, but the arrival at Naples undoes her. Everything changes as suddenly the author bombards us with what are for us, and for Gabriella, exotic details of the Italian scene. For Mrs. Serto, whose ancient mother meets her on the pier, however, it is all one complex, glorious, and unexpected invitation to resume once more her own role of daughter; and resume it she does, leaving Gabriella slightly bewildered but wiser in her temporary displacement.

Tangible clay makes no such dramatic entry in "The Bride of the Innisfallen." It is there from the beginning. The consciousness at the center of this story is that of a young American girl in London who is running away from her husband. Through her senses we get the details of the murky, rain-dreary Paddington Station and the collection of characters she encounters on her long ride through southern England and Wales into the night. Then there is the tedious crossing of the choppy Irish Sea, the smoky lounge of the *Innisfallen,* and finally the arrival at Cork, with the sights and sounds of the awakening city in the bright light of morning as the boat glides up the river Lee. Like the American girl making her escape, we grope for meaning in this tantalizing succession of data and almost pass by the one bit that seems to have power to bring much of it into focus.

Just as the *Innisfallen* is about to dock, someone on the pier shouts, "There's a bride on board!" And "Sure enough, a girl who had not yet showed herself in public now appeared by the rail in a white spring hat and, over her hands, a little old-fashioned white bunny muff." The bride we suddenly see, however, is the sad young wife, who has seemed lost in the aimlessness symbolized by the plethora of precise detail that has marked her progress westward during the preceding hours. The girl lets the incident pass without special notice, until she stares at the chalk marks that the customs officer leaves on her suitcase, "like a gypsy's sign found on her own front door." "A rabbit ran over my grave," she thinks, and, leaving her suitcase in the parcel room, she walks forthwith into the streets of Cork.

There Easter and suggestions of new life are all about her: rhododendrons swimming in light, boughs bursting with leaves, little girls in confirmation dresses racing up and down the streets like "animated paper snowflakes." She tries unsuccessfully to compose a message to send to her abandoned husband but decides to let the past go. The image of the bride has done its work. This is her Easter, her confirmation, and her new land. Hearing animated talk in a nearby pub, she turns and walks "into the lovely room full of strangers."

The ending of "No Place for You, My Love" is less happy. This is the first story in the collection; it is also probably the best. The title suggests the theme of it, and the text reads like a descent into hell. Two strangers figure in the story: a married man from Syracuse and a young woman from Toledo who is having an affair with another married man. The place is New Orleans on a Sunday in summer — "those hours of afternoon that seem Time Out in New Orleans." The two meet by accident in a restaurant, go for a ride southward from the city, all the way to the Gulf, through a section that is unlike anything else in the southern United States. There they find Cajuns, mosquitoes, crawfish, snakes, and at the end a shack where they can buy beer and sandwiches. Above all there is heat — heat everywhere, with the road running through it like a quivering nerve — but no love do they find, and their abortive relationship expires with a shriek as they return to the city.

The drive back to New Orleans is the revealing part of the story. Above them are the stars of the southern sky, and about them in all directions the red glows of smudge fires. It is on this half of the excursion that he makes the one attempt to come to terms with her, but the kissing is futile and it is not repeated. Finally he sees where they are — riding across "a face, a head, far down here in the South — south of South, below it. A whole giant body sprawled downward then, on and on, always, constant as a constellation or an angel. Flaming and perhaps falling, he thought." Only Milton has described it better. What it all amounts to for the woman we never know. For the man from Syracuse it marks the end forever of his youthful expectations of romantic love.

This story found a conspicuous place for display in the second edition of Brooks and Warren's popular *Understanding Fiction,* and that may help keep attention turned in the direction of *The Bride of the Innisfallen* until the other stories, too, receive some of the critical attention they deserve. The essay "How I Write," reprinted with the story, may also remind readers that Eudora Welty has produced a small but respectable body of criticism along with her fiction. Three more essays, "Place in Fiction," "Words into Fiction," and "The Short Story," have been collected in a Smith College pamphlet, and the first and last of these three have been published separately. Most readers, however, will find it easiest to look for the critical studies in the periodicals in which they first appeared. In addition, she has done reviews of fiction by other writers, Henry Green, William Faulkner, Isak Dinesen, and William Sansom; and she has written a fine essay in praise of Katherine Anne Porter, "The Eye of the Story," which, as might be expected, contains some of her own more important observations about fiction.

Most of Eudora Welty's criticism belongs in the category of apology. Fiction is a mystery like any other kind of human creativity, she maintains, and it cannot be explained. For her, writing means beginning with something definitely known and disentangling the significance from it. This process necessarily involves selection and alteration; but if the writer is gifted and his activity is part of a general concern for human beings, the end of it all will be a truth, human understanding, and another act of communication between people. As for critical analysis, she prefers that that be considered a different kind of thing: "Criticism can be an art too," she says in "How I Write"; but she adds, "It's a mistake to think you can stalk back a story by analysis's footprints and even dream that's the original coming through the woods." Like Faulkner she refuses to write extended theoretical discussions of her art or confer upon it a spurious dignity by playing the role of artist in public. She remarked to Miss Porter many years ago that she was "underfoot locally"; and if reports may be believed, she is still very much that way, underfoot and involved in whatever concerns the lives of those who share soil, air, and water with her. This is her distinction and strength.

In her own way she has also been involved in Mississippi's troubles of the 1960's. Clearly the murder of Medgar Evars outraged her, as it outraged honest people everywhere; and it prompted her to write a short sketch for the *New Yorker* — "Where

Is the Voice Coming From?"—which represented an unnamed redneck explaining how he shot from ambush a defenseless Negro. Two years later she replied to criticism by friends from outside the state, some of whom had expected a more forthright commitment of her talents, in an essay "Must the Novelist Crusade?" Briefly her answer was that a crusading novelist is a contradiction in terms. Like any other human being a novelist must love his fellow man and seek justice; but his way of doing that is to show rather than to argue—to let us see our feelings and face our actions rather than to beat drums and deliver judgments. The novelist writes out of concern, and he writes with passion; but he does not distort a work of passion for the sake of a cause. "To write honestly and with all our powers," she says, "is the least we can do, and the most."

A fictional complement to this answer was "The Demonstrators," published in the *New Yorker* late in 1966. This is not one of Miss Welty's best stories, but it is certainly one of her most interesting. A young physician, whose politically liberal wife has recently left him, on a single evening ministers to an old schoolteacher and to a young Negro couple who have given one another fatal wounds with an ice pick. The mode of the young doctor's existence is symbolized by the persistence that keeps the dying teacher alive; and his dilemma, by his recognition of a cup of fine china in the hand of the Negro who brings him water at the deathbed of the girl. Afterwards he broods in the morning sunlight and reads a vulgar and condescending account of the affair in a local paper; but he cannot bring himself to leave the community. A sentimentalist might suggest that the author has here projected her own frustration. This could be so. Nevertheless, Miss Welty's artistic conscience is probably clear, and she seems not to have despaired yet either for Mississippi or for the human race.

A more ambitious piece, "The Optimist's Daughter," appeared in the *New Yorker* for March 15, 1969. (Miss Welty has since published a revised and slightly longer version of *The Optimist's Daughter* in book form [Random House, 1972].) The title of this long short story, or novelette, is ironic; for the optimist is a retired Mississippi judge, Clinton McKelva, who has deliberately chosen optimism as the only attitude that can enable him to face such things as the helpless and angry fatal decline of his first wife, Becky, the disappointing ineptitude and vulgarity of a second and much younger spouse, Wanda Fay, and finally his own fatal illness. The story comes to us through the consciousness of Judge McKelva's widowed daughter, Laurel, who has flown down from Chicago to comfort her father during what turns out to be a futile attempt to repair a detached retina and then, after his death, stays on to see that the funeral is conducted with full respect to him and to the expectations of his contemporaries. Unlike her father, Laurel is not an optimist; and her responses reflect the agonizing pressure of some of the realities that her father's pose had enabled him to endure.

The story has four movements. First, there is the long vigil in the New Orleans hospital, which ends abruptly when Wanda Fay in an act of childish desperation precipitates prematurely the old man's death. Then there is the Mississippi home funeral, reminiscent in its predictable proprieties and anecdotes of the one in *The Golden Apples* of twenty years before and, in the appearance of Wanda Fay's relatives from Texas, of the bizarre Peacock funeral in *The Ponder Heart*. After that there is an interval during which Wanda Fay returns to Texas for a visit with her parents and Laurel stays on temporarily in the house, preparing to surrender it to Wanda Fay, who is now "the last of the McKelvas." It is during this period that the optimist's daughter's renewed association with the house enables her to recall the Becky Clinton who fiercely resented the removal from West Virginia that her "good" marriage had forced upon her. Laurel now understands the hostility with which her mother in the last years of life expressed her frustration at the irreconcilable contradictions of her attachments to house, artifacts, husband, and childhood memories; and as the story nears an end, Laurel too experiences a similar surge of anger when she comes suddenly upon her mother's breadboard, now ruined by Wanda Fay's cracking walnuts on it with a hammer. She even comes close to striking Wanda Fay as the stupid girl arrogantly returns from Texas to claim her rights as a McKelva, but she forbears. After this unpleasantness Laurel returns to Chicago, carrying with her a painful sense of emptiness and loss, knowing something about human love that she did not know before, and perhaps sensing that her father's optimism may have had its uses.

The novel that Miss Welty published in 1970 was even more impressive than this novelette of 1969. In *Delta Wedding* of 1948 she had presented a brief glimpse, and that at second hand, of a Mississippi beyond the rich delta land. In this later novel, *Losing Battles*, she focuses her attention on the hill country in the northeastern part of the state, with its hills, gullies, undeveloped roads, and second-growth timber. The time is summer, in the 1930's; and the place, the community of Banner, Mississippi. Here as in *Delta Wedding* we get a detailed and loving look at one of those ceremonial occasions by which stable families and communities everywhere routinely affirm and renew their identity. The occasion in *Losing Battles* is ninety-year-old Granny Vaughn's birthday, an event regularly observed by great numbers of relatives, mostly Beechams (though Granny now lives with the Renfro family of her granddaughter Beulah), who live within driving distance. The special thing about this particular reunion is that it marks the return of young Jack Renfro from serving a sentence at the state penitentiary at Parchman and his reunion with his wife, Gloria, and their infant daughter, Lady May. For Jack Renfro, thus, there are two reunions; and the purpose of the action of the novel is to weld them into one.

As Granny Vaughn's clan gathers in the hill home to make its affirmation of unity, another powerful force is leaving the Banner scene. This is Miss Julia Mortimer, retired schoolmistress, who gave her life in an effort to make the sons and daughters of Banner look beyond their Mississippi microcosm. Much of the tension in the story is a consequence of Miss Julia's unremitting efforts to improve the natives of Banner and what she considers to be the primitive mode of life they cling to. For the most part her efforts have miscarried and simply caused the more promising young people to seek their fortunes elsewhere. This is why her last thoughts have been on Gloria, an orphan and prize pupil who did stay in Banner and even succeeded her mentor as local teacher but who married, to Miss Julia's dying dismay, Jack Renfro. Gloria genuinely loves her young husband, but she cannot comprehend at first what it means to belong to a family, any more than Miss Julia could. Thus she resists full adoption into the clan until the vexed Beechams initiate her with a bath and force-feeding of fresh watermelon that seems to have disturbed, quite unnecessarily, even some of Miss Welty's more sympathetic reviewers. Understandably after such boisterous treatment, however, Gloria continues to feel alienated for a time; but slowly the fact of her acceptance begins to sink in, and eventually the fund of charity in Jack Renfro tips the balance to make her consent to be one of them.

Taken singly, the members of the Banner clan are like any other group of human beings — varied in talent and temperament, and for the most part neither saintly nor very bad. Taken together they are far more admirable than they are individually — probably because in their roles as members of a group they lose some of that selfishness that lies at the root of human ugliness. This is what the intellectually proud but lonely Miss Julia has never fully understood: individually the Renfros and the Beechams may be stupid, petty, or mean; as a group they can be amazingly generous, capable of loving their enemies on occasion, and almost always capable of reaching out to take in the lonely, the estranged, and if necessary even the willfully eccentric. Thus the battles that the characters in this novel wage and lose are battles they wage in the hope of being able to remain alone, as isolated individuals. For example, Miss Julia, who wanted to be buried in solitary dignity under the steps of the schoolhouse, loses her last battle in death when the Banner people claim her for their own and honor her with burial in the community graveyard. Gloria surrenders the dream that Miss Julia has tried to give her, accepts the childlike Jack fully, as he accepts her, and returns to live with him in the house with Granny Vaughn and the other Renfros. The paradox is that, whether they know it or not, all these people are infinitely richer for having submitted to the ties that bind; and the strength they find is a direct consequence of the concession they have made. It is altogether appropriate that the novel should end with a rejoicing Jack Renfro, who has lost most of his battles since well before the novel began, bursting into the old evangelical hymn of victory "Bringing in the Sheaves."

Comparisons of Eudora Welty with other writers in the southern United States have been fairly frequent. In choice of subject, of course, she resembles all those who have written accurately about Mississippi, and she also has demonstrable affinities with those modern authors who have written of other states in the deep South. Being a southern woman, she is also often compared with Katherine Anne Porter, Caroline Gordon, Carson McCullers, and Flannery O'Connor. Being southern, however, is at once the most important and the least important thing about

Eudora Welty. Mississippi has been her sustenance for so long that one can scarcely conceive what she would have become had she fed elsewhere. Whatever her place, she would have been a maker of something, for that is her nature. She has, as she herself confessed, a visual imagination and a penchant for seeing things in their connectedness; and the simultaneous unraveling and compounding of the networks she finds in life about her produces those complex pieces that more often than not seem to have grown like crystals from simple sketches into the strange new entities that are her stories. Occasionally her tendency to see things in terms of other things has got her into trouble. Some of the descriptions in *A Curtain of Green*, especially, invite the term "baroque" because of uncontrolled and nonfunctional metaphors. The stories there have a few warts on them. In recent years these lapses have not occurred. As for structure, that has been present in Eudora Welty's work from the beginning.

Miss Welty is not without the southern writer's sense of the past or feeling for the metaphysical, but she has never allowed her writing to play a partisan's role in either of these areas. Her one story about the Civil War could have been told with the same truth about almost any war, and her tales of the Natchez Trace would have much the same validity if told about the Wilderness Road or the path westward left by Lewis and Clark. That is, she is historically minded without being antiquarian. Her sense of the metaphysical is frequently but unobtrusively displayed for readers who may be tuned in to it. We can see it at work in Mrs. Larkin's strange perversity, in the intimations that come to William Wallace during the river dragging, in the roles that Livvie and Jenny Lockhart and several of the characters in *The Golden Apples* unknowingly assume, and in the pathetic frustration of the semi-divine Circe with her realization that silly mortals have a divinity all their own, though they themselves may be unaware of it. Some readers may regard these intimations of transcendence as aspects of an outdated provincialism; but they are pervasive enough to make one suspect that for this writer such things represent the ground of her being. And, at any rate, the tangible is always there, too, and very much in focus.

Selected Bibliography

Principal Works of Eudora Welty

A Curtain of Green and Other Stories. New York: Doubleday, Doran, 1941.
The Robber Bridegroom. New York: Doubleday, Doran, 1942.
The Wide Net and Other Stories. New York: Harcourt, Brace, 1943.
Delta Wedding. New York: Harcourt, Brace, 1946.
The Golden Apples. New York: Harcourt, Brace, 1949.
The Ponder Heart. New York: Harcourt, Brace, 1954. Originally published in the *New Yorker*, 29:47–138 (December 5, 1953).
The Bride of the Innisfallen. New York: Harcourt, Brace, 1955.
Three Papers on Fiction. Northampton, Mass.: Smith College, 1962. (Contains "Place in Fiction," originally in *South Atlantic Quarterly*, 55:57–72 (January 1956), and later published in a limited edition, New York: House of Books, 1957; "Words into Fiction"; and "The Short Story," originally in *Atlantic Monthly* (as "The Reading and Writing of Short Stories"), 183:54–58 (February 1949) and 46–49 (March 1949), and separately by Harcourt, Brace, 1950.)
The Shoe Bird. New York: Harcourt, Brace and World, 1964.
Losing Battles. New York: Random House, 1970.
The Optimist's Daughter. New York: Random House, 1972.

Selected Uncollected Items

"Ida M'Toy," *Accent*, 2:214–22 (Summer 1942). (Sketch.)
"Pageant of Birds," *New Republic*, 109:565–67 (October 25, 1943). (Sketch.)
"A Sketching Trip," *Atlantic Monthly*, 175:62–70 (June 1945). (Story.)
"Hello and Goodbye," *Atlantic Monthly*, 180:37–40 (July 1947). (Story.)
"In Yoknapatawpha," *Hudson Review*, 1:596–98 (Winter 1949). (Review, William Faulkner.)
"How I Write," *Virginia Quarterly Review*, 31:240–51 (Spring 1955). Reprinted in Cleanth Brooks and R. P. Warren, *Understanding Fiction*, 2nd ed. New York: Appleton-Century-Crofts, 1959. Pp. 545–53. (Essay.)
"A Flock of Guinea Hens Seen from a Car," *New Yorker*, 33:35 (April 20, 1957). (Poem.)
"A Touch That's Magic," *New York Times Book Review*, November 3, 1957, p. 5. (Review, Isak Dinesen.)
"Henry Green: A Novelist of the Imagination," *Texas Quarterly*, 4:246–56 (Autumn 1961). (Essay.)

212

"Time and Place — and Suspense," *New York Times Book Review*, June 30, 1963, pp. 5, 27. (Review, William Sansom.)

"Where Is the Voice Coming From?" *New Yorker*, 39:24–25 (July 6, 1963). (Sketch.)

"The Eye of the Story," *Yale Review*, 55:265–74 (Winter 1965). (Essay.)

"Must the Novelist Crusade?" *Atlantic Monthly*, 216:104–8 (October 1965). (Essay.)

"The Demonstrators," *New Yorker*, 42:56–63 (November 26, 1966). (Story.)

Bibliography

Gross, Seymour L. "Eudora Welty: A Bibliography of Criticism and Comment." *Secretary's News Sheet* (Bibliographical Society, University of Virginia), 45:1–32 (April 1960).

Critical Studies

Appel, Alfred, Jr. *A Season of Dreams*. Baton Rouge: Louisiana State University Press, 1965.

Glenn, Eunice. "Fantasy in the Fiction of Eudora Welty," *A Southern Vanguard*, edited by Allen Tate. New York: Prentice-Hall, 1947. Pp. 78–91. Reprinted in *Critiques and Essays in Modern Fiction, 1920–1951*, edited by John Aldridge. New York: Ronald Press, 1952. Pp. 506–17.

Hardy, John E. "*Delta Wedding* as Region and Symbol," *Sewanee Review*, 60:397–417 (Summer 1952).

Morris, Harry C. "Eudora Welty's Use of Mythology," *Shenandoah*, 6:34–40 (Spring 1955).

Ransom, John Crowe. "Delta Fiction," *Kenyon Review*, 8:503–7 (Summer 1946).

Rubin, Louis D., Jr. "The Golden Apples of the Sun," in *The Faraway Country: Writers of the Modern South*. Seattle: University of Washington Press, 1963. Pp. 131–54.

Vande Kieft, Ruth M. *Eudora Welty*. New York: Twayne, 1962.

Warren, Robert Penn. "The Love and the Separateness in Miss Welty," *Kenyon Review*, 6:246–59 (Spring 1944). Reprinted in R. P. Warren, *Selected Essays*. New York: Random House, 1958. Pp. 156–69.

Mary McCarthy

Mary McCarthy has so far written six novels, as well as thirteen books of other kinds, and though all the novels are not equally successful, each has so much life and truth, and is written in a prose so spare, vigorous, and natural, and yet at the same time so witty, graceful, and, in a certain way, poetic, that it becomes a matter for wonder that she is not generally named among the finest American novelists of her period. She is much admired, of course, and has achieved a best seller, but that is not the same thing. The reason, I think, is that she is a sort of neoclassicist in a country of romantics. The sprightliness and detachment of her prose, her preference for sense over sensibility, her satirical eye for the hidden ego in our intellectual pretensions are qualities we are not comfortable with in this country. They may amuse, but they also antagonize. And they don't, among all our heaven-storming Titans, seem Important. At any rate, whatever the reason, the qualities and meanings that lie beneath her sparkling surface tend, even by admiring critics, to be misconceived. Her novels have been called "essayistic," for instance — designed to persuade us of ideas rather than to present living characters and felt experiences. And their subject is often supposed to be a supercilious, zestfully destructive view of people she dislikes, a view unredeemed by any examples of the humanly admirable — except in the heroines who represent herself. These charges are so common, in fact, that it may be useful to begin with a preliminary answer to each.

As to the first, though she has written mainly about her own class of American intellectuals, people who try to live by ideas or to give the appearance of doing so, and has therefore naturally admitted the play of ideas into her stories, her chief concerns have always been psychological, emotional, above all moral, the concerns of the novelist. Whenever her characters express ideas, something of more urgent human interest is also going on, whether they know it or not. And though her novels, like most of those which are nowadays taken seriously, are meaningfully organized, it is no simple polemical formula that turns out to be their meaning. It is rather the kind of vision, precisely the novelist's, which moves us, which enlarges our sympathies, and which brings us closer to a complex reality. The fact is, if one remembers her novels freshly at all, it is surely characters and not ideas which their titles bring first to mind — the man in the Brooks Brothers shirt, Macdougal Macdermott, Will Taub, Henry Mulcahy, Domna Rejnev, Miles Murphy, Warren Coe, the girls in "the group" and certain of their men and their parents. In novels these days, Miss McCarthy has complained, "there are hardly any people," only "sensibility" and "sensation," but her own have been an exception. Moreover, though she is of course right in noting the enormous difference between her art and that of the novelist she says she would most like to resemble, Tolstoy, yet her admiration for the godlike realist is reflected at least in the way her intentions are always buried deep inside a flesh of vividly rendered particulars. The concrete world of her people, their tics of behavior, their ways of talking — a precise notation of these gives her work throughout the special authority of the visible and the audible. Indeed, her eye for the particular qualities of things makes half the charm of her style, where it adds to the more sober virtues deriving from her intelligence and honesty a flashing witty poetry of metaphor.

As for that other notion, that she is a heartless satirist whose chief interest is to demonstrate her own superiority to the silliness of her victims — this is just as mistaken. While she does indeed make characters out of people she regards as morally weak or ugly or dangerous, and makes them with a bold thrust toward grotesque extremes that recalls another writer she admires, Dickens, the norms of sense or decency which such people violate are equally vivid in her novels. We see these norms both in the passionate indignation between her lines and in the large number of her characters who cannot live without struggling toward them or becoming their champions. In fact, it is precisely one of her distinctions that she has succeeded in creating good people — even out of twentieth-century intellectuals! — who are at once convincing and attractive. It should be added, however, that the characters she values are not necessarily intellectuals. On the contrary, they may be, like Warren Coe, the kind of people at whom her clever, learned heroines tend to smile. And we must add also, what is equally true and equally unnoticed by the run of her critics, that the heroine who represents herself is often, for all her cleverness, the character most roughly treated by the ironical author. If she ends by coming out all right, it is with a rightness earned by much agonizing error, and itself riddled with imperfections sadly accepted.

Amid the criticism of fiction fashionable during her career, a kind which has concentrated so hard on technique or symbols that it often bypassed what they were intended to serve, Miss McCarthy's ideas on the subject have been liberatingly sensible. Here (from "Settling the Colonel's Hash" in *On the Contrary*) is a remark that may be taken as an introduction to the present study:

It is now considered very old-fashioned and tasteless to speak of an author's "philosophy of life" as something that can be harvested from his work. Actually, most of the great authors did have a "philosophy of life" which they were eager to communicate to the public; this was one of their motives for writing. And to disentangle a moral philosophy from a work that evidently contains one is far less damaging to the author's purpose and the integrity of his art than to violate his imagery by symbol-hunting, as though reading a novel were a sort of paper-chase.

The images of a novel or a story belong, as it were, to a family, very closely knit and inseparable from each other; the parent "idea" of a story or a novel generates events and images all bearing a strong family resemblance. And to understand a story or a novel, you must look for the parent "idea," which is usually in plain view, if you read quite carefully and literally what the author says.

The same thing is surely true of the serious writer's total oeuvre: all his works will, for the same reason, show this family resemblance. Since Miss McCarthy, in spite of the abundant social reality in her novels, is as autobiographical a novelist as Fitzgerald or Hemingway, we can best approach the "parent idea" underlying her career by beginning with her life. And the first point to make is that it has been a life blessed — and cursed — with an unusual amount of freedom. Orphaned at six, she was taken care of for years by coldly cruel guardians and later by grandparents who were kind but detached. Doris Grumbach tells us that a former Vassar classmate, now a psychiatrist, remembers that at college Mary McCarthy was "'aloof, independent, irrelevant . . . lonely,' seemingly rootless because she, unlike most of the others, had no real family she had to please. 'She appeared to be much freer than we were and this fascinated and frightened us.'" Such freedom resembles, it is true, the freedom to think and do as they wish that many clever young people of our time claim as a right, but for the orphaned Mary McCarthy it was a condition more serious than a bright student's pose. She was really free, and had to experience what this meant in her deepest nature. And the kind of freedom that comes from having no family to please — is it not a freedom from those pressures, loyalties, urgencies of feeling that, though they hamper us, also give us a sense of who we are, of what is real, of what is right? To lack such direction can mean one is at the mercy of merely plausible ideas on such matters, ideas which decent people hope to choose according to their truth, of course, but which, amid the multiple "truths" life offers, even the best of us are in danger of choosing with our vanity, or our fear, or our lust. To be directed by external authority has its own dangers; these are the dangers of freedom.

Her work is about the painful mixed blessing of freedom for her kind of people — for intellectuals — and in particular, about how hard it has been for intellectuals in our time to behave decently and humanly. For to be free and clever has often meant only to be able to escape from difficult, limiting reality into the realm of flattering abstractions. And yet — for I have said that to speak of what she dislikes is to speak of only half her subject — if she shows what makes her kind go wrong, she shows just as vividly what makes them go right. She shows that sometimes, even in intellectuals free to please themselves, there arises a love for reality that is greater than love of self. This development, because it means that the self must be willing to suffer for something it values more than its own ease, can be one of the moving and beautiful events of a human life — it can be heroic. At any rate, the conflict between these two tendencies of the mind is at the center of all Miss McCarthy's novels. Because this conflict is her own, her reports on it have the variety, complexity, and intensity of personal experience. But because the freedom to live by ideas, ideas which may lead away from the real as well as toward it, is what distinguishes the whole class of twentieth-century intellectuals, her tales of the troubled Mary McCarthy heroine have developed naturally into social satire.

The exquisitely written *Memories of a Catholic Girlhood* (1957) reveals how deeply rooted Miss McCarthy's stories are in her own life. She tells us that she was born in Seattle in 1912 to a Protestant mother, whose own mother was Jewish and who accepted her husband's religion, and a Catholic father. The mother was beautiful. The father was a partial invalid, irresponsible as a breadwinner, but handsome, charming, a delight to his children with his stories and presents. When she was six both parents died in one week from flu. The rich McCarthy grandparents, whose Catholicism was a "sour and baleful doctrine in which old hates and rancors had been stewing for generations, with ignorance proudly stirring the pot," placed her and her three brothers in a house as poor as their own was luxurious and under the guardianship of a couple of Dickensian monsters, a great-aunt and a German-American husband. The theme of the first chapters of *Memories* is injustice, and Miss McCarthy describes the needless poverty, the ugliness, the sadistic, self-righteous beatings with an unaccustomed, if controlled, intensity of rage and pity.

At the age of eleven she was rescued and taken to Seattle by her other grandfather, also rich, but a model of the Protestant virtues. To cite qualities she later found he shared with Julius Caesar, Grandfather Preston was "just, laconic, severe, magnanimous, detached." She was no longer wretched, but she remained an outsider —in her new home, whose moral standards were oppressively high; in the Catholic convent school she went to first, where she lost her faith; later in a public school, among the school "hearties"; finally in an Episcopal boarding school, where she was set apart by her "brilliance" and her independence. And here, at sixteen, she underwent experiences which, as described in the chapter of *Memories* called "The Figures in the Clock," clearly foreshadow the characteristic moral vision, and even the organizing "conflicts," of the fiction to come.

In this chapter it is a conflict between the wicked conspirator Catiline and Julius Caesar. Acting the part of Catiline in a play written by her Latin teacher, she made a sensation by reading her lines so as to *vindicate* the rebel, to champion his self-willed brilliance — and thereby her own — against mere dull law and order. Shortly after this, however, a strange thing happened. Under the guidance of Miss Gowrie (the fictitious name she gives her teacher), the girl fell in love with Julius Caesar! "The sensation was utterly confounding. All my previous crushes had been products of my will, constructs of my personal convention, or projections of myself, the way Catiline was. This came from without and seized me . . . the first piercing contact with an impersonal reality happened to me through Caesar." She and her teacher loved that mind "immersed in practical life as in some ingenious detective novel, that wished always to show you how anything was done and under what disadvantages . . . the spirit of justice and scientific inquiry that reigned over the *Commentaries*." "Justice, good will, moderation, and *uncommon fidelity*," why, she asks, quoting Caesar's praise of a conquered Gaul loyal to himself, "should these substantives of virtue have stirred the Seminary's Catiline? At the time I was sublimely unaware that my fortifications had been breached, that the forces of law and order were pacifying the city while the rebel standard still waved on the ramparts."

What she loved in Caesar hints not only at the moral values in the novels to come, but at their art — their way with details and their way with sentences. But we are not done with the meaning of this rich chapter. Another insight alternates with the first "like the two little wooden weather figures in a German clock, one of which steps out as the other swings back into the works, in response to atmospheric pressures." The "good Gaul" whose loyalty to Caesar she and Miss Gowrie admired was after all a "quisling," traitorously loyal to his people's conqueror. Later, when "bad Gauls" merged in her mind with those who resisted Hitler, she was angry with her Latin teacher for having steered her wrong. But then, later still, it came to her that it had been Miss Gowrie who had seen to it that her Catiline costume was espe-

cially gorgeous — she has at last "an eerie sense that Miss Gowrie,
unsuspected by me, was my co-conspirator." It appears that
for her teacher too that preference for Caesar, for "impersonal reality" and law and order over the lawless ego, was haunted by the
contradictory possibility that the ego can have a self-justifying
beauty, or that law and order, with changes in "atmospheric pressure," that is, in the context, may serve error, and the self-asserting
individual be in the right. And in her note to the chapter Miss
McCarthy tells us that this conflict is rooted in her inheritance.
"Caesar, of course, was my [Preston] grandfather . . . Catiline
was my McCarthy ancestors . . . To my surprise, I chose Caesar
and the rule of law. This does not mean that the seesaw between
these two opposed forces terminated; one might say, in fact, that
it only began during my last years in the Seminary when I recognized the beauty of an ablative absolute and of a rigorous code of
conduct."

A word about her life after the Seminary. For a summer she
studied acting; then, from 1929 to 1933, she attended Vassar College. In 1933 she married the actor and unsuccessful playwright
Harold Johnsrud, and began to write reviews for the *New Republic* and the *Nation*. Her essay "My Confession" tells how at this
time she was drawn into political controversy by her indignation
at the smug dishonesty of American Communists and especially by
their defense of the "Moscow trials," in which the exiled Trotsky
was being discredited by an elaborate structure of lies. In 1936, her
marriage dissolved, she lived in Greenwich Village, wrote reviews,
and worked for an art dealer. A year later she began to write
a monthly "Theater Chronicle" for the recently revived *Partisan
Review*. In these essays there was much good sense and some affected and excessive rigidity of principle, as she herself admits in a
preface to the book *Sights and Spectacles* (1956) in which they were
later collected. In 1938 she married the critic Edmund Wilson.

The marriage ended after seven years, but he was the father of her only child Reuel, and it was at Wilson's suggestion that she began to write fiction. Her first story, "Cruel and Barbarous Treatment," became the opening chapter of *The Company She Keeps*. For two years she was a college teacher — at Bard in 1945–46 and at Sarah Lawrence in 1948–49 — and her history since then, aside from her marriage to Bowden Broadwater, which lasted from 1946 to 1961, and to James West in 1961, is mainly the history of her books.

In 1956, along with *Sights and Spectacles*, she published the first of two works on Italian cities, *Venice Observed*, and in 1959 the second, *The Stones of Florence*. Each book is an account of the city's history, architecture, art, and people. The first is the slighter, the more personal and anecdotal, the second the more sober and scholarly, and at the same time the more passionate: The art and architecture of Florence moved her intensely. This latter book, in fact, is surprisingly readable for so scholarly a work, and the reason is only in part the lively, taut, and elegant style. Even more important is her clear concern throughout with the "human interest" of the history and the art.

In 1962 the essays she had been writing since 1946 on a variety of subjects were collected in the volume *On the Contrary*. These differ in quality. Most valuable are her contributions to the political debates of the time — on the Moscow trials, on McCarthyism, on Communists in the schools — and her essays on fiction and drama, "Settling the Colonel's Hash," "The Fact in Fiction," "Characters in Fiction," and "The American Realist Playwrights." Of the latter group it is enough to say here that they constitute, by implication, a defense of the kind of art she herself has practiced. This is a realistic art, which gives us what might usefully be called *samples* of reality rather than *symbols* of it. (She herself speaks of "natural symbolism.") For the reader to do justice to such work, he needs to be alert rather to human matters — the psychological or moral meaning of actions or tones — than to literary allusions and strategies.

We are now ready for the novels, on which her permanent reputation will surely rest. The first of these, *The Company She Keeps* (1942), consists of six chapters published originally as stories in magazines. In a very interesting and useful *Paris Review* interview, Miss McCarthy has said that though she had originally intended them as separate stories, "about halfway through I began to think of them as a kind of unified story. The same character kept reappearing, and so on. I decided finally to call it a novel in that it does in a sense tell *a* story, one story." The reappearing character is Margaret Sargent, of whom we learn at the end that she was the daughter of a tolerant, intelligent Protestant father and a beautiful Catholic mother, and was brought up as a Catholic, after her mother's early death, by a vulgar and bigoted Catholic aunt. Not only has Miss McCarthy given her heroine a background substantially like her own; she has told us herself that the stories are all autobiographical except one, "Portrait of the Intellectual as a Yale Man." In fact, the book is remarkable for the honesty of its self-exposure, an exposure which dares to include the ignoble and the humiliating and which shows a kind of reckless passion for the truth that is to remain an important element of her talent.

This passion for the truth not only provides the motive power behind the self-exposure in these tales. It turns out to be their underlying subject as well. The author has suggested, and it has been repeated by many critics, that the "one story" of the book is that of the heroine's vain search, amid her many identities, for some real identity underlying them all. But this search seems actually to be less important than her moral development, a development of which the ultimate goal is not to know what she is but to behave as an adult should. What we mainly watch as her story unfolds is Miss Sargent's increasingly desperate struggle, against all the temptations to falsehood in the intellectual life of her time, to stop lying and to live by the truth.

She begins far enough from any truth. In the first chapter, "Cruel and Barbarous Treatment," which is not so much a story as a witty satire on nameless generalized types and their typical behavior, she is a married "Woman With a Secret" delighting in an affair with a "Young Man" chiefly because it "was an opportunity, unparalleled in her experience, for exercising feelings of superiority over others." Play-acting irresponsibly with life's realities, she reduces them to fashionable clichés that minister to her vanity. The second chapter, "Rogue's Gallery," in which Miss Sargent works for a rogue who runs an art gallery and appears as a naive, good-natured foil for her colorful con man of a boss, seems a mere exercise in the Dickensian picturesque. But in the third the book's deeper story continues: the heroine's play-acting is complicated by an opposing impulse. "The Man in the Brooks Brothers Shirt" is an account of how Miss Sargent, now seen in the role of poised, sophisticated New York intellectual, is drawn into an affair with a businessman on a cross-country train trip because she enjoys playing that role before such an audience. And yet, showing off an advance copy of a new book, she wonders uneasily "if her whole way of life had been assumed for purposes of ostentation." When the man speaks shrewdly about her past, she leans forward. "Perhaps at last she had found him, the one she kept looking for, the one who could tell her what she was really like. . . . If she once knew, she had no doubt that she could behave perfectly." Then there is her horrified shame, when she awakens in his compartment, at the drunken sex of the night before which she gradually remembers. (This is the first of those cool "shocking" notations of the unattractive particulars of "romantic" episodes for which Miss McCarthy has won a certain notoriety, though far from being exploitations of sex, they seem expressions of a puritanical disgust.)

Finally, she becomes aware of a reluctance to leave the man, who, falling in love with her, had changed in her eyes from the vulgar businessman type to an actual and attractive person; and at this "a pang of joy went through her as she examined her own sorrow and found it to be real." The affair dies away after the trip, and the story ends with both falling back into the stereotypes from which they had briefly emerged, but Margaret Sargent has acquired substance as a character with the disclosure that she is divided, like the rest of us, and that the hunger of her intellectual's vanity is opposed by a hunger for reality.

In "The Genial Host" we see this new Miss Sargent again. She is now the dinner guest of one Pflaumen, who is shown as having repressed both his natural tendency to fat and hairiness and his natural personality of a Jewish paterfamilias to become the elegant familiar and host of clever, fashionable, successful people. Moreover, this reality-avoider collects his guests for their "allegorical possibilities," that is, for the chic intellectual positions to which they have sacrificed their own reality. Thus, Margaret, hotly defending Trotsky against the party's Stalinist, and delighted at the effect she is making, is horrified to note that Pflaumen is beaming at her for performing as expected, while the party's one honest man, a poor young Jewish lawyer, is applauding ironically. The story ends in another capitulation: she dare not yet rebel against Pflaumen and the falsenesses by which she sings for her suppers, she is still too "poor, loverless, lonely." But in the next, "Portrait of the Intellectual as a Yale Man," though she is still in need, she has ceased to capitulate.

This story is mainly about the Yale Man, who, though naive and second rate, has been welcomed onto the Stalinist-dominated weekly magazine the *Liberal* because he comes as a healthy, happy, clean-cut, average American, a type rare among them. This was a time — the thirties — when out of loyalty to the ideal of communism a large proportion of the intellectual establishment had accepted so many of the lies and brutalities of the Stalin dictatorship that they had lost the sense of the relevance to politics, and even to life, of the ordinary decencies. Such people lied in defense of the Communist party's shifts in policy or vilified the opposition rather than debate with it, and did both with a sincere feeling of virtue. Jim Barnett, the Yale Man, is not one of these; he tries to be honest, but he is able to make a living as a radical political commentator only because his shallowness is precisely suited to the intellectual climate of this milieu, from which the Stalinists have largely excluded reality.

Margaret Sargent was put into this story, says Miss McCarthy, "because she had to be in it," that is, for the sake of the unity of the book to come, but her role turns out to be crucial, for she is there as an eruption of integrity into that world of blur and lies. Now when she defends Trotsky, it is among Stalinist editors who can fire her from the magazine job she needs. "You had to admire her courage," Jim thinks, "for undertaking something that cost her so much." Even her way of taking Jim for a lover is significantly different from her past behavior. She submits to this married man's sudden overpowering lust — and perhaps to her own as well — with a "disconsolate smile" — no play-acting here. Jim quits his job indignantly when she is fired, and in this time of proud excitement, he gets an idea for an important book. But the effort to write the book and to live on that moral peak is really beyond his means. He gives up both, gets a handsome job on the conservative magazine *Destiny*, and though he continues to send checks to the American Civil Liberties Union, he grows increasingly impatient with opinionated unsuccessful left-wing intellectuals. And for Margaret he comes to feel a kind of hatred. Pathetic though she is in her "too tense" clinging to her truth, in her unsuccess, she is somehow triumphant. In the story's beautifully written last pages she haunts him as a reminder of the dead illusion of his youth, the illusion that he could be free of "the cage of his own nature" and better than himself.

In the last story "Ghostly Father, I Confess," after five years of an unhappy second marriage to an architect apparently congenial but really authoritarian and unimaginative, Margaret is spending an hour on a psychoanalyst's couch. She has been sent by her husband, who is fed up with the way she uses her "wonderful scruples as an excuse for acting like a bitch." And now, though she disapproves of psychoanalysis, whose conclusions can never be proved wrong since all disagreement is mere resistance, and considers her doctor a limited man, she finds herself drawn into an agonizing search for the cause of her misery and bad behavior, for it is also a search for the "meaning" that will redeem her life from "gibberish." The story is crammed with the up-welling, emotion-charged facts of her life —from the childhood passed between her father's rationalism and her aunt's vulgarities to the second marriage, in which she feels herself suffocating amid such stylish middle-class culture-objects as "her white pots of ivy, her Venetian blinds, her open copy of a novel by Kafka. . . . each in its own patina of social anxiety." Miss McCarthy seems to have thrown boldly into the story the whole confusion of her own life. Yet it moves with a nightmarish coherence amid the chaos, and, in fact, what she understands at the end makes the story a unity and a fitting conclusion to the book's whole development.

The story is about the pressure on Margaret Sargent to accept the life of the intellectually sophisticated middle class which she detests. And for that life she is now to be made fit by a mode of "therapy" which is presented as the most insidious of all its ways of avoiding reality. The object of the therapy is to perform a "perfectly simple little operation." First the consciousness is put to sleep by "the sweet, optimistic laughing-gas of science (you are not bad, you are merely unhappy . . . poor Hitler is a paranoiac, and that dirty fornication in a hotel room, why, that, dear Miss Sargent, is a 'relationship')." Then the doctor cuts out "the festering conscience, which was of no use to you at all, and was only making you suffer." But to have a conscience is to remain aware of what is outside one's own wishes, that is, of a difference between truth, however painful, and lies, however gratifying. Under the pressure of the idea that she is unhappy merely because she is ill, "her own sense of truth was weakening. This and her wonderful scruples were all she had in the world, and they were slipping away." And it is this that makes her most miserable. She can't behave as she should, but not to know when she does evil, and not to mind, is to lose her grip on reality and to shrink from a healthy adult into an invalid or a child.

The story ends with an apparent inconclusiveness that is really, as I have said, a sufficient conclusion, both to the story and the book. She is almost persuaded by her doctor that she can be good and free and strong inside her marriage, which is to say, that all can yet be well at no painful cost, when she remembers a dream she had begun to tell him earlier. In this dream she had enabled herself to accept the embraces of a Nazi type by pretending that he was really rather Byronic. As she walks away from the doctor's office, feeling the hateful expected tug of an attraction to him, she suddenly understands the dream. It has told her that all will *not* be well, that unable to love herself except through the love of men, she will again seek a new love to rescue her from past failures and will again snatch at it blindly and perhaps unscrupulously. But though in the dream she pretended the Nazi was a Byron, "she could still detect her own frauds. At the end of the dream, her eyes were closed, but the inner eye had remained alert. . . . 'Oh my God,' she said . . . 'do not let them take this away from me. If the flesh must be blind, let the spirit see. Preserve me in disunity.'"

228

Thus is completed the "one story" of Margaret Sargent. Beginning as a manipulator and falsifier of reality, she is now its true lover, who would rather suffer than pretend and whose suffering, because it means the clarity of mind to see the truth and the courage to face it, is the measure of a new dignity.

It is no doubt true, as Elizabeth Hardwick has suggested, that all such "frank" confession is in part self-exculpation. But Miss McCarthy's frankness in confessing weakness and error in this book seems to earn her the right to move on, for a completer truth indeed, to the virtues of her defects. At any rate, the portrait of Margaret Sargent carries conviction, and her struggle toward honesty has a permanent relevance to our experience.

Certain themes in the first book are repeated in *Cast a Cold Eye* (1950), a collection of four stories and three early versions of chapters of her *Memories*. In "The Weeds" is treated somberly, and in "The Friend of the Family" with bitter humor, the sort of marriage seen in "Ghostly Father." It is the marriage that destroys the individual's integrity, his troublesome loyalty to the truth of his own nature. "The Old Men," less successful than the other two but interesting for its meanings, tells how a young man who has long been uncertain of his own identity comes to feel that the self is no more than a *"point du depart"* for "impersonations," and that reality, the actual, is "pornography" and to be avoided. At this, "blithe and ready to live, selfishly and inconsiderately," he sings out the Yeats epitaph which gives the book its title, and shortly afterward, as if for want of any reason to live, he abruptly dies. It thus appears that the "cold eye" which reviewers have generally supposed the author meant as her own is meant in fact to describe what she most reprobates, that indifference to what is outside the self which deprives the self of reality and makes life pointless.

Miss McCarthy has defended *The Oasis* (1949) from the charge that it is not a novel by insisting that it was not intended to be, that it is a *conte philosophique*. This explains its lack of action, for instead of plot we have slight episodes explored for their large meanings and characters revealed less by what they do than in long satirical descriptions. But it cannot eliminate the sense that the tale's developments, which ought after all to arise by an inner necessity, are sometimes arbitrarily asserted, as if to get things moving. And yet the reminder of an elegant eighteenth-century prose form does point to qualities that will keep the tale, in spite of its imperfections, interesting for a long time. The satirical descriptions do not merely imitate but genuinely duplicate the qualities of eighteenth-century prose masters — the psychological insight, the general wisdom, the witty, epigrammatic, gracefully balanced sentences.

The Oasis is the story of a group of New York intellectuals — based apparently on well-known friends of the author, but to the rest of us quite recognizable as contemporary types — who, shortly after World War II, form a colony called Utopia in the Taconic Mountains of New York State. The colonists fall mainly into two factions. The "purists" hope the colony will illustrate "certain notions of justice, freedom, and sociability" derived from their Founder, a saintly Italian anarchist lost in "a darkened city of Europe." This group is led by Macdougal Macdermott, a man who rightly senses that he does not naturally belong to "that world of the spirit" which he yearns to enter, but who, "ten years before . . . had made the leap into faith and sacrificed $20,000 a year and a secure career as a paid journalist for the intangible values that eluded his empirical grasp. He had moved down town into Bohemia, painted his walls indigo, dropped the use of capital letters and the practice of wearing a vest" and become the editor of a "libertarian magazine." The "realists," on the other hand, have come only for a holiday from the pressures of real life. They look upon "conspicuous goodness" like the Founder's as a "form of simple-mindedness on a par with vegetarianism, and would have refused admission to Heaven on the ground that it was full of greenhorns and cranks." Moreover, they find absurd the assumption of "human freedom" which underlies all that the purists believe, for they are inheritors of Marxian "scientific socialism," and though they had discarded the dialectic and repudiated the Russian Revolution, "the right of a human being to *think* that he could resist history, environment, class structure, psychic conditioning was something they denied him with all the ferocity of their own pent-up natures and disappointed hopes." And since "ideological supremacy" has become "essential to their existence," they look forward with pleasure to the colony's failure. They do, however, wish it to fail convincingly, of its own foolishness, and this seduces them into unusually good behavior. Soon Will Taub, their leader, finds that he participates "in the forms of equity with increasing confidence, and though of course he did not take any of it *seriously*, his heavy and rather lowering nature performed the unaccustomed libertarian movements with a feeling of real sprightliness and wondering self-admiration, as if he had been learning to dance."

In Will Taub we have the first full-fledged example of the enemy in Miss McCarthy's world, the Other to all that she values. He is one who is at home only in the realm of ideas, who is flat-footed in his behavior with children, women — in all non-intellectual relations — who feels pain at the very word "Jew" because "his Jewishness [was] a thing about himself which he was powerless to alter and which seemed to reduce him therefore to a curious dependency on the given." And this rejection of the "given," the real, on behalf of a world of ideas where he can reign supreme involves too a rejection of moral responsibility. It is for the realists a felt oddity in Utopia that "here they were answerable for their deeds to someone and not simply to an historical process." And

Taub is even capable, like the later Henry Mulcahy, of beginning to believe his own lie (that an embarrassingly cowardly reaction of his is due to former police persecution) in order to maintain his cherished supremacy.

These two characters, and Joe Lockman, the go-getting businessman who comes to Utopia determined to get more spiritual profit out of it than anyone else, are the tale's most vivid portraits. But it is a fourth, Katy Norell, to whom its chief events tend to happen and out of whose responses its meanings emerge. Katy, a teacher of Greek, suffers from "a strong will and a weak character," an awkward compulsion to tell the truth even when it aggravates her problems, and a readiness to feel guilty when things go wrong. Though it was her "instinctive opinion . . . that the past could be altered and actions, like words, 'taken back,'" her husband's disgust with her, on one occasion when it seems serious, gives her a frightening glimpse of life "as a black chain of consequence, in which nothing was lost, forgot, forgiven, redeemed, in which the past was permanent and the present slipping away from her." This character, weak but scrupulous, who wishes life were easy but can't shut out the perception that it is hard, is, of course, a sister of Margaret Sargent as well as of the later Martha Sinnott, though, unlike the others, she pays for representing her author's inner life by being one of the less vivid characters in her book. But it is out of her inner contradictions that the book's closing insights come. These insights are initiated by the last of several challenges to the colony's "sociability" — the stealing of their strawberries by some rough interlopers, whom Katy herself, frightened when her pleading is answered with threatening gestures, demands be ejected by force. Taub taunts her with her contradiction, her yielding to "human nature," and at this, lulled or liberated by the dinner wine, she begins to understand. They did wrong, she thinks, to cling to the strawberries without needing them — it was only the idea of the strawberries they really cared about. They had let "mental images" possess them as the idea of sex dominates the mind in pornography. But the mind should stick to its own objects, "love, formal beauty, virtue"; they should not have tried to make real things dance to the mind's tune. And this is only a small example of their fundamental error. As the tale draws to an end, she realizes that Utopia is going to fail because of their wish to "*embody* virtue." If they had been content to manufacture, not virtue, but furniture, it might have survived.

It is a rueful, if not tragic, conclusion. To replace the stubborn complexity of people and society with ideas is the mistake of both parties in Utopia. The cynics who insist that our behavior is determined by history and the "idealists" who believe so easily that man can be what he wishes to be are shown to be equally removed from the life we actually live. And yet those like Katy Norell, who see through this error, who feel and suffer life up close, are better off, if at all, only because it is better to understand. For their superiority consists mainly in desiring a virtue they know they can never attain.

"And search for truth amid the groves of academe" — this quotation from Horace prefaces Miss McCarthy's next novel. The search for truth, and the human defects that hinder it, we have seen to be her permanent subject. Now again the private concern becomes a way of understanding the large public matters that her life has brought before her: this time the political liberalism of the "witch-hunting" era of Joseph McCarthy (the 1950's), when the reactionary right, not the Communist left, frightened or confused intellectuals into self-betrayal; and progressive education, with its own less obvious hindrances to the search for truth. But *The Groves of Academe* (1952) is her first real or completely successful novel because now, for the first time, she has found a setting, characters, and a plot that dramatize both her private and her public subjects in one lively story. With this novel, moreover, her resemblance to Jane Austen, already evident in the irony, sanity, and grace of her prose, and the combination of moral concern and tough intelligence in her approach to people, grows even more striking. She gives us now, in that same prose, a group of characters vividly and comically idiosyncratic, with a wonderful comic villain in the center. She gives us a plot which evolves with perfect illuminating logic from the moral qualities of the characters. And she gives us the peculiarly Austenish pleasure of watching good, intelligent, and articulate people work their way through much painful error to the relief of shared understanding.

The plot is a most ingenious stroke of wit. Its humor is based on the fact that where in the outside, non-intellectual world it had become dangerous in this period to have once been a Communist, in the world of liberal intellectuals a man persecuted for a Communist past has become almost a holy martyr and entitled to defense. Miss McCarthy's joke is that when the incompetent, irresponsible (though learned and brilliant) Henry Mulcahy is about to be let go by the liberal president of Jocelyn College, he is able to win the support of his colleagues by pretending to have *been* a Communist. The joke reaches its climax when an old anarchist acquaintance of Mulcahy's is interrogated by President Hoar and a faculty committee about whether their colleague really had this claim on their respect and protection, and the anarchist, who "sings," betrays the shocking secret that Mulcahy's Communist past had been a lie. Upon which, in an explosion of topsy-turveyness, Mulcahy comes raging to Hoar like the righteous victim of a witch-hunt, and using the secret investigation as evidence that the president has betrayed his liberal principles, forces *him* to resign.

It is a pity to tell the punch line of such a story, but the fault is less grave than it might be because the fun here lies in the characters and in the fine detail by which they and their world are kept always very much alive. Most of all the story belongs to the magnificently repulsive Henry Mulcahy, in whom the kind of intellectual dishonor which we have already begun to recognize as Miss McCarthy's chief target is carried to breathtaking extremes. It is moreover a special triumph of the book that she has shown us this comic monster from the inside (she calls the technique "ventriloquism," as George Henry Lewes once wrote of Jane Austen's "dramatic ventriloquism"), mimicking his mode of thought so fully and felicitously that it is impossible, for all his excesses, not to recognize him as real.

In Henry Mulcahy, a pear-shaped, soft-bellied father of four, Ph.D., contributor to serious magazines, Guggenheim Fellow, etc., the intellectual's besetting sins — his lust for supremacy and his preference for flattering ideas over mere facts — undergo a marvelous efflorescence. He not only identifies himself with Joyce, Kafka, and other "sacred untouchables of the modern martyrology"; he comes to regard disloyalty to himself as "apostasy," and the dismayed Domna Rejnev discovers that "behind Joyce . . . is the identification with Christ." At the same time his great lie is to him the work of an artist, who creates out of life's raw material "a figurative truth more true than the data of reality." (Remembering vaguely that he had once heard the phrase "heart murmur" used of someone in his family, he is soon exclaiming to himself — sincerely! — that he holds Hoar "personally responsible for the life of his wife and/or son.") And when the defeated president finally asks him, "Are you a conscious liar or a self-deluded hypocrite?" Mulcahy replies, "A Cretan says, all Cretans are liars." Having thus put in question the very possibility of finding truth, he frankly declares, "I'm not concerned with truth. . . . I'm concerned with justice."

The faculty for whom Mulcahy has thus set a special problem in truth-seeking are all sharply realized, but those who share the center of the stage with Mulcahy are two teachers who are most different from him, and who bring what Miss McCarthy honors as effectively to life as he re-creates what she despises. Domna Rejnev and John Bentkoop are also intellectuals but to them the truth matters more than their own success and comfort. In Miss Rejnev, beautiful twenty-three-year-old daughter of Russian emigrés, whose "finely cut, mobile nostrils quivered during a banal conversation as though, literally, seeking air," and who, in a crisis, asks herself "What would Tolstoy say?" this intellectual passion is endearingly childlike in its ardor and even in its vanity. The ardor we see when she hears of Mulcahy's "persecution": "Her strange, intent eyes were shining; she tossed her head angrily and the dark, clean hair bobbed; she clicked her pocket-lighter and drew in on a cigarette. 'This cannot be permitted to happen,' she declared quickly, amid puffs of smoke. 'One simply refuses it and tells Maynard Hoar so.' She jumped up, knocking a book off the desk, and seized her polo coat from the coatrack. 'I shall do it myself at once to set an example.' "

And we see the vanity when she warmly praises Mulcahy's learning to silent colleagues out of her pleasure in honoring excellence. "She rather enjoyed the idea that she was sufficiently spendthrift (that is, sufficiently rich in resources)." But this pride is so far from the smug confidence of the self-worshippers that a colleague lets her pour out a passionate argument without interrupting "because he knew her to be honest and presumed that therefore, before she had finished, a doubt would suddenly dart out of her like a mouse from its hole." Sure enough, it is her agonizing recognition not only that she had been wrong about Mulcahy, but that she had been seduced into pretending not to know defects in him which she did know, into a sort of lying, that is to be her climactic experience in the book.

236

The deep, the metaphysical opposition between Mulcahy's kind and hers emerges during a painful dinner at the Mulcahy home when Domna suddenly learns she has been defending a liar. Uneasy, he tries to recoup by suggesting that, being handsome, she is a "monist," but that unattractive people like himself "know that appearances are fickle. We look to somebody else to discover our imperishable essence." And he asks her if she could love a leper, meaning, as she understands, himself. "If you mean a moral leper, no," she says. "Fair without and foul within has no charm for me. Nor the reverse, for that matter. . . . People whose inside contradicts their outside . . . have neither essence nor existence." Mulcahy, in short, can feel virtuous when he does evil and entitled to loyalty even by those whom he betrays because he believes instinctively in a sort of dualism according to which the concrete world, where actions have consequences and entail responsibilities, can be regarded as mere "appearance" — of secondary importance beside those abstractions (Norine Schmittlapp of *The Group* will call them "intangibles") which his ego can manipulate. The others are like Domna — or like Virginia Bentkoop, who, in a charming touch, though "she had met Domna only once, at a college lecture . . . divined correctly that her feet were wet." They are people who notice and respect the actualities of the world.

This, however, is a progressive college, and these are liberals of the fifties, and the combination has guaranteed Mulcahy's triumph. For, as the novel has also been suggesting, and as one teacher puts it at the end, progressive education means a concern with "faith and individual salvation" — that is, the student's inner quality is considered to be more important than his demonstrated mastery, through hard work, of real subject matter. This has a sinister resemblance to Mulcahy's self-defense that "appearance" — the mere concrete facts of what one is and does — is somehow less important than one's invisible "essence." And it is a view that is plainly akin to the tendency of many liberals of the era to separate "justice," in the words of Mulcahy again, from "truth," to consider scruples that interfered with work for a "good cause" mere ivory tower pedantry. Not that Miss McCarthy fails to make clear that the progressive college and its liberal faculty are right and attractive in many ways, and create a world in which good things can grow as well as bad. But her story makes it even clearer that there is no safety in good intentions when their pursuit requires us to ignore the truth.

Because *The Groves of Academe* is about college teachers, much of its drama comes to us in the clash of explicit ideas amid explicit descriptions of the college world and its intellectual character. For some readers this may sometimes clog or confuse the otherwise lively story. There can be no such objection to *A Charmed Life* (1955), for though this novel is equally rich in meaning, its meaning is more centrally human and expressed more completely by the rushing story alone. And the style, having to argue and explain less, having only to serve the urgent events and emotions, seems lighter, swifter, and richer in Miss McCarthy's characteristic poetry.

Perhaps too the novel is her best so far, the most poignant and powerful under the usual ironic control, because she has here found a subject which dramatizes the conflict among her own most cherished values — that "seesaw" between the demands of the self and those of "impersonal reality" — and which therefore taps her own strongest feelings. This conflict is foreshadowed in a new twist given to her familiar heroine. Martha Sinnott is another woman of mind, another lover of that "impersonal reality," but an element in the type hitherto regarded as only a source of difficulty is now permitted to present fully its own case. For this very clever and learned young playwright is also a woman, as her husband tells us, with "an obstinate childish heart," one to whom reality speaks a "little language" and who cannot bear that it ever utter, in her marriage, what is not true and beautiful and good. She not only insists that life conform to her dream, but, to make it conform, she dares to act as if, in the words of Katy Norell in her weakness, "the past could be altered and actions, like words, 'taken back.'" Miss McCarthy herself tells us that the novel is about "doubt," and it is true that the doubt which, among contemporary intellectuals, automatically dogs every dream and every piety is important in the story. But even more important is the "obstinate childish heart" by which the doubt is opposed. It is her heroine's "romanticism" that is now this "neoclassic" novelist's subject, and it is that romanticism's tormenting ambiguity which gives the story its wealth of meaning and its almost desperate intensity.

The romantic demand which Martha Sinnott (her last name suggests the McCarthy heroine's usual vain wish) makes upon life acquires a special urgency as the story opens because she has, to finish a play, come back with her second husband to the same Cape Cod town where she had once lived with her first — that is, to a place where her new love and new hope are in danger. New Leeds is dangerous for two reasons. First, because it is a contemporary Bohemia, full of artists and intellectuals who live in a state of freedom from tradition, convention, morality, and regular work. These are people who are always divorcing and remarrying, sinking into alcoholism or fighting it, falling down flights of stairs or into wells, and who yet seem to bear a charmed life — nothing seems to hurt them. The reason for this grows clear when Martha, in a moment of near hysteria, cries out that though the New Leedsian will never "admit to knowing anything, until it's been proved," and though he is always setting himself free to do as he pleases by demanding, "Explain to me why not. Give me one reason why not," the fact is, "you don't really doubt. You just ask questions, like a machine. . . . Nobody is really curious because nobody cares what the truth is." The New Leedsian's life is charmed into unreality by his moral indifference. Nothing really matters to him and so nothing can really hurt him. And that she is right to fear this moral casualness emerges when her husband goes out of town for a night and she is brought together by a friend — for the fun of it — with her ex-husband Miles Murphy.

Miles is the second danger she fears. He is not quite a typical New Leedsian, since he is capable of disciplined study and work (he is a writer and a psychologist). But he shares with the others their moral qualities. He is unscrupulous, and can cheat not only an insurance company but a friend. And he is brutally self-regarding and self-assertive: Martha had never been able to resist his utter inability to doubt himself.

The promise in all this is fulfilled when Miles takes her home from the party. After a struggle in which she yields partly to force but even more to the pressure of Mile's conviction that it isn't worth fighting — there is no "reason why not" — she lets him have her. One reason soon appears. Shortly afterward she finds herself pregnant. And though for the ordinary New Leedsian this would not have mattered, since her husband need never know what happened, for Martha it matters to the point of anguish. She cannot bear to have a child of whose paternity she must always be in doubt, or who might give the awful Miles a claim on her, and she cannot bear to base her life with John upon a lie. She decides to have an abortion. And it is in her struggle to determine whether this is right or wrong that we come upon that ambiguity already mentioned.

Such a way of making everything beautiful again has, to begin with, an unsettling resemblance to the ordinary New Leedsian's tendency to evade the consequences of his mistakes, to shirk responsibility. And yet the romantic dream need not always be self-indulgent fantasy. It may be the faith — the religion — which directs and ennobles our lives. In fact, Martha's inner struggle is sometimes described in religious terms. During one terrible night she is besieged and tempted by the devil himself, and at her blackest hour she finds rising to her lips the cry, "Father, let this cup pass from me." *Her* devil, of course, is a New Leedsian. "The medieval temptations, with all the allures of gluttony and concupiscence could not, Martha thought, have been half so trying as the sheer dentist-drill boredom of listening to the arguments of the devil as a modern quasi-intellectual." He utters now all the bright ideas of contemporary sophistication, and his object is to convince her that her vision of the good cannot stand up under rational cross-examination. (In the voice of the psychologist Miles the devil whispers that she doesn't really want a baby and is merely seizing this pretext to get rid of it.)

Her dream is thus opposed by the devil because it is a dream of living for what is right and not for what is merely pleasant. Indeed, among her weapons, as she struggles, is a sense of how the right makes itself known that would have won the approval of the author of *Pilgrim's Progress*. It is worth quoting for its bold recapitulation of an unfashionable morality, as well as for its prose.

Yet all the while the moral part of Martha knew that she would have to have an abortion because all her inclinations were the other way. The hardest course was the right one; in her experience, this was an almost invariable law. If her nature shrank from the task, if it hid and cried piteously for mercy, that was a sign that she was in the presence of the ethical. She knew this also from the fact that she felt no need to seek advice; what anyone else would do under the circumstances had no bearing. The moral part of her seemed to square its shoulders dissociating itself from the mass of weakness that remained. It was almost a social question, she observed with wan interest: the moral part of her would stop speaking if she did not do what it commanded. But how, she cried out, weeping. How am I to do it, all by myself? There was no answer. The rest of her, the low part, apparently, was supposed to devise the methods. The lawgiver was impractical, a real lady, disdaining to soil its hands, leaving the details to its servants. Martha could have laughed aloud, except for the pride and awe she felt in the acquaintance. She would not have guessed she had so much integrity. In the midst of her squirming and anguish, there was a sensation of pleased surprise.

Thus the past-canceling abortion, which might well have seemed a New Leedsian act, takes on the character of an act of moral heroism, of faith.

Having won the inner battle, she gets the external help she needs from the artist Warren Coe. Warren, a beautifully realized comic character who listens with enormous respect to the "deep" talk of people like Martha and seems created to be her butt, turns out to be her very counterpart in what matters most. What he is and what the others are and, indeed, what the whole story is about is suggested in a delightful discussion of Racine's *Bérénice* which is read aloud at that fateful New Leeds party. This play, in which the newly crowned emperor Titus must renounce forever his beloved Hebrew queen because a Roman may not marry a foreign monarch, is a tragedy about the conflict between love and duty. And though Miles and Martha came together at first like brilliant equals among ordinary people, it soon appears that it is Warren and not Miles whose ideas she shares. Miles thinks "love is for boys and women," at which Martha raises her brows and Warren, hearing his wife blandly agree, declares, "I could eat that *rug*." When Warren wants to give a hypothetical man who likes to murder old women a reason not to, Martha sympathizes with his wish for universal principles outside the self's wishes, but Miles thinks we do what we can get away with. "The electric chair . . . that's the reason we give him," he tells Warren, and then adds a remark for which one is tempted to forgive him all his crimes: "For you, it's an academic question. If you don't want to murder old women, let it go at that. Don't worry about the other fellow. Live selfishly." The play itself illuminates Martha's position by contrast. It is Racine's view that one can't live the moral life and have one's heart's desire as well. But Martha wants honor *and* she wants her love, she wants both together again as if her one lapse had never occurred; and in the world of Mary McCarthy, as well as of Racine, such a wish has to be vain.

As Martha is driving home from the Coes' with Warren's loan for the abortion in her pocketbook, her husband, who thinks her recent preoccupation has been due to her worry about buying him a proper Christmas present, leaves a note in her typewriter: "Martha, I love you, but life is serious. You must not spend any money on Christmas." And in this moving touch we are surely intended to see that John is not as mistaken in the nature of her errand as he appears on the surface. She does want to buy him a present, and she is buying him something only an "obstinate childish heart," impatient of adult seriousness, would dare to fix on. Moreover, she turns out to be childishly extravagant too — she pays with her life. She is killed in a head-on collision with another car. This death has been called arbitrary, but it is, with a sort of playfulness, given roots in the tale. The other car is driven by a woman who significantly resembles Martha, a woman with a past, a writer, an intellectual, and a "cautionary example of everything Martha was trying not to be," and she is driving — of course — on the wrong side of the road. It is clearly because Martha has been such a woman that she is now at the woman's mercy. With this death, the real, with its chain of ineluctable consequences, asserts its dominion over her romantic dream.

And yet — is Martha only another New Leedsian after all? Obviously, she is not — she bears no charmed life. The saving difference is that she cares, "cares about the truth," and cares enough— Miss McCarthy tells us this in the *Paris Review* — to "put up a real stake." We read near the end, "The past *could* be undone, in certain conditions. It could be bought back, paid for by suffering. That is, it could be redeemed." In fact, what makes her happy in her last moments is the conviction that she is earning back, by means of her suffering, the right to her husband's trust, that whether or not she later tells him what she has done, her ordeal would restore "truth between them again," and "it would be all right." It is apparently thus, and thus alone, that the romantic's "obstinate childish heart" can be reconciled, in the world of Mary McCarthy, with her implacable devotion to "impersonal reality."

The Group (1963) was Miss McCarthy's first best seller, but to many critics it was an embarrassing failure. There were two main objections to the book. The first was that it exhibited a descent, surprising in so "intellectual" a writer, to the preoccupations and the language of women's magazines. The second was that its characters were "dummies," all alike and all created merely to be "humiliated." Now it is true that the success of the book is not uniform throughout, but to speak of that kind of "descent" was possible only to those who took literally what was intended as irony, who ascribed to the author preoccupations and language of which the whole point is that they testify to the limitations of the characters. (Miss McCarthy herself has said that the novel is "as far as I can go in ventriloquism," and that almost all of it is enclosed in "invisible quotation marks.") And that same inattention to significant detail probably accounts for the failure to notice that the novel's many characters are, in fact, sharply distinct from each other. The truth is, *The Group* differs from her early work mainly in its scope. Where each previous novel had been about some problem of a committed intellectual (though her heroines did indeed yearn toward the more centrally human), *The Group* is about the characteristic attitudes and life patterns of a whole social class, as shown in the loves, jobs, marriages, and housekeeping, as well as the clichés of thought and language, of a group of more or less ordinary girls.

To this one must immediately add, however, that the girls in her group *are* upper-middle-class college graduates of the thirties, which is to say they belong to a species one of whose main characteristics is a pride in keeping up with advanced ideas. In fact, these girls are a suitable subject for their author because their chief problem is another version of Miss McCarthy's permanent problem: the danger to the emotional and moral life, when the guidance of family ties and traditions has disappeared, of the freedom to live by ideas. Miss McCarthy has said the novel is about "the loss of faith in progress." This must refer to the author's own loss of such faith, since the characters who have it keep it to the end; it might be more exact to say that the novel shows the poisonous effects of that faith — of the confidence of most of these ordinary girls that they know better how to manage their lives than people ever knew before. In general, their troubles result from the fact that they are cut off by their advanced ideas from the realities of life and their own nature; less up-to-date, they might well have been better and happier people.

The novel consists of chapters written from the viewpoint and in the language of the chief members of a group of Vassar friends (class of '33), and what unifies their varied, interweaving histories is the story of one of them, Kay Strong. It is at Kay's marriage to Harald Petersen in 1933 that we first meet them, at her funeral seven years later that we see them together for the last time, and it is mainly because of her, her parties and her often grotesquely pitiful troubles, that the girls keep coming together during the years between. A sketch of what the girls are like and of what they represent should make clear both the qualities and the meaning of the novel.

Kay seems at times an oddly confused conception. Miss Mc-

Carthy apparently began by thinking of her as another "sister" to Margaret Sargent; at least, her college personality and her life seem clearly autobiographical. An attractive girl, she came to Vassar from out West, dominated her college friends with her crushing analytical cleverness, was interested in the theater, married a would-be playwright whose bullying made her miserable, longed to be admired and was often awkwardly honest. But the girl whose troubles we now follow — this later Kay quite convincing and alive — lacks any kind of intellectual distinction or even interests and could not conceivably dominate anyone. In fact, her tragedy is precisely that she is a childlike creature, "a stranger and a sojourner" in this time and place, and pathetically driven by a snobbish longing for "nice" things, who depends for her ideas and for her prospects of acquiring identity, self-respect, admiration on a husband who totally fails her. This husband is another of Miss McCarthy's fine monsters of egoism. A second-rate talent whose ambition is due mainly to jealousy of the rich and the successful and whose cheap brilliance is used for self-display, self-exculpation, or the sadistic pleasure of exercising his power over his vulnerable wife, he is shaped to be the perfect frustration of her needs. He denies, for instance, with his ill-bred, outsider's contempt for all tradition, Kay's need for traditional elegance in the home and at the table. Some funny and horrible moments come from their warring ideas of a proper meal.

Priss and Libby are simpler, less interesting types. The first is mousy and stammering, loves neatness and order, and is easily mastered by tidy theories and confident men. Seeing a stain on a friend's dress, she mentally applies Energine ("her neat little soul scrubbed away"), and it is she who is the book's ardent New Deal Democrat, eager to make society too conform to an ideal of the reasonable. (Her pediatrician husband is an anti-Roosevelt Republican, but he is infatuated with his own new deal in the form

246

of up-to-date theories of infant care, theories he forces on his screaming baby and equally suffering wife with inhuman rigidity.) Libby, on the other hand, is not interested in bettering the world but in rising in it, her need to be the envied heroine of every encounter so frantic that she is incapable of even thinking the truth, and her chattering mouth seems to Polly like a "running wound."

With Dottie we come to a more original creation. Dottie is a shy, humorless, literal-minded girl, who is most at home in cosy chats with "Mother" and whose shyness conceals a great power of love, sexual and emotional. Her story is a tragicomedy in which a girl clearly made to be happy with old-fashioned romance and marriage but ready to behave as the new epoch thinks right is coolly and efficiently deflowered and then sent to be fitted for a pessary by a lover who doesn't even kiss her, let alone pretend that the "affair" has anything to do with love. (Docile little student of the *Zeitgeist* though she is, that omitted kiss does bother her.) Later, in one of the novel's wittiest and most touching scenes it is her *mother* who, with a timidly "bold" respect for love which is already out of date, presses Dottie to seek out that first lover. Dottie, scorning those old attitudes (and her own emotions), insists on going through with a practical marriage.

In Norine Schmittlapp Blake, occasional mistress of Kay's husband, Miss McCarthy gives us another example of that perversion of the life of the mind to which clever people are liable — this time as it appears among ordinary college graduates. Her mind and her talk are wholly given up to advanced ideas — her very apartment, painted black as Macdermott's was painted indigo, is a "dogmatic lair," all its furnishings "pontificating . . . articles of belief." She is so quick to display her superior progressiveness that it is she who announces near the end the change from one epoch and style of intellectual cliché to another by declaring that of course "No first-rate mind can accept the concept of progress any more." As before in Miss McCarthy's work, the reason for such a love of "ideas" is an inability to see, let alone to value, real things, an inability that is almost literally a blindness. This was foreshadowed in college, where she declared that a Cézanne still life (which the coldly knowing Lakey called "the formal arrangement of shapes") presented "the spirit of the apples." That phrase, with its implied scorn for the concrete, becomes her *Leitmotif*, and we find her later feeling pleasantly superior to people like the sensible Helena, who seems to shrink from "imponderables" and "intangibles." (It is part of the same indictment that her husband Putnam is a fund-raiser and publicist for labor organizations, that is, not a real laborer at anything, but a manipulator of notions and "images" for causes that entitle him to feel virtuous even if he lies — and that he is impotent.) Not only is Norine's apartment so filthy that poor Helena experiences an awkward block when she goes to her bathroom; her preference for lofty "intangibles" over mere realities enables her to feel superior in virtue while she is up to her neck in moral nastiness. This is carried to a comic climax when Helena asks her pointedly where Kay had been while Norine and Kay's husband were, as Norine put it, with her fine intellectual disdain for middle-class euphemisms, "fornicating" on her couch. " 'Kay [a Macy's employee] was working,' said Norine. 'The stores don't observe Lincoln's Birthday. They cash in on the fact that the other wage slaves get the day off. It's a big white-collar shopping spree. When do you think a forty-eight-hour-week stenographer gets a chance to buy herself a dress? Unless she goes without her lunch? Probably you've never thought.' "

This extreme example of the mode of life and thought Miss McCarthy detests evokes, in one of the novel's best scenes, à wonderful explosion of the other mode by which she has always opposed it. It is Helena who explodes, the rich girl to whose parents Miss McCarthy gave her own Protestant grandfather's wealth and his passion for education, and whose encyclopedic knowledge and many accomplishments have left her wry, unassertive, good-natured — passionate about nothing but the truth. The simple concreteness of what she says when at last she can stomach Norine's falseness and ugliness no more, though it is intended literally, is also intended as samples of larger things, and her outburst is worth quoting at length because it is so funny and true and because it can be taken as implying the fundamental McCarthy creed.

". . . if I were a socialist, I would try to be a good person. . . . You say your husband can't sleep with you because you're a 'good woman.' . . . Tell him what you do with Harald. . . . That ought to get his pecker up. And have him take a look at this apartment. And at the ring around your neck. If a man slept with you, you'd leave a ring around him. Like your bathtub. . . . I'd get some toilet paper. There isn't any in the bathroom. And some Clorox for the garbage pail and the toilet bowl. And boil out that dishcloth or get a new one. . . . I'd unchain the dog and take him for a walk. And while I was at it, I'd change his name." "You don't like Nietzsche?" "No," said Helena, dryly. "I'd call him something like Rover." Norine gave her terse laugh. "I get it," she said appreciatively. "God, Helena, you're wonderful! Go on. Should I give him a bath to christen him?" Helena considered. "Not in this weather. He might catch cold. Take a bath yourself, instead . . . And buy some real food — not in cans. If it's only hamburger and fresh vegetables and oranges." Norine nodded. "Fine. But now tell me something more basic." . . . "I'd paint this room another color." . . . "Is that what you'd call basic?" she demanded. "Certainly," said Helena. "You don't want people to think you're a fascist, do you?" she added, with guile. "God, you're dead right," said Norine. "I guess I'm too close to these things. . . . Next?" "I'd take some real books out of the library." "What do you mean, 'real books'?" said Norine, with a wary glance at her shelves. [Earlier we had been told that these shelves contained "few full-size books, except for Marx's *Capital*, Pareto, Spengler, *Ten Days That Shook the World, Axel's Castle*, and Lincoln Steffens," all trademarks, as it were, of the radical intellectuals of the time.]

"Literature," retorted Helena. "Jane Austen. George Eliot. Flau-
bert. Lady Murasaki. Dickens. Shakespeare. Sophocles. Aristoph-
anes. Swift." "But those aren't seminal," said Norine, frowning.
"So much the better," said Helena. . . . "Is that all?" said Norine.
Helena shook her head. Her eyes met Norine's. "I'd stop seeing
Harald," she said.

Two members of the group remain to be mentioned, aside
from fat comfortable Pokey, who is most valuable for bringing
into the story her funny parents, absolutely stupefied with their
wealth and self-importance, and their even funnier butler, Hat-
ton, whose mastery of his profession entitles him to a self-importance greater, if possible, than that of his employers. These other
two rank with Helena among the characters respected by their
author, and with them the novel comes to an end.

Helena, Lakey, and Polly have Miss McCarthy's respect because,
like other characters she has valued, they are honest, incapable of
hurting or using others for their own advantage, and attentive to
what is outside themselves — they notice things. But they differ significantly too. In Helena and Lakey intellectual development has
crippled ordinary humanity. Helena is so enormously cultivated,
so utterly knowing, that she is incapable of passion — except, as
I've said, for the truth. She is cool, virginal, she even looks like
a boy rather than a woman — charming to talk to, in short, but
not a girl to marry. In Lakey it is her sensibility that has suffered
the crippling overdevelopment. She is aware of failures of tact
or artistic taste to the point, at times, of torture. It is fitting
that she becomes an expatriate, spending years as a rich student
and connoisseur of art in Europe, and that, though her exquisite
refinement is housed, appropriately enough, in a person of exquisite beauty, she too turns out to be a girl one doesn't marry.
She startles her friends by returning from Europe with a woman
lover, as if, for the most scrupulous feminine sensibility, the male

is too gross. This is not shown as a degradation. She is now obviously attractive as a human being, able to wince at her past snobberies, and so on. But she is also obviously incomplete. Polly Andrews alone is all that a woman ought to be, and this may be why she is referred to several times as a creature out of a fairy tale.

Polly seems, in fact, to be an audacious embodiment of a McCarthy daydream, the author's "ideal," the sort of person the little daughter of her gay invalid father and beautiful mother might have become if her hair were long and golden, if her parents had lived, and if her happy childhood had fulfilled itself, after the inevitable fairy tale trials, in a properly happy ending. For Polly's childhood too was delightful with games and presents. Her father too — one of Miss McCarthy's most successful comic creations — is a gay, fun-dispensing invalid. (He is a manic-depressive.) In her poor apartment house, Polly seems to her first lover "a girl in a story book — a fairy tale. A girl with long fair hair who lives in a special room surrounded by kindly dwarfs." What is this fairy tale creature like? She takes pleasure in the work of the kitchen, and even the laundry, she makes her own Christmas presents, she is happy and generous in love, she has a sense of humor — in short, she has the gift of being able to live enjoyably in the real world. Then, as we have found before, this openness to the real has a moral dimension. She is not only honest and morally conscientious — often to comic and troublesome extremes — she is a nurse: her profession is to help people. When she decides to marry a handsome doctor, her chief praise of him is that he is "good." (An oddly foreign word to people in her world — her mother says, "I suppose you mean he's a bit of an idealist.") And yet — her Jim is a psychiatrist. But no, this turns out to be only a spell put on him by the evil spirits of the *Zeitgeist*. He took up psychiatry, he explains, under the mistaken impression that it was a science, but he is changing to research. He will study "brain chemistry" — that is, the reader of Mary McCarthy will by now understand, he will give up the delusive freedom of psychiatry, a freedom to deal masterfully in untestable ideas, and work instead with concrete "impersonal" realities. Polly marries this good man, and taking her father to stay with them — to the horror of all their up-to-date friends — they live happily, for all we know, ever after.

As I have said, *The Group* is not perfectly successful. A defect of its method is that characters whose human importance is comparatively trifling (Libby) or who are of mainly sociological interest (Priss) are treated as fully as those who engage the author more deeply; with such characters, though they are often amusing, the narrative urgency slackens. And there are Polly's two lovers, who seem created only to make points with or to serve the plot. Nevertheless, the book is mainly a pleasure to read. The pleasure comes from the characters (most of them), so pathetic and comic, so true, in their struggle to live up to their advanced ideas or to cling to reality amid the general falsenesses; from the continuous vivifying detail of their setting, appearance, tone, and gesture; and from the sheer quantity of people and experiences the story brings to life.

Four years after *The Group*, in 1967, Miss McCarthy published *Vietnam*, a report of her visit to that country and of her impressions of the war which the United States had been waging there for eight years. The book shows this war to have been an unwarranted and brutal intervention into Vietnam's internal affairs; and, against a current emphasis on certain practical problems of American withdrawal, it insists that the problem is a moral one, to be solved by doing not what is practical, but what is right. "Either it is *morally* wrong for the United States to bomb a small and virtually defenseless country or it is not," she declares, "and a student picketing the Pentagon is just as great an expert in that realm, to say the least, as [Secretary of State] Dean Rusk or [the newspaper columnist] Joseph Alsop."

Such undercutting of the theories of the "sophisticated" — intellectuals, "experts" — by a return to the human realities which the theories obscure is, we have seen, the primary action of Miss McCarthy's mind. It is in this sense that she is a "realist," and this is why realism, which it is nowadays fashionable to consider a worked-out vein, has shown in her fiction undiminished possibilities of intelligence, feeling, wit, and grace. She herself remarks in the *Paris Review* that she can't help "a sort of distortion, a sort of writing on the bias, seeing things with a swerve and a swoop, a sort of extravagance." But though, like any serious artist, she offers her own kind of data to serve her own vision, her stories are surely intended as true examples of the experience of our time. That "swerve and swoop" are only the wit, play, and poetry in her manner of conveying what she has seen, and these qualities are not more important in her work than her accuracy. Like the "philosophy of life" it expresses, her art comes from her loyalty to the life we actually live, her pleasure in the concrete particulars of people and the world, her refusal to be seduced away from them by ideas, however fashionable or however flattering. She is, in fact, one of several current novelists and critics — Saul Bellow, with his boisterous insistence on the life of feeling, is one; the late Lionel Trilling, with his critique of what he called the "second environment," that cosy conformist world of received ideas inhabited by so many "nonconformists," was another — who write out of impatience with their own class of intellectuals. Different though they are in so many ways (Bellow, for instance, quite as "romantic" as Miss McCarthy is "neoclassic") , they stand together against the intellectual's tendency to value chic ideas more than the human experience or the human ends they are supposed to serve, or, worse still, to conceal from himself, with the help of such ideas, realities he prefers not to see.

As for the contempt thought by many to be her sole motive

power, the cutting satire supposed to be her main quality, these, as I have tried to make clear, are by-products of something more fundamental. They come not from an intellectual's superciliousness but from an intellectual's hunger for the ordinary decencies and delights of life. When she strikes out, it is precisely at the kind of people who think cleverness is better. What has given Miss McCarthy's work its deepest interest is that, with all her "brilliance," she knows very well how little the mind's accomplishments may be worth in the face of life's agonizing difficulties, and that before the non-intellectual virtues — kindness, honesty, conscientiousness, the ability to take pleasure in people and the world — she lowers willingly her formidable weapons.

Since 1968, when the above (aside from small changes) was written, Miss McCarthy has published six more books. She continued her exposé of the Vietnam War in *Hanoi* (1968), a report of her visit to the capital of North Vietnam; in *Medina* (1972), about the trial and acquittal of the officer in charge of the 1968 mission into the village of My Lai which resulted in the massacre of unarmed civilians by American soldiers (Captain Calley, who actually led the mission, had already been found guilty) ; and in *The Seventeenth Degree* (1974), which reprinted her previous Vietnam writing, as well as a long review of a recent bestseller on how the war was handled by our presidents and their associates in Washington, D.C., and which is prefaced by an intimate memoir of her experiences while acting and writing against the war. In *The Mask of State: Watergate Portraits* (1974) she reported the televised (Senator) Ervin Committee hearings into the political scandal which ended in the resignation of President Nixon. Those four books are mainly vivid on-the-spot journalism. The other two, *The Writing on the Wall and Literary Essays* (1970) and the novel *Birds of America* (1971), are literature.

These last-named works confirm one's sense that she belongs among those especially interesting writers whose self-exploration becomes more and more a way of understanding the world. For many of the essays, though devoted to other writers, turn out to be about her own deepest preoccupations. And the idea in her previous novels that "freedom for her kind of people — for intellectuals" has often led only to "escape from difficult, limiting reality into the realm of flattering abstraction" has become in both books a frankly gloomy vision of the whole drift of contemporary civilization.

The three most recent essays in *The Writing on the Wall* — on Ivy Compton-Burnett, Orwell, and Nature — are full of what might almost be notes for *Birds of America*. Compton-Burnett is seen to be obsessed by the ambiguities and contradictions in "two insistent words . . . : Nature and Equality." Orwell is shown as a man who felt "obliged to believe in progress," but who loved "some simpler form of life" and "hated the technology he counted on to liberate the majority." And in "One Touch of Nature" she finds that Nature has ceased to determine values, but "has become subject to opinion" and "is no longer the human home." *Birds of America* is, in fact, a rich study of the contradictions within and between those two ideas, Nature and Equality, which we have dreamed we can bring together, and of how the latter, given irresistible power by technology, is destroying the values associated with the former. The contradictions are brought to life in the relationship of nineteen-year-old Peter Levi and his much divorced artist (harpsichordist) mother, Rosamund Brown, who, though the story and its point of view are his, remains a sort of loved and opposed other self throughout.

Peter and his mother have returned to Rocky Port, Massachusetts, for the 1964 summer holiday preceding his junior year abroad, and the story begins with his memory of their first visit four years earlier, the happiest time of his life. In that earlier period he was "deeply in love with his mother," and he also loved Nature, which meant then the New England countryside and above all its wild birds. Of his mother we see chiefly what she can share with Peter — her delight in the pleasures and customs of her childhood and of an earlier, simpler America, and in particular, in cooking real food. Since she is "a hopeless romantic" who "turned everything into a game," she decides to cook only American recipes from an old Fanny Farmer cookbook, and nothing that has been "naturalized" less than a hundred years. The story is in part the funny spectacle of her difficulties as she struggles to cook the old recipes with the proper ingredients and utensils in a town whose shops "get no call" for such things any more, and of Peter's "mature" irony at a childish intensity and lack of logic he really enjoys. But it is also about the pleasure they take in their food, their walks, their games. And above all, it is the story of their love, the love of two people who "notice things" with exceptional sensitivity and hence are always scrupulously just both for and against each other and themselves, and of the playful delicacies by which they express, or conceal, their feelings. When the flashback ends and we return to the 1964 Rocky Port, we find it buried four years deeper under the "improvements" of technology. The mother's struggle for old-time reality in the kitchen has grown a bit frenzied: she wants "fowl" rather than fryers because they're cheaper and "economy is contact with reality. I love reality, Peter. I hope you will too" — but spends gallons of gas hunting for real jelly glasses. Peter, less simply "in love" and more aware of the outside world — civil rights workers vanishing in Mississippi — begins to wonder if she isn't "making too much of the minutiae." He has become, moreover, a devotee of the ethics of Kant, whose categorical imperative — perform no action whose principle you would not accept as a universal law — is his supreme commandment, and so is uneasy about the aristocratic refinement of taste by which his artist-mother instinctively decides what is good and right. The rest of the novel, though its tone stays mostly light or ironic, draws out for Peter the increasingly painful implications of the battle these two fought with Rocky Port, each other, and themselves.

The absurd idea of some reviewers, resembling a kind of tone deafness, that Peter is a "prig," without "passions or contradictions," and Rosamund is an "overcultivated cipher," seems to rest on the assumption that passion must be sexual — or at least noisy — and that characters with intelligence, wit, and learning, especially if their manners are reserved, must be unreal. But "the mightiest of the passions," as Shaw's Jack Tanner declares, is "moral passion." And what chiefly characterizes Peter and his mother, what makes them funny and touching, is the unremitting intensity of their moral concern, their way of seeing moral issues in minutiae. As for contradictions, it is precisely Peter's inner tug-of-war that is the point of his story. And this keeps it alive as fiction even when "story" of the usual kind is, in varying degrees, abandoned.

The adverse reviews say the novel turns into an "essay" and imply that its fictional vitality disappears. Now, it is true that except in these first two chapters, another in the middle, and the last, the book is not a conventional realistic novel: what we are given of characters and their relationships is mainly what can serve a development in ideas, and the wide and witty application of the ideas certainly makes for a good deal of the fun. But if "essay" means a kind of writing in which the author merely announces her own worked-out conclusions, then all the chapters, even that of Peter's long philosophic letter to his mother, are clearly something else, and this a something else which retains precisely the reality peculiar to fiction. For fiction restores reality to ideas by giving up the pretense that they exist apart from particular persons in particular situations and that they are static. In *Birds of America* all the ideas emerge from the mental life of *Peter*, whom we have come to know in non-intellectual ways as well; in her mimicry of idiom, tone, and personal style Miss McCarthy is as amusingly accurate with this American boy of the 1960's as she has been with so many other characters. Moreover, his mental life is a constant struggle among ideas that actively contend with each other. In short, the novel gives us ideas in their living state. For, as Gide's Edouard affirms so passionately, ideas "live; they fight; they perish like men." Edouard admits that "ideas exist only because of men; but that's what's so pathetic; they live at their expense."

So Peter's encounter in a train to Paris with some Midwest American schoolmarms, as kind and neighborly as they are naïve and vulgar, becomes a squirming inner battle between the taste, intellect, and need for privacy he shares with his mother and his American egalitarian sense of justice. So, though his letter to his mother begins by rejecting her ethics of "taste" as those of a "snob," it goes on to tell of a battle he fights to keep clean the public toilet of his Paris lodgings which others leave disgustingly filthy, a battle which leads him to a devastating possibility: "Could humanity be divided into people who noticed and people who didn't? If so there was no common world." And later it is his own reactionary tendencies that are jolted. After smiling at an elderly Italian's old-fashioned faith in the power of American technology to free men from slavery and want, he is reminded that the picturesque European simplicities he prefers are only the way slavery and want look to the comfortable outsider — Mistrust the picturesque, the man says. It stinks.

The climax of this conflict occurs in the next to last chapter when Peter argues in the Sistine Chapel with the novel's chief spokesman for contemporary American civilization, his sociologist faculty adviser. This man, named with Dickensian appropriateness Mr. Small, had earlier reduced Peter's complex dissatisfactions to neurotic symptoms easy to "explain" and advise. He now has a foundation grant to study the flight patterns of the new, and mainly American, flying creature, the tourist. Not only does Small defend against Peter's "elitist" objections both American capitalism and the technology by which, at some temporary cost here and there, it spreads the good things of life more and more widely; he also demonstrates the new "anti-elitist" trend in American education in his belief that the great frescoes are really in essence abstractions — Norine Schmittlapp's "intangibles" — accessible to all with the right feelings. To him Peter's insistence that they say something in a language which a little education would illuminate is only the old business of shutting out the "disadvantaged." Finally, he tries to share their lunch check equally, though he in fact ate more than Peter, and then, with the "warmth" of the new "with-it" teacher, gives Peter a farewell hug to show their differences don't matter, a neat illustration of that blurring of distinguishing particulars some egalitarians call justice — or love.

The last chapter is again pure — and poignant — fiction. It depicts a series of betrayals. First, Peter finds sleeping on his lodging stairs one cold winter night a stinking, drink-stupefied woman, a *clocharde*, waiting for him "like a big package with his name on it: Peter Levi, Esq., Noted Humanitarian." Taking her to his room for a night's shelter, he experiences all the little self-betrayals generated by moral actions that make one's flesh crawl: if one doesn't act, one feels guilty, but if one does, one feels hypocritical, for no action is ever enough to make up for the irrepressible reservations. Then President Johnson betrays his election promises to keep America out of war by bombing North Vietnam; when

Peter goes to the zoo for comfort in his horror and despair, an angry swan wounds the bird-lover with a beak dripping with polluted water; in a hospital afterwards technology almost kills him with penicillin, to which he is allergic; and finally his mother tells him she will play in Poland for the U.S. State Department because "it's only music." He knows he can reawaken her moral common sense, but the fact that he should need to destroys her authority for him forever — a small sample of the division between the generations in the 1960's. And the book ends with a brief but tellingly described dream visit by Kant, who announces gravely that, not God, whom men have long managed without, but "Nature is dead."

This bold statement of the book's "message" in its last line, far from flattening the closing emotional effect, oddly intensifies it. We feel an earnestness in the author that drives her to abandon the usual coyness of fiction. The fact is, for Mary McCarthy the death of Nature, in spite of her Kant's disclaimer, is very much like the death of God announced by Nietzsche. Her Nature (as the capital letter suggests) is only the line to which God has lately retreated; both serve, in Arnold's phrase, as that reality not ourselves which makes for righteousness — as well as sanity, health, beauty. And the tragedy at the heart of her novel is not only that Nature is dead, but that it has been murdered by an ideal she also values, the ideal of Equality.

The novel has shown why the fact that these are in conflict is — for Peter and his mother and their enlightened contemporary readers — at once painful to admit and hard to deny. We like to think that nature supports our humanitarian bias, that being the same for all and in all, it teaches that all should be treated alike. But nature is actually the realm of minute particulars, and every real relationship to these must also be minutely particular; that is, it is the realm of differences and inequalities, both in things and in our power to notice, appreciate, and possess them. For this reason, if people are to share in all life's goods, these goods must be stripped of the particulars that limit their accessibility. They must be "processed" into easily reproducible and portable (also inexact and tasteless) approximations of the real thing — and this applies to products of the mind as well as to those of nature. Nor is it only those two kinds of products that make for inequality and call for such processing. There are also the particulars of custom and tradition that have evolved out of the history of nations, neighborhoods, families. These give us our unique childhoods, the sources and objects of our emotional lives, our identities, but they do keep us apart. Equality therefore demands that such uniqueness be replaced by a generalized humanity we can share. In a single sentence, the pursuit of equality is an attempt to live by an idea, and so, however "self-evident," beautiful, and irresistible the idea, a constant flight from reality. Hence the quotation which serves as a motto for the book: "to attempt to embody the Idea in an example, as one might embody the wise man in a novel, is unseemly . . . for our natural limitations, which persistently interfere with the perfection of the Idea, forbid all illusion about such an attempt. . . ."

The ego-serving manipulation of reality Miss McCarthy has always detested in intellectuals (including herself) thus turns out to have been only her personal near-at-hand example of the process of technology. Since this process serves the idea of equality, she cannot of course reject it, but her novel is a record of what it costs. With the growing power of technology there is no longer any reality not ourselves. Not only has it replaced Nature, and our "second nature," custom, with life-reducing conveniences and abstractions, but, far worse, by giving man control over what once controlled and educated him, it has put our whole world at the mercy of the ego-driven human will.

IRVIN STOCK

A sad conclusion. And though many of us refuse to give up a sort of animal faith in the power of human creativity to save us yet again — even from the human will — the pessimism of this rich and moving novel is certainly an appropriate response to the world we now inhabit.

Selected Bibliography

Works of Mary McCarthy

FICTION

The Company She Keeps. New York: Simon and Schuster, 1942.
The Oasis. New York: Random House, 1949.
Cast a Cold Eye. New York: Harcourt, Brace, and World, 1950.
The Groves of Academe. New York: Harcourt, Brace, and World, 1952.
A Charmed Life. New York: Harcourt, Brace, and World, 1955.
The Group. New York: Harcourt, Brace, and World, 1963.
"The Hounds of Summer," *New Yorker*, 30:47–50 (September 14, 1963).
"Birds of America," *Southern Review*, 1(n.s.):644–83 (July 1965).

NONFICTION

Sights and Spectacles: 1937–1956. New York: Farrar, Straus, and Company, 1956.
Venice Observed. New York: Reynal and Company, 1956.
Memories of a Catholic Girlhood. New York: Harcourt, Brace, and World, 1957.
The Stones of Florence. New York: Harcourt, Brace, and World, 1959.
On the Contrary: Articles of Belief, 1946–1961. New York: Noonday Press, 1962.
Mary McCarthy's Theatre Chronicles, 1937–1962. New York: Noonday Press, 1963.
Vietnam. New York: Harcourt, Brace, and World, 1967.
Hanoi. New York: Harcourt, Brace & World, 1968.
The Writing on the Wall and Literary Essays. New York: Harcourt, Brace & World, 1970.
Medina. New York: Harcourt Brace Jovanovich, 1972.
The Mask of State: Watergate Portraits. New York: Harcourt Brace Jovanovich, 1974.
The Seventeenth Degree. New York: Harcourt Brace Jovanovich, 1974.

Bibliography

Goldman, Sherli Evens. *Mary McCarthy: A Bibliography*. New York: Harcourt, Brace, and World, 1968.

IRVIN STOCK

Critical and Biographical Studies

Auchincloss, Louis. "Mary McCarthy," in *Pioneers and Caretakers*. Minneapolis: University of Minnesota Press, 1965.

Brower, Brock. "Mary McCarthyism," *Esquire*, 58:62–67, 113 (July 1962).

Grumbach, Doris. *The Company She Kept*. New York: Coward-McCann, 1967.

Hardwick, Elizabeth. "Mary McCarthy," in *A View of My Own: Essays in Literature and Society*. New York: Noonday Press, 1963.

Kazin, Alfred. *Starting Out in the Thirties*. Boston: Little Brown, 1965. Pp. 155 et seq.

Mailer, Norman. "The Case against McCarthy: A Review of *The Group*," in *Cannibals and Christians*. New York: Dial Press, 1966.

McKenzie, Barbara. *Mary McCarthy*. New York: Twayne Publishers, 1966.

Niebuhr, Elisabeth. "The Art of Fiction XXVII," *Paris Review*, 27:58–94 (Winter–Spring 1962).

264

Carson McCullers

SINCE CARSON MCCULLERS' gifts as a novelist are essentially celebratory and elegiac, it is appropriate that the simple facts of her life should evoke both wonder and melancholy. She was born Lula Carson Smith in Columbus, Georgia, on February 19, 1917. Lemar Smith, her father, was a watch repairman whose family had recently come South from Connecticut; her mother, Marguerite Waters, proudly traced her ancestry to Irish settlers in South Carolina before the Revolutionary War.

From an early age, Carson was recognized as an odd, brooding, solitary girl, obsessed with music, reading, fantasy, and making up stories. For much of her childhood, she dreamed of becoming a concert pianist, but in adolesence literary ambitions took pride of place. As she was later to recall: "My first effort at writing was a play. At that phase my idol was Eugene O'Neill and this first masterpiece was thick with incest, lunacy, and murder. The first scene was laid in a graveyard and the last was a catafalque. I tried to put it on in the family sitting room, but only my mother and my eleven-year-old sister would cooperate. . . . After that I dashed off a few more plays, a novel, and some rather queer poetry that nobody could make out, including the author." Among those vanished adolescent works were *The Faucet*, a play set in New Zealand (where anything was likely to happen) ; *The Fire of Life*, a two-character verse play in which Christ debates with Nietzsche; and *A Reed of Pan*, a novel about a musician seduced by jazz.

Supported by funds from the sale of a valued family ring, Carson at seventeen traveled to New York to study at the Juilliard

School of Music and take writing courses at Columbia. She had planned to room with a girl from Georgia, but in a confused sequence of events, the tuition money was lost or stolen, and she soon found herself on her own in the city. Loneliness, financial worries, ill-health, and the bleakness of Manhattan in the depression made this a stressful time for a girl so young and sensitive; but she stuck with the courses at Columbia and New York University, and worked feverishly at her stories. Most of her apprentice fiction did not appear in print until after her death (*The Mortgaged Heart*, 1971); but "Wunderkind" — the tale of a prodigy's failure — appeared just before her twentieth birthday in the December 1936 issue of *Story* magazine. By this time, she was going steady with Reeves McCullers, whom she had met two summers earlier and would marry the following fall.

During her stay in New York, Carson suffered a recurrence of a childhood illness that was to exercise so powerful and poignant an influence on her life. She had always been a frail girl (suffering from respiratory problems, pleurisy, and other ailments), but after having experienced a severe attack of rheumatic fever in the winter of 1936–37, she began her third decade in a vulnerable state of health. Her literary ambitions, however, remained fierce, and when she married Reeves McCullers in September 1937, she was already at work on a novel called *The Mute*.

The couple lived first in Charlotte, then in Fayetteville, North Carolina, where Reeves worked as a credit investigator. Although the early months were happy, they soon found their roles in the marriage a source of severe strain. Thinking of herself only as an artist, Carson paid little attention to the demands of domestic life; Reeves — with writing ambitions of his own — soon capitulated and performed the house chores as well as his job outside. When Carson received a contract from Houghton Mifflin for six chapters and an outline of her novel, Reeves felt more intensely the threat of her devouring ambitiousness. Heavy drinking, sexual tensions, and the dreariness of small-town living added to their demoralization; and after Carson finished *The Mute*, recuperated in Columbus, and swiftly wrote *Army Post*, the couple decided to move permanently to New York.

They arrived in the city in June 1940, soon after the retitled *Mute* was published as *The Heart Is a Lonely Hunter*; and a few weeks later Carson McCullers was famous. Many influential reviewers praised her novel as a formidable achievement in its own right, but the age of the author was too startling to minimize. For a twenty-three-year-old woman to probe at such length the passionate idealism of half-a-dozen adult characters was an astonishing act of imaginative sympathy; and Carson was heralded as one of the most promising new writers in America.

Fame was exhilarating but quickly propelled her into situations she was too inexperienced and unstable to handle. In the early summer, she met Klaus and Erika Mann, W. H. Auden, and other distinguished members of European emigré circles in New York. She fell instantly, hurtfully in love with Annemarie Clarac-Schwarzenbach, a beautiful, sophisticated, neurotic Swiss writer, who did not return her passion. In August, at the Bread Loaf Writers' Conference, she drank too much, became involved with Louis Untermeyer, and even among artists was tagged as an uncommonly strange bird of passage. By September, she was back with Reeves, restless, discontent, anxious to write more and to move faster among literary celebrities, maimed by the rejection of Annemarie, and eager for other lesbian relationships. They talked of divorce but decided for the moment to separate.

Earlier that summer Carson had been asked by George Davis, literary editor of *Harper's Bazaar*, to join an experiment in cooperative living at 7 Middagh Street in Brooklyn Heights, New York. No one with a desire to mingle with talent and genius could have resisted the invitation. Auden became more or less the manager and at different times rooms were occupied by Gypsy Rose Lee, Richard Wright, the designer Oliver Smith, Chester Kallman, Paul and Jane Bowles, Benjamin Britten, and Peter Pears. During the early years of the second World War, a visitor to the house might find any one of the transient charter members, or such guests as Aaron Copland playing the piano, or Salvador Dali decorating the walls with a mural.

For a young woman from the provinces, 7 Middagh Street provided unusually spirited company and singular material for novels and stories. A strutting hunchback who came each evening to a bar near the Brooklyn Navy Yard now lives in "The Ballad of the Sad Café," and a New York fire engine played a role in the birth of Frankie Addams. After meditating for weeks on the disjointed elements in a story of an adolescent girl, Mrs. McCullers heard a siren, followed Gypsy Rose Lee out of the door, and was oddly inspired to shout: "Frankie is in love with her brother and his bride and wants to become a member of the wedding."

The early 1940's — when she lived at 7 Middagh Street, in New York, Saratoga Springs, and occasionally Columbus — proved to be Mrs. McCullers' most productive period. *Army Post*, retitled *Reflections in a Golden Eye*, appeared in *Harper's Bazaar* in the fall of 1940, and in book form the following February. "A Tree. A Rock. A Cloud" was chosen for the *O'Henry Prize Stories* in 1942 and "The Ballad of the Sad Café" for *Best American Stories* two years later. Encouraged by fellowships from the Yaddo colony, the Guggenheim Foundation, and the American Academy of Arts and Letters, she continued to work on the manuscript of *The Member of the Wedding*.

At the same time her personal life seemed more unruly than ever. Many people who knew her in those days have since testified to the wild, unresolvable contradictions of her nature. By

268

turns and sometimes even all at once, she could be shy and expansive, honest and untruthful, generous and vindictive, amusing and morose, feverish and serene. Emotionally (if not literally) promiscuous, she had an insatiable need for attention and love, but was so often suspicious, anxiety-ridden, compulsive, and self-dramatizing that she could rarely respond in a sustained way to the needs of other people. As Rosamond Lehmann once put it: "I found her fascinating and lovable, but at the same time a terrific psychic drain. She made enormous emotional demands."

For the short story writer Edward Newhouse, Carson was "*childlike*, although people who didn't like her thought her *childish*. She could drop people suddenly or pick them up with a tremendous show of affection." Other friends described her as a frightened bird, a wounded sparrow, a crippled deer, "a sick wildcat caught in the garden"; but Arnold Saint Subber — objecting to the persistent emphasis on fragility — christened her "the iron butterfly." In his brief acquaintanceship, Alfred Kazin found her "unhappy to the point of catastrophe — and [yet] when we met I was so grateful for her sympathy, as for her art, that it was great being together." Summarizing paradoxes often noted by friends, Elizabeth Bowen recalled that she "always felt Carson was a destroyer; for which reason I chose never to be closely involved with her. Affection for her I *did* feel, and she also gave off an aura of genius — unmistakable — which one had to respect. . . . Carson remains in my mind as a child genius, though her art, as we know, was great, sombre, and above all, extremely mature. I remember her face, her being, her bearing with a pang of affection — and always shall."

As these comments and others like them suggest, the story of Carson McCullers' many friendships, infatuations, rivalries, and feuds is immensely tangled — too tangled to be described briefly here; but it can be read in Virginia Spencer Carr's meticulous, admiring biography, *The Lonely Hunter*, published by Doubleday in 1975.

In the years just after the second World War, Mrs. McCullers was still considered an exceptionally promising, ambitious writer plagued by ill-health and a chaotic personal life. In 1945 she and Reeves remarried; a year later she published *The Member of the Wedding*, won another Guggenheim, and began a life-long friendship with Tennessee Williams; in 1947 — just past thirty — she suffered two paralyzing strokes; in 1948 her marriage broke up again and sunk in desperation she tried to commit suicide. In 1949 she was back with Reeves and adapting *Member of the Wedding* for the stage.

This most turbulent decade ended, however, with a moment of triumph. On the night of January 5, 1950, *The Member of the Wedding* opened at the Empire Theatre in New York to the extravagant praise of the audience and newspaper critics. In the *World-Telegram*, William Hawkins spoke for the majority: "I have never before heard what happened last night at the curtain calls for *Member of the Wedding* when hundreds cried out as if with one voice for Ethel Waters and Julie Harris." When the season ended, the play won both the Donaldson Award and the prize of the Drama Critics Circle; and after running for 501 performances it was filmed by Stanley Kramer.

On the crest of her popular and critical success, Houghton Mifflin the following year published Mrs. McCullers' three novels and seven stories in an omnibus volume. Reviewing the British edition, V. S. Pritchett called its author "a genius . . . and the most remarkable novelist to come out of America for a generation." At thirty-four, Mrs. McCullers was, in Gore Vidal's recollection, "*the* young writer" of the period, "an American legend from the beginning." Even critics like Edmund Wilson and Diana Trilling, while expressing serious reservations about her talent, were likely to talk of her youth and the undeniably rich promise of her future. If, Joseph Frank wrote, Mrs. McCullers could, like Dostoevski, place her characters in a situation where their grotesqueness takes on symbolic value, "American Literature may find itself with a really important writer on its hands."

From this point on, however, the life story of Carson McCullers becomes the history of declining health and talent. The promise, which in the 1940's was on everybody's lips, was never fulfilled. If she had moments of triumph, she had months of misery and despair. In 1952, she and her husband bought a house at Bach-villers, near Paris, where they lived on and off for two years; but domestic calamities made much of the interlude a nightmare. They both drank heavily and could not deal with their mutual bisexuality. Reeves took drugs and fell into fits of wild, almost maniacal abusiveness. Mrs. McCullers, terrified, returned alone to Nyack, New York, where her widowed mother had recently bought a house. Soon afterwards, while visiting Lillian Smith in Georgia, Carson learned that Reeves had committed suicide.

Other personal disasters weakened her resistance: the death of a favorite aunt in 1953 was followed less than two years later by the loss of her mother, on whom she had always been unhappily overdependent. Given the severity of the stresses under which she labored, the play and the novel Mrs. McCullers published in 1958 and 1961 were triumphs of stoicism but, unfortunately, failures of art. *The Square Root of Wonderful,* a maladroit comedy of manners, closed after forty-five performances in New York; and *Clock Without Hands,* an ambitious, long-studied novel about race, was devoid both of energy and plausible social observation. But despite these disappointments, her earlier work continued to be widely read and appreciated. Each of the first four volumes sold more than half-a-million copies in hard- and soft-covered editions and adaptors were eager to translate her books into other media. Edward Albee dramatized "The Ballad of the Sad Café" in 1963; John Huston filmed Marlon Brando and Elizabeth Taylor in *Reflections in a Golden Eye* (1967); and Robert Ellis Miller directed Alan Arkin and Sondra Locke in the film version of *The Heart Is a Lonely Hunter* (1968).

Against the physical afflictions of her last decade, Mrs. McCullers responded with stubborn gallantry and spirit. A heart attack, breast cancer, pneumonia, and a bone-crushing fall occurred in grim succession from 1958 to 1964; and yet she traveled, received guests, and worked fitfully on unfinished manuscripts. Her relationships with friends and family remained as turbulent and unpredictable as ever; but she did establish one important new friendship with Dr. Mary Mercer, a specialist in child psychiatry, who cared for her in the closing years of her life. In August 1967, Mrs. McCullers was felled by still another stroke and lapsed into a coma from which she never regained full consciousness. She died on September 29, 1967.

Any reader who wishes to determine the characteristic strengths and limitations of Carson McCullers as a writer could do no better than to begin with *The Heart Is a Lonely Hunter*. Not only is this first novel an admirably complete introduction to her themes and subject matter, but it raises in a complex and provocative way the major critical issues posed by all her important work. The scene is the deep South; the characters are estranged and disadvantaged; and the theme is loneliness and the inevitable frustrations of love.

When the book opens, John Singer and Spiros Antonapoulos, two deaf-mutes, have been joined for ten years in a close but enigmatic friendship. The active and quick-witted Singer has been entirely infatuated with his impassive and feebleminded friend. Although most of the other people in this depressed factory town are isolated, the two mutes never seem lonely at all.

Singer gives; his friend receives; and each seems absorbed in his role as lover and beloved. But suddenly Antonapoulos becomes mysteriously ill and a social menace, stealing silverware, jostling strangers, urinating in public places. Despite his distress and passionate concern, Singer can do nothing; the deranged Greek is packed off to an asylum two hundred miles away. At this point, still very early in the story, Singer involuntarily enters the life of the community by renting a room in the Kelly house and taking his meals at the New York Café.

During the course of the next few months, Singer unwittingly becomes the focal point of the lives of four other people, who, visiting his room, see in him a mysterious figure to complete their own obsessive but fragmentary dreams. For Mick Kelly, a twelve-year-old tomboy with a blossoming gift for music, Singer's imagined harmony of spirit brings Mozart to mind. To the crusading Negro doctor Benedict Copeland, the mute symbolizes an all-too-rare instance of white compassion. For Jake Blount, a haggard radical agitator with a greater gift for talk than action, Singer is divine because he listens. For Biff Brannon, the café owner who self-consciously observes the human pageant, Singer is a fit subject for contemplation because of the attention paid to him by others. None of these dreamers knows of Singer's love for Antonapoulos; nor are they aware of the bewilderment with which he observes their interest in him. When Antonapoulos dies, Singer commits suicide, and the disciples are left to ponder and to grieve.

From the opening pages of *The Heart Is a Lonely Hunter* one is aware that this strange and absorbing story is designed to be read both as a realistic tale of a half-dozen displaced southerners and as a generalized parable on the nature of human illusion and love. And, at the start at least, each level operates satisfactorily with the other. All the carefully observed details needed to authenticate the mutes are present. Antonapoulos, fat and slovenly, works in a fruit store; Singer, tall and immaculately dressed, engraves silver for a local jeweler. Their routine is carefully set, odd perhaps in its regularity, but entirely credible: they play at chess, and go once a week to the library, to the movies, and to a local photography store. As we move on, characters read *Popular Mechanics* and write letters to Jeanette MacDonald; they sing "Love's Old Sweet Song" and "K-K-K-Katie," smoke Target tobacco and speak of Joe Louis and Man Mountain Dean. Behind the exotic Georgian passion play stand Chamberlain, Munich, and the Danzig Corridor, and when Mrs. McCullers stops to describe a character from the viewpoint of Biff Brannon, she writes with the specificity familiar in traditional realistic fiction.

Yet along with the virtues of specification go the vaguer promptings of allegory. The symmetrical obsessions of Singer's four admirers quickly make him a special case, more interesting as a catalyst than as a complex human being; and soon afterwards the admirers themselves take on generalized significance: the adolescent, the idealistic Negro, the failed reformer, the philosophical student of human affairs. Through the passion with which each constructs the god he needs, he bears ironical witness to the many and wayward forms of human mythmaking.

For the first one hundred pages of *The Heart Is a Lonely Hunter*, Mrs. McCullers is able to persuade us that contemporary reality and legendary story are one; but soon afterwards her technique falters and the novel becomes increasingly unsatisfactory both as document and as myth. On the literal level the difficulties center on implausible psychology and faulty observation of character. Biff Brannon is introduced as a man with a rare gift for disinterested observation and described in such a way as to suggest that he should function as Mrs. McCullers' *raisonneur*, the one person to make objective sense of the action. As a café owner, he can see more of the drama than anyone else and he is sympathetic to a wide range of emotional grotesques; as a male with a strong feminine strain, he is able to temper the chill of analysis with the warmth of an intuitive compassion. Following the presentation of Singer, Biff is the first of the main characters to be introduced, and his reflections form the coda that brings the novel to an end.

Throughout the early pages, Biff is described as thoughtful, inquisitive, and alert; whenever something happens, he is often the first, perhaps the only, person to notice. As the pattern of the action evolves, however, Biff is of little use beyond his ability to tell us things we have already established on our own. Sometimes, his vaunted insight is merely banal: "By nature all people are of both sexes. So that marriage and the bed is not all by any means. The proof? Real youth and old age. Because often old men's voices grow high and reedy and they take on a mincing walk." But most often his discoveries are posed in terms of coils, puzzles, unanswered questions; after rubbing his nose, narrowing his eyes, fixing his stare, he is most likely to come up with this: "How Singer had been before was not important. The thing that mattered was the way Blount and Mick made of him a sort of homemade God. Owing to the fact he was a mute they were able to give him all the qualities they wanted him to have. Yes. But how could such a strange thing come about? And why?"

It is just "how it came about" and "why" that Biff is never able to tell us, and — on many of the more important matters — neither can Mrs. McCullers. In this respect, the fundamental weakness of *The Heart Is a Lonely Hunter* is that past midpoint, the central theme (men make strange gods in their own image) is not so much developed as embroidered by still another fancy but no more enlightening illustration.

Related to this inadequacy is Mrs. McCullers' failure to establish a satisfactory relationship between the various idealizations of Singer and what actually happens to each dreamer in the novel. A number of commentators have insisted that the forlorn fate of each character at the end of the book is prompted by Singer's suicide. When the Kelly family is pressed by poverty, Mick quits school to work in the dime store, her musical promise thwarted. Copeland, devastated by the bestial white torture of his prisoner son, goes in broken health to live with relatives who ignore his message. But these events are not causally related to Singer's death. The Kelly family is impoverished because of damages they must pay to the mother of a child their son injured, and Mick took the dime store job while Singer was still alive; in fact, he approved the choice. Copeland is shattered not by anything related to Singer, but by impotence, frozen incomprehension, and the obvious failure of his dream.

There is a growing sense, toward the close of the novel, that the death of God is anticlimactic, or perhaps even beside the point. The dreamers would have been doomed to frustration had the mute never lived, and the kind of fierce inevitability that so beautifully links a Kurtz to a Marlow, a Clarissa to a Lovelace, or Ahab to his own white whale does not bind the characters to Singer in *The Heart Is a Lonely Hunter*.

On a realistic level there are other small problems as well. Several of the episodes in the middle section of the novel are either irrelevant or gratuitous to the main lines of the action (I am thinking of the shooting of Baby Wilson, Blount's encounter with the crazed evangelist, the riot at the amusement park; but others could be mentioned). Occasionally, characters are given dialogue so preposterous that it would bring high color to the face of a Victorian melodramatist: Copeland, who reads Spinoza and Shakespeare, says "Pshaw and double pshaw" when goaded into anger. Several times in the novel people express frustration and rage by hitting their heads against walls, fists against tables, thighs against stones. And, finally, climactic scenes collapse because the writer is too busy establishing lofty poetic meaning to notice the absurdity of a literal image. Here, for instance, is Biff's final recognition on the last page of the book: "Between the two worlds he was suspended. He saw that he was looking at his own face in the counter glass before him. Sweat glistened on his temples and his face was contorted. One eye was opened wider than the other. The left eye delved narrowly into the past while the right gazed wide and affrighted into a future of blackness, error, and ruin. And he was suspended between radiance and darkness. Between bitter irony and faith." Like the legendary student who wrote of Petrarch standing with one foot in the Renaissance while with the other he spanned the Middle Ages, Mrs. McCullers has forgotten the classic rule: specify first; signify later.

When one remembers, however, that *The Heart Is a Lonely Hunter* is the work of a twenty-two-year-old girl, the realistic lapses are understandable; they could easily be corrected by more careful observation and growth. But the failures on the level of fable are more troublesome because they point to an ambivalence that was a permanent feature of Mrs. McCullers' sensibility. There existed in her nature a continuing conflict between her nearer and her further vision, between her desire to document the world and a desire to give it evocative poetic significance. Like Edward Albee (who — in Philip Roth's fine phrase — was "born Maupassant but wished to be Plato") she seemed to waver in her own evaluation of her gifts, and sometimes would express contradictory allegiances almost in the same breath. The most remarkable and revealing example of this occurs in a set of notes on writing, "The Flowering Dream," published in *Esquire* in 1959. First, she tells an anecdote that confirms her existence on a plane beyond mundane reality: "What to know and what not to know? John Brown, from the American Embassy, was here to visit, and he pointed his long forefinger and said, 'I admire you, Carson, for your ignorance.' I said, 'Why?' He asked, 'When was the Battle of Hastings, and what was it about? . . . I said, 'John, I don't think I care much.' He said, 'That's what I mean. You don't clutter your mind with the facts of life.' " But then, two paragraphs later, comes this expression of the ultimate supremacy of living facts in fiction: "Every day, I read the *New York Daily News*, and very soberly. It is interesting to know the name of the lover's lane where the stabbing took place, and the circumstances which the *New York Times* never reports. In that unsolved murder in Staten Island, it is interesting to know that the doctor and his wife, when they were stabbed, were wearing Mormon nightgowns, three-quarter length. Lizzie Borden's breakfast, on the sweltering summer day she killed her father, was mutton soup. Always details provoke more ideas than any generality could furnish. When Christ was pierced in His *left side*, it is more moving and evocative than if He were just pierced."

The trouble with the symbolism of *The Heart Is a Lonely Hunter* begins with Mrs. McCullers' inability to decide whether Singer is pierced on his left side, just pierced, or never pierced at all. The characters themselves are rarely in doubt. For Mick Kelly, the thought of God conjures up an image of Mr. Singer with a long white sheet around him, and she whispers: "Lord forgiveth me, for I knoweth not what I do." Preparing her lesson for the Sunday school, Alice Brannon chooses the text "All men seek for Thee"; and a moment later, reflecting on the gathering of the disciples, her husband thinks of the mute. Gradually, however, the correspondences become rather murky. Copeland's daughter, Portia, claims that Singer's shirts are as white as if John the Baptist wore them; and as the plot thickens, the mute becomes poignantly and comically all things to all men: a Jew to the Hebrews, a Turk to the Turks, a wizard to the ignorant. Obviously, Mrs. McCullers wants us to see Singer as an ironic God figure, a product of mass wish-fulfillment; but even an ironic symbol runs the danger of becoming too indiscriminately resonant. Part of the problem stems from Mrs. McCullers' flawed control over the implications of the symbol itself. Usually, the insistence on Singer's religious nature is made by one of his blinded admirers, but sometimes the objective narrator seems to confirm their romantic obsessions. Singer, Mrs. McCullers writes, has "the look of peace that is seen most often in those who are very wise or very sorrowful." And finally, the mute is thirty-three when he dies, a detail chosen not by Blount or Mick Kelly, but by the author.

Some of the same uneasiness must greet the frequent assertion that *The Heart Is a Lonely Hunter* is an allegory about fascism. Although Mrs. McCullers has given this reading her guarded blessing, its origin is difficult to pinpoint. I suspect, however, that it may have grown from the casual remark of Clifton Fadiman, who — in his early notice — confessed to seeing signs of a myth of fascist and anti-fascist forces in the human soul. Yet, even if we recall Mrs. McCullers' cautious disclaimer ("the word is used here in its very broadest terms . . . the spiritual rather than the political side of that phenomenon") the analogy has no roots in the narrative. In what sense does Singer actively tyrannize anyone; who is being regimented, and to what degree? Can Christ and Hitler live comfortably within the confines of the same myth?

What we have here, I think, is early evidence of Mrs. McCullers' susceptibility to portent, her tendency to glide irresistibly toward any beckoning abstraction so long as it is somber, suggestive, and poetic. She never wrote a book that was not to some degree weakened by this inclination, and only once (in "The Ballad of the Sad Café") was she able to put dark fancy to the service of a compelling and powerful literal truth. In *The Member of the*

Wedding, her finest achievement, there is less aberrant symboliz-
ing than in any of her other works.

Yet even after all the damaging charges have been made, *The
Heart Is a Lonely Hunter* remains what it was in 1940: "a queer
sad book that sticks in the mind." The original design is brilliant
enough not to be wholly dimmed by the failure of the performance. If the inflated myth finally collapses, the sense of small-
town meanness holds up. Few books of the 1930's communicate as
well the stagnancy of life in a depressed textile community and the
inevitable frustration for those who try to stir free from it. "Find
an octopus and put socks on it," says Blount in a phrase that sums
up a generation. If the solemnity of the novel palls, the flashes of
shrewd country humor remain bright: the antics of Grandpa
Copeland and his ancient mule Lee Jackson; the fancies of Bub-
ber Kelly, who prefers fairy tales that have something to eat in
them. If Brannon and Copeland seem flat, Mick Kelly is about as
round as a twelve-year-old can be. Laughter has always been the
finest defense against pretentiousness, and in her treatment of
several minor characters and of Mick herself, Mrs. McCullers reveals an affectionate gaiety that provides wholesome leavening
for the pessimism so pervasive in this first novel.

The portrait of Mick Kelly is a charming evocation of the
sensitivity and thickness, the exuberance and boredom, the ease
of flight and quickness of descent that mark a familiar period in
early adolescence. Like so many characters in Mrs. McCullers'
books, Mick is defined by the extremity of her isolation and the
fever of her fantasy life. Although she wants desperately to connect with other people, she cultivates those qualities of talent
and personality that might bring her increased separateness as
well as applause. Excitement keeps her imagination at boiling
point. To escape the squalor of her slum environment, she climbs
a ladder to the roof of a house being built nearby and sits reflect-

ing on the possibilities of celebrity and fortune. In her inventor's phase, she hopes to market radios the size of green peas that people could stick in their ears and to provide flying machines to fit comfortably on a voyager's back. During her heroic period, she expresses her desires in murals of natural and human catastrophe, "Town Burning," or "Sea Gull with Back Broken in Storm." In her interlude as a composer, she hopes to rival Mozart in symphony and song, but since her family cannot afford an instrument, she tries to make a violin out of a broken ukulele. Her tunes, dissonant and intense, carry titles like "Africa," "The Snowstorm," "A Big Fight." The magniloquent but unfinished "This Thing I Want, I Know Not What" is her masterpiece.

As the conflict worsens between the world and her imagination, Mick constructs her most elaborate and personal defense: "She sat down on the steps and laid her head on her knees. She went into the inside room. With her it was like there was two places — the inside room and the outside room. School and the family and the things that happened every day were in the outside room. Mister Singer was in both rooms. Foreign countries and plans and music were in the inside room. The songs she thought about were there. And the symphony." A moment later, Mrs. McCullers conveys the transparent frailty of her defense with the sentence: "Spareribs stuck his dirty hand up to her eyes because she had been staring off at space. She slapped him."

Although Mick is irrepressibly creative, she is by no means free from an egotism strident enough to injure others. When her brother accidently shoots Baby Wilson, she torments him with visions of Sing Sing and hellfire; and we are told earlier that she had continually hit him whenever she noticed his hands in his pants, so that now he never "peed normal like other kids" but with his hands behind him. Although Mick is a virtuoso of escape, her artistry is rarely effective, and at the end of the novel she feels the disquiet of being barred from the inside room. She does, however, manage to express a qualified affirmation, which – in its vernacular familiarity – is one of the most convincing moments of celebration in the novel:

> But maybe it would be true about the piano and turn out O.K. Maybe she would get a chance soon. Else what the hell good had it all been – the way she felt about music and the plans she had made in the inside room? It had to be some good if anything made sense. . . .
> All right!
> O.K.!
> Some good.

Part of Mick's appeal rests in her indomitability and it is this sense of a human being refusing to accept meanness that Mrs. McCullers is able to celebrate so skillfully. Singer talking blissfully with his hands to an incomprehending Antonapoulos; the feuding Kelly family joined for a short while in loyalty and love; the weary Copeland hearing "rich, dark sounds" from the pages of Spinoza – these are moments of beauty as well as pathos. Rage, anger, and indignation are often in this story the other side of love, for Mrs. McCullers – like Keats – believed that a street fight is ugly, but the energies displayed can be beautiful.

No such beauty exists in *Reflections in a Golden Eye*, the most pompous and disagreeable of all her books. Almost as if to spite those critics who complained of the squalor of her subject matter, Mrs. McCullers created a swamp where no light shines and no people live. In 1941, when the novel first appeared, reviewers intensified their earlier objections to the morbidity of her materials: perversion, voyeurism, mutilation, and murder; but now, three decades and many a Gothic novel later, the objection is not to the luridness of the subject, but rather to lack of artistry in Mrs. McCullers' treatment. *Reflections in a Golden Eye* is a muddled, pretentious book that promises to illuminate shadowy places of the human psyche, but manages only to exploit them.

The scene is an army camp in the deep South during the late 1930's, and the characters (to quote the best line in the book) are "two officers, a soldier, two women, a Filipino, and a horse." One officer is Captain Penderton, a tightly repressed latent homosexual, infatuated with his wife's lovers; the other is Major Langdon, an easygoing charmboy who bedded the lusty Leonora Penderton in a blackberry patch two hours after their first meeting. The soldier, a moronic naif named Williams, sees Mrs. Penderton framed nude in a window and begins tiptoeing into her bedroom to worship her while she sleeps. The other woman, Alison Langdon, frail and neurasthenic, has recently clipped off her nipples with a garden shears, and now finds solace in the company of a prancing houseboy, Anacleto. The horse, Firebird, is tended by Williams, adored by Leonora, and despised by her husband. After a series of violent, inconclusive adventures, Penderton is drawn in love and hate toward the silent Williams; but when he finds that the private has eyes only for his wife, he murders him.

After such action, what explanation but fantasy? And recently a number of critics have argued that *Reflections in a Golden Eye* is not supposed to be read literally, but rather as a deliberately extravagant symbolic prose poem, true not to the real world but to the vagaries of abnormal psychology. In its charity, however, this argument ignores the fact that the novel never establishes credible connections with any world, literal or fantastic, and that its understanding of human pathology is misty to the point of meaninglessness. As often happens in Mrs. McCullers' weakest books, the fatal devils are an overriding ambition and something less than full clarity of intention. Her basic subject is clear enough: the ravages of dammed-up sexual energies; but in a desire to marry Faulkner to Flaubert and D. H. Lawrence, she takes three mutually contradictory attitudes toward her subject matter. First, as an objective narrator, she introduces the action in a detached and formal manner: short sentences, sculptured paragraphs, a poised monotonic response to everything miraculous and mundane. Designed to establish the verisimilitude of the story, this style depends on a great many details drawn from a firsthand experience of army life — matters of rank, architecture, armor, and so on. Existing simultaneously with the reporter is a satirist, whose aim is to demolish everyone in sight for the assorted vices of pride, moral vacancy, and self-deceit. Leonora is shown to be so dim-witted that the demands of writing a thank-you note reduce her to nervous exhaustion; her husband, a storehouse of technical information, cannot put two facts together to make an idea, and is entirely blind to the most obvious of his own physiological impulses; the mindless Major Langdon orders his life on the premise that only two things matter: "to be a good animal and to serve my country"; and young Williams, when driven to the point of action, finds "the vaporish impressions within him condensed to a thought." The third voice in the novel belongs to a mythopoeic explorer who sees in this grotesque domestic drama a monumental conflict of will against instinct, the artificial against the natural, and death against life.

The journalist and the satirist do their work only too well. By concentrating on the facts of the physical and social scene, Mrs. McCullers makes it impossible for us not to ask that her human beings remain plausible; but by insisting that the people are pathological types, and by damning them with such relentless sarcasm, she makes it difficult for us to care for their inhumanities. There is excessive malice, too, in the mockery. Usually, satire achieves force by aiming at targets that represent some universal yet remedial failing (the self-interest of politicians, the heartlessness of society women, the greed of bankers); but Mrs. McCullers' satire deals with perverse emotional failures of which the characters themselves are unaware, or about which they can do nothing (Penderton's unconscious desire for a handsome young primitive; Williams' witlessness, and so on).

It is, however, only when the poet takes over that Mrs. Mc-Cullers reveals the full inadequacy of her conception, since she has neither the language nor the depth of insight to give the sordid drama the elemental force of myth. Different as they are, the voices of the realist, the satirist, and the mythmaker can exist compatibly in a single work (*St. Mawr* and *Heart of Darkness* are modern examples) but in Lawrence and Conrad the ordinary people are free agents and the narrator's analysis of their situation is weighty enough to give them a significance beyond the realm of the natural. In Mrs. McCullers' book, the people are caricatures and the narrator's commentary is a triumph of adjectives over analysis, reminiscent of the worst in Poe rather than the best in Lawrence. Penderton and Williams continually move in states between stupor and somnambulism, experiencing rootless terror and dark, unspeakable desires. When the captain is near the private, he suffers "a curious lapse of sensory impressions" and finds himself "unable to see or hear properly"; and Williams often stands silent staring ominously into space "in the attitude of one who listens to a call from a long distance." Unfortunately, the call never comes through for Williams, or for the reader; the menace remains obscure and Mrs. McCullers' promptings stir only laughter and disbelief.

In the last analysis, *Reflections in a Golden Eye* provides no genuine insight into sexual pathologies, but merely an arbitrary series of gaudy, melodramatic episodes that shock without illuminating and never coalesce into larger patterns of action or meaning. Penderton may drop a kitten into a freezing mailbox, but his sadism seems less significant than his stupidity. Williams, standing over the sleeping body of Leonora, finishes her half-eaten piece of chicken; we may remember the gesture, but not the true nature of the man who made it. When Alison sees the soldier hiding in the shadows of the Penderton house, she feels "an eerie shock," closes her eyes, and counts "by sevens to two hundred and eighty." People counting by seven to two hundred and eighty — this is a useful image to describe what goes on in *Reflections in a Golden Eye* — strange, oddly provocative, but not very enlightening about human character and conduct.

"The Ballad of the Sad Café" is a good deal more rewarding. Instead of trying to compete with writers of much greater psychological awareness and architechtonic skill, Mrs. McCullers here wisely moves in a limited area more suited to her talents — the alien, elemental world of legend and romance. Like all good ballads, her story is urgent, atmospheric, and primitive, and yet, in its melodramatic swiftness and simplicity, tells us more things memorable about human life than all the devious sophisticated posturings of *Reflections in a Golden Eye*.

In the background are the physical facts of life that count for so much in the ballad world: a dingy southern town cut off from the accommodations of civilized society, boundaries of swamps and cold black pinewood, weather that is raw in winter and white with the glare of heat in summer. Only those who must come here: the tax collector to bother the rich; an investigator to refuse credit to Ryan, the weaver; a lost traveler to find his way back to his destination. Decayed buildings lean in imminent collapse and intimations of mortality are everywhere. The moon makes "dim, twisted shadows on the blossoming peach trees," and the odor of sweet spring grass mingles with the warm, sour smell of a nearby lagoon. Strangers arrive suddenly, often at night, and they have intimate ties with the twilight world of animals. The hunchback's hands are like "dirty sparrow claws," and he perches on a railing the way "a sick bird huddles on a telephone wire," to "grieve publicly." Much depends on the cycle of the seasons and the climactic events of the plot often have their effective climatic correspondences. Autumn begins with cool days of a "clean bright sweetness," but when the villain comes home from prison, the weather turns sticky, sultry, and rotten. A month before the famous wrestling match that brings the story to a close, snow falls for the first time in living memory.

The boldness and precision with which she creates the sense of a town estranged from the rest of the world is the first of Mrs. McCullers' successes in "The Ballad of the Sad Café." Unlike those narrators in the earlier novels who move uneasily from realism to myth and back again, the invented voice in this story has an obvious authority and grace. Beginning simply in the present, she tells us that things are dismal now but once upon a time there was gaiety and color in the human landscape. No attempt is made to mask the calamitous outcome; ruin is announced at the start; our interest will be entirely in how it was accomplished. Since she is confident in her grasp of the moment and the milieu, Mrs. McCullers assumes a relaxed, colloquial style, punctuating the narrative with phrases like "time must pass" and "so do not forget."

Knowing that her gruesome story might, if too solemnly told, seem wildly melodramatic, she skillfully uses folk humor to sweeten the Gothic tale. When the shambling, toothless Merlie Ryan spreads the rumor that Amelia has murdered the newly arrived Lymon, Mrs. McCullers casually reports: "It was a fierce and sickly tale the town built up that day. In it were all the things which cause the heart to shiver — a hunchback, a midnight burial in the swamp, the dragging of Miss Amelia through the streets of the town . . ." But then, moments later, she parades her little peacock proudly down the stairs. Throughout the narrative, understatement and playfulness humanize the actors and make their behavior seem less morbid. Often, in dialogue, they use an idiom full of the comic hyperbole so common in country speech. Amelia claims to have slept as soundly as if she were drowned in axle grease, and when she is dizzy with apprehension and love, the neighbors speak of her being "well on her way . . . up fools' hill," and they can't wait to see how the affair will turn out.

It turns out badly. "The Ballad of the Sad Café" is the story of Miss Amelia Evans, a quirky amazon who sells feed, guano, and domestic staples in the town's only thriving store. Tall, dark, and unapproachable in a rough, masculine way, Amelia is an uncompromising merchant with a passion for vindictive lawsuits and a beneficent witch doctor with a genuine desire to ease human pain. Both her business acumen and her healing powers are legendary; what she shrewdly extracts in trade she gives back in the free and effective dispensation of a hundred different cures. Since her liquors relieve melancholy, her foods hunger, and her folk remedies pain, this perverse cross between Ceres, Bacchus, and the neighborhood medicine man is the one indispensable person in town.

That the hard-fisted Amelia has the living touch is demonstrated at the arrival of a sniveling hunchbacked dwarf who asks for food and shelter. His worth, he claims, is based on the urgency of kinship, and his weird unraveling of cousins, half sisters, and third husbands is a neat parody of the mysterious genealogical links in ballad and romance. Miss Amelia immediately acknowledges the tie, lightly touches his hump, and offers him liquor, dinner, and a bed. Soon, Cousin Lymon is installed in Amelia's sanctuary, sharing rooms rarely seen by living eyes, and a bizarre relationship, very much like love, transforms them both. As lover, she becomes softened, graceful, communicative, eager to extend the rewards of companionship to others; he, the beloved, becomes proud, perky, aristocratic. Even the townspeople benefit. The liquor that Miss Amelia used to dispense on her doorstep is now served inside, and gradually the store evolves into a café featuring the exotic hunchback and some palatable food and drink. Warmth, affectionate fellowship, "a certain gaiety and grace of behavior," momentarily replace suspicion, loneliness, egotism, and rough-hewn malice — the rigorous truths of the world outside. Niggardly Amelia puts free crackers on the counter, customers share their liquor, and the flourishing café provides the one bright page in the history of this melancholy town.

Unhappily, the festive interlude lasts only six years before the sins of the past exact their tribute and the catastrophe announced at the start is set in motion. Some years before the appearance of Lymon, the young Amelia had been married for ten stormy days to Marvin Macy. Handsome, mercurial, vicious, and cunning, Macy had been a most notable young scoundrel, the demon lover of every "soft-eyed" young girl in town. Miraculously enough, *he* had fallen passionately in love with the haggard Amelia and became her long-suffering romantic knight. As a disdainful mistress, Amelia needed little instruction; after their marriage, she rejected his advances, sold his presents, and battered his face with her punches. Macy, disconsolate and swearing vengeance, ran off to a life of crime and an eventual stretch in the Atlanta penitentiary. Afterwards, Miss Amelia cut up his Klansman's robe to cover her tobacco plants.

Once Macy reappears in town, the tempo quickens and everyone prepares for the inevitable confrontation of the two epic antagonists. Most of the wise money is on Amelia, for she had beaten more than her weight several times before. The twist, however, in this tale is provided by Cousin Lymon, who completes the eccentric triangle of love relationships by falling desperately for the roguish Macy. This time it is Amelia's turn to suffer at the hands of a capricious beloved. While Lymon slavishly follows the scornful Macy about town, she becomes increasingly distraught at the turn in his affections; but nothing can be done. Lymon announces that Macy will move in with them and Amelia comes to the mournful recognition that "once you have lived with another . . . it is better to take in your mortal enemy than face the terror of living alone."

Step by step, Amelia and Macy prepare for the hand-to-hand combat that everyone knows must come. On the second of February, when a bloody-breasted hawk gives the signal by flying over Amelia's house, all the townspeople move as spectators toward the café. At seven o'clock, the two contestants begin to pound one another with hundreds of bone-cracking blows. After a savage half-hour, when boxing has turned to wrestling, Amelia puts her triumphant hands to the throat of her fallen adversary; but with astonishing swiftness, Cousin Lymon flies at her back, pulls her off, and gives the victory to Macy. That night, to celebrate their triumph, the two men smash up Amelia's property and disappear. In the months that follow, Amelia lets the café and her healing practice fall into ruin, and she eventually becomes a recluse. The town returns to its desolate, mechanical ways; "the soul rots with boredom"; and the tale ends with the swelling song of a chain gang.

Much of what is permanently haunting in this grotesque little story is the product of Mrs. McCullers' easy relationship with the properties of the ballad world. Experience heightened far beyond the realm of plausibility is given a valid, poetic truth by the propriety of those conventions that make the miraculous seem oddly real. Dreams, superstitions, omens, numbers, musical motifs, all operate here to provide an authentic atmosphere for this perverse triangle of passions, and to make the inexplicable longings of the characters seem like dark elemental forces in the natural world. Enigmatic melodies are heard in the night: wild, high voices singing songs that never end. Macy, the demon lover, plays the guitar, and when he sings the tunes glide "slowly from his throat like eels." As a doctor, Amelia depends on a stunning variety of secret herbs; her Kroup Kure, made from whiskey, rock candy, and an unnamed third power, is a wonder drug, while her liquor has been known to bring up messages from the bottom of the human soul. When she guards the low fire of her ritual still, Amelia likes to untie knots in rope, and in her parlor cabinet she keeps an acorn and two small stones. The acorn she picked from the ground the day her father died, and the stones had once been removed from her kidney. If she wants Lymon to come along to Cheehaw, she asks him seven times and when he continually refuses, she draws a heavy line with a stick around the barbecue pit and orders him not to trespass that limit. Naturally, when the time must be set for the epic fight, seven o'clock is chosen. Miss Amelia is not the only character to be given a powerful armory of signs and talismans. Lymon sits regularly on a sack of guano and is rarely without his snuffbox. Years earlier, Macy had courted his love with a bunch of swamp flowers, a sack of chitterlings, and a silver ring; and when he returns from prison the neighbors fear him as more dangerous than ever because while put away he "must have learned the method of laying charms." Always called devilish, Macy never sweats, not even in August, and that — Mrs. McCullers reminds us — is surely "a sign worth pondering."

By relying so heavily on charms and rituals, the characters emphasize the fated, irrational quality of so many of their decisive acts. Like most works in its traditional genre, "The Ballad of the Sad Café" illustrates the consequences of moral choice but does not probe it; analysis is less vital than the starkness of dramatic presentation. Yet an evocative atmosphere and a strong story line would not in themselves ensure success if the illustration were not thematically absorbing as well. The richly patterned, sinister dance in which Macy, Amelia, and Lymon play at different times the roles of lover and beloved dramatizes the wayward nature of human passion and the irreconcilable antagonism inherent in every love relationship.

At one point in his poem "Prayer for My Daughter," William

Butler Yeats, speaking of the splendid contrariety with which females choose their lovers, describes how beautiful women sometimes eat "a crazy salad with their meat." "The Ballad of the Sad Café" is about the "crazy salad" of every man: ugly and beautiful, heiress and outlaw, dwarf and amazon — they all choose love objects in ways that demonstrate that passion is the most permanent and amazing of all the human mysteries. In the McCullers world, the lover occupies the highest seat in the pantheon, for he has the restlessness and imagination to wish to break free from the constrictive prison of ego and connect with another person. His choices are often arbitrary and improbable, but once made he worships them with a constancy that can only inspire amazement. Everyone wants to be a lover because the lover is the archetypal creative spirit: dreamer, quester, romantic idealist. If love compels, it can also soften. When Macy is smitten with Amelia, he becomes improved in civility; and Amelia's passion for Lymon not only refines her temperament and reduces her lawsuits, but results in the establishment of the café. Product of her love, the café is the symbol of the ability of human affection to create intimacy and delight where only barrenness existed before. Yet, if love can sweeten and refine, it can also leave the lover defenseless. Having created the beloved in the image of his own desperate desire, the lover is open to rebuff and betrayal, for he tempts the one permanent quality of any beloved — his cruelty. In "The Ballad of the Sad Café," the beloved is a static figure, chosen by someone else. Easily resentful of being considered a token, he is also quick to recognize the assailability of his admirer and the extent of his own manipulative powers.

In Mrs. McCullers' triangle, each character is revealed successively in the roles of lover and beloved. In his suit of Amelia, Macy is meek with longing and easily swayed by others: he saves his wages, abandons fornication, and goes regularly to church. But in response to Amelia's chilling rejection, he becomes more brutally antisocial than he had ever been before. On his return to town, cast as his wife's revenger and Lymon's beloved, he alternates between abusiveness and complete indifference, calling the sullen dwarf "Brokeback" at one moment and ignoring him the next. Like Macy, Lymon is also violently contradictory in both roles. Admired by Amelia, he gains forceful self-assurance, but also learns to exercise the hateful tyranny of a spoiled child. Finicky, boastful, self-absorbed, he becomes wildly obsessive in his demands for personal gratification. Yet when he falls for Macy, his reversal is perhaps even more disagreeable. Obsessed now by his desire to attract Macy's attention, he flaps his ears and mopes about pathetically like a small dog sick for love.

The most memorable metamorphosis, however, is experienced by Amelia. Chosen by Macy at nineteen, she spits in contempt and strikes out fiercely at every opportunity. Hardhearted, peremptory, and self-sufficient, she does not let her rage affect her capacity to turn a deal in her own favor, and she quickly strips her husband of everything he owns. At thirty, however, when she chooses Lymon, a remarkable change occurs. The rudest misanthrope in town turns genial, even cheerful, moving easily among people, sharing her liquor, forgetting to bolt the door at night. Instead of overalls and swampboots, she occasionally dons a soft red dress, and as she rubs Lymon twice a day with pot liquor to give him strength, her hatred of physicality relaxes. Suddenly nostalgic about the past, she turns candid about the present, confiding in the dwarf about trade secrets and the size of her bank account. As lover for the first time in her life, Amelia takes emotional risks by putting herself in a position of extreme vulnerability. Staring at Lymon, her face wears the fascinating expression of "pain, perplexity, and uncertain joy" — the lonesome look of the lover. When she learns that Macy may return, she — in her pride — miscalculates Lymon's fickleness and her own power over his life; and after his affection is alienated, she becomes frightfully distracted, pursuing those contradictory courses that lead to her downfall.

Because she has the capacity to change and the energy to pursue her awakened desire for companionship, Amelia turns from a harridan evoking awe to a woman worthy of compassion. By learning to love she has become more human — more tender, gracious, amiable, perceptive; but also more obviously exposed to the inevitable stings of loneliness, betrayal, and suffering. As healer, hostess, and lover, she is — despite her rudeness and suspicion — a force for good in the community, and the destruction of her dream is a cause for genuine mourning. "The Ballad of the Sad Café" is an elegy for Amelia Evans, and it has all the brooding eloquence and eccentricity to stand as a fitting tribute to that very peculiar lady.

Although "The Ballad of the Sad Café" is by far the best of Mrs. McCullers' excursions into the grotesque, it is not without reminders of the penumbral insistence that mars her worst work. Too much is occasionally made of dark nights of the soul and of things going on there that only God can understand. Because the things that go on in *The Member of the Wedding* are available to everyone and are recorded with vivacity by an artist who understands them, it is the best of all her books.

Like a number of other carefully patterned modern novels (*Nostromo, A Passage to India, To the Lighthouse, The Sun Also Rises*), *The Member of the Wedding* is divided into three parts to call special attention to the rhythmical quality of the action. In Hemingway's book, for instance, a false sense of movement is established by having Brett go off with Robert Cohn at the close of the first part and with Pedro Romero at the close of the second. Part III, however, ends as it should with Brett and Jake, sterile as ever, sitting in a stationary taxi. In Mrs. McCullers' book, the rhythm — different but equally self-conscious — follows the familiar journey of adolescent initiation: the stirrings of dissatisfaction, jubilant hope founded on misplaced idealism, and disillusionment accompanied by a new wisdom about the limits of human life.

In Part I, we are introduced to the world of Frankie Addams, a tall, gawky, motherless, twelve-year-old tomboy with cropped hair and the scars of wildness decorating her feet. Ever since April, Frankie has been in the press of a vague but powerful discontent, and now — in the heat of August — she approaches her first serious teen-age crisis. As Diana Trilling has remarked, summer is the most disquieting time of the child's year because the end of school throws him back "so completely on his own incoherent resources"; and Frankie validates this observation both by the range of her resources and by the charming extremity of her incoherence. Often she is an agile, quick-witted girl, her language able to reveal the quality of her mind and sensibility. Thinking of her brother and Janice, his fiancée, she can coin the phrase "they are the we of me"; and she has the wit to dramatize her passion for "hopping-john" (a mixture of peas and rice) by asking her cousin to wave a plate under her nose when she lies in her coffin, for if a breath of life is left her she will sit up and eat. At the edge of adolescence, however, she doesn't quite know what she is going to say until she says it, and she continually falls back on words like "curious," "queer," "puzzling," and on such affected literary borrowings as "I am sick unto death." Her main complaint is separateness; she is "an unjoined person" and "a member of nothing in the world."

Since Frankie now feels far more than she is able to express, Mrs. McCullers wisely uses a narrative technique similar to the Jamesian point of view in *The Ambassadors,* following the girl around, reporting what she does and sees, but speaking of her only in the author's third-person voice. Thus, she is able to achieve sympathy and a certain distance, to convey the vivid, poetic, but essentially unformed quality of Frankie's fantasy life. And Frankie is nothing if not a fantast. In the heat of the Georgia summer, she dreams and writes little plays about polar bears and igloos, and when she puts seashells to her ear, she has no trouble hearing tides in the Gulf of Mexico. Thinking of the warmth and conviviality of family life, she imagines people around a hearth talking with "woven voices." And in her finest performance, she sits with eyes half-closed at the kitchen table conjuring up the wedding of Jarvis and Janice in a snow-covered, silent church — the bride and groom with luminous blankness where their faces should be.

The first part of *The Member of the Wedding* fills in the details of this fine portrait of twelve going on thirteen: the blend of prescience and infantilism; the edginess, indecision, continual bluster; the brooding inarticulateness mixed with the wackiest kind of exactitude. Although Frankie cannot describe her convulsive feelings about life, she has figured out with frightful precision that if her present growth continues she will be just over nine feet tall at her eighteenth birthday. By turns solemn and giddy, she does anything that impulse drives her to do, but whatever she does is always wrong and not at all what she actually would like to do. In the most effective instance of this muddle, she picks up a knife to have something to hold on to, but soon flings it across the kitchen to scare the bewildered cook and to demonstrate her claim to be the finest knife thrower in town. (Amusingly enough, this point was transformed in the stage version, when — to keep Julie Harris from having to perform as a virtuoso every night — Mrs. McCullers had the knife miss the beam and Frankie exclaim: "I *used* to be the best knife thrower in town.")

A significant part of our response to Frankie is complicated
and controlled by the setting in which she is placed and the people with whom she has to deal. The kitchen in the ramshackle
house at 124 Grove Street, where most of the action takes place, is
a stale, ugly square room decorated fitfully with the odd draw-
ings of children. In the background, a radio, crossing several stations, blends war reports with advertisements and the music of a
honky-tonk band. In the foreground is the imposing figure of
Berenice Sadie Brown. At thirty-five or thereabouts (she is described as cagey about her age in the novel, and as forty-five in the
play), Berenice gives off an air of power and tranquillity. Short,
broad-shouldered, and very black, she speaks with a slow, measured cadence that suggests a wisdom painstakingly earned; and
her stock of folk sayings ("it is a known truth that gray-eyed people are jealous," "I believe the sun has fried your brains") reveals
both an earthy common sense and a gift for high-flown metaphor-
ical language. For much of the novel, Berenice's clarity and
bluntness serve as a genial check on Frankie's foggy romanticism,
and she spends a good deal of her time calling the girl back to
the things of the real world. This mild, yet affectionate antagonism between Frankie and Berenice is the source of some of the
most delicate comedy in the novel, and Mrs. McCullers' steady
gift for recording its turns and counterturns is an index to her
mastery of these homely materials.

Yet Berenice would not be so memorable a character if she did
not also embody in her own personality a complementary response to realism, for she is a woman with a profound romantic
strain that has not been extinguished by those very disappointments on which her most mature stoicism is based. The physical
sign of Berenice's fascination is her false eye, the glittering blue
counterpart of her real eye, which is melancholy and dark. That
this black woman should want a bright blue eye is a mystery to
Frankie but not to us, for it symbolizes her powerful desire to

break free from the fated conditions of her birth and social position. The moral sign of Berenice's exoticism is implicit in the history of her four marriages, a story that she tells with the leisure and formulaic vividness of an ancient bard. When she sits in the dreary Addams kitchen and begins the narrative that Frankie has heard countless times before, she seems to the girl "a colored queen unwinding a bolt of cloth of gold." The first husband had been Ludie Freeman, a brickmason with whom she lived happily for nine passionate years, and when he died suddenly in November 1931, she embarked on an unconscious voyage to find his equal in other, less satisfactory, men. Ludie had been a handsome fellow with only one touch of ugliness — a bruised and disfigured thumb. One day, half a year after his death, Berenice was astounded to see a replica of that thumb on a man sitting next to her at church. Transfixed by the sign, she married Jamie Beale, who soon turned out to be alcoholic and worthless. Henry Johnson, the third husband, was also created in the image of the beloved Ludie. He had bought the dead man's coat at a second-hand clothing store and hypnotized Berenice by the familiarity of the fine figure he made. But poor Johnson, lacking his share of good sense, began to dream of eating while asleep, and after he swallowed a swatch of the bed sheet, Berenice felt compelled to try her luck elsewhere. The fourth husband, Willis Rhodes, gouged out her eye, stole her furniture, and ended up in jail, but his resemblance to Ludie never quite comes clear, since Berenice insists that the tale is not fit for adolescent ears.

Because of Berenice's legendary history, Frankie's response to her is properly double. She is fascinated by the shining blue eye and by thoughts of marital melodrama, but she is suspicious of Berenice's hard-won, untheatrical stoicism. After Berenice presses a gaudy dress that she had previously ridiculed, Frankie "would have liked for her expression to be split into two parts, so that one eye stared at Berenice in an accusing way, and the other eye thanked her with a grateful look. But the human face does not divide like this, and the two expressions canceled out each other." This combination of hostility and admiration is also revealed in Frankie's response to the kitchen itself, and to the third member of its daily triumvirate, her little cousin, John Henry. The ritual of the kitchen — the protracted dinners, the ragged card games, the repetitious, rhythmical conversation — is comforting and disquieting; and the room itself (in the words of Gerald Weales) is both a sanctuary and a prison. The droll and elfin John Henry may be able to draw Picasso-like profiles of the telephone man, with one eye measured just above the nose and another just below; but the harsh reality of the kitchen is less than gentle with his dreams. He makes a wonderful, original biscuit man, with a little grinning raisin mouth, but when it comes out of the oven it looks just like any biscuit man ever made by a child, the fine, eccentric work of John Henry having been baked out. The boy, still an innocent six-year-old sensualist, stares through his glasses, wipes the biscuit man with a napkin, and butters his left foot. For Frankie, however, the kitchen is more threatening. Although she recognizes the genuine warmth and protection to be found there (the way human voices can "bloom like flowers"), she instinctively realizes that her final destiny is elsewhere. If Berenice takes her pleasure mainly in the past, and John Henry entirely in the present, then Frankie must place her fondest hopes on the promise of the future; and at the close of Part I she makes her triumphant announcement that she will become a member of her brother's wedding.

The opening pages of Part II (in which Mrs. McCullers describes the joy of a girl who seems to be walking just outside paradise) is one of the finest examples of her powers as a celebratory novelist. By inventing a bold conceit and then convincing us of

its inevitability and aptness, she effectively dramatizes the para-
doxical freedom to be found in human solidarity. Inspired by her
new sense of belonging, Frankie finds the day before the wedding
magical and unique because the familiar, not the unexpected,
strikes her "with a strange surprise." To communicate this
"twisted sense of the astonishing," Mrs. McCullers relies heavily
on a series of fresh metaphors that catch Frankie's bright new
perception of her ordinary world. In the old days, Frankie was
like Uncle Charles's blindered mule, moving laboriously in the
same deadening circle, lingering on street corners, browsing at
the dime store, passing time at the local movie; but now —
rechristened F. Jasmine — she is an exotic animal set free to
wander in places she has never seen before. When F. Jasmine
wakes up on this unforgettable Saturday morning, she feels as if
"her brother and the bride had slept . . . on the bottom of her
heart," and she immediately thinks of the Sunday wedding.
Forgoing her usual outfit of mismatched clothing, she enhances a
neat pink dress with lipstick and a new perfume. Downstairs at
breakfast, she gives another demonstration of the benevolent
powers of human connection. Exhilarated by the thought of her
role at the wedding, she is able for the first time to understand
the mundane ritual of her father's life. Watching him across the
kitchen, she breaks free from the prison of her ego, and feels a
new tenderness for this bluff, good-hearted widower. Mrs. Mc-
Cullers, realistic and anxious to avoid sentimentality, has Frankie's expression of love throttled by her father's demand for a
monkey wrench and screwdriver.

Once wandering through town, F. Jasmine feels the quickness
and enthusiasm of a voyager in an enchanted land. For the first
time in her life, the shouts of neighborhood children have an in-
effable sweetness, and she feels a heightened sensitivity to every
passing object and human being. In this new state of gladness,

her perceptions are of an almost visionary intensity. When an old colored man glances at her from atop a wagon, she feels a vibrant sense of connection and can immediately conjure up a mental image of his home and his field. Like the Ancient Mariner obsessed with a story he must share with others, F. Jasmine is compelled to tell people about the wedding; but instead of interrupting a marriage feast with a morbid tale, she amuses passersby with a sweet one. To her first listener, a sullen Portuguese café owner, she begins the narrative like "a circus dog" breaking through a paper hoop; and later, spilling her story to an old lady sweeping a porch, she discovers that the tale has "an end and a beginning, a shape like a song." Starting like a march tune, it softens to a dreamy melody that slows her footsteps to a wander. Over drinks with a soldier, her aural hallucinations turn visual again, and she suddenly sees herself walking with her brother and his bride "beneath a cold Alaskan sky, along the sea where green ice waves lay frozen and folded on the shore." When they climb a glacier, friends call in Alaskan their "JA" names. A few minutes later, on the way home, she sees Janice and Jarvis again in a startling burst of light, but when the brightness fades, the reality turns out to be two colored boys standing in an alley.

The early morning bliss that F. Jasmine feels at no longer being separate from herself and from other people is powerful but temporary, and in the remainder of Part II the facts of the ordinary world gradually reassert themselves. As soon as she returns home, "the afternoon was like the center of the cake that Berenice had baked last Monday, a cake which failed"; and in several long and revealing conversations, Berenice's blunt but eloquent common sense punctures F. Jasmine's romantic pretensions. But the girl keeps dodging past the truth, and when she finds it hard to argue with the obvious facts, she slides off with "You wait and see," or some equally transparent evasion.

The rhythm established in the middle section of *The Member of the Wedding* depends on F. Jasmine's incorrigible gift for flight and Berenice's unerring ability to bring her spinning back down to the ground. F. Jasmine, anxious to leave her childish identity behind her, argues that a person can change his nature by changing his name, but Berenice insists that things are always accumulating around one's name, and that "We all of us somehow caught. We born this way or that way and we don't know why. But we caught anyhow. I born Berenice. You born Frankie. John Henry born John Henry. And maybe we wants to widen and bust free. But no matter what we do we still caught. Me is me and you is you and he is he. We each one of us somehow caught all by ourself."

F. Jasmine's proud refusal to accept the accuracy of Berenice's simple equation "me is me" is carried into the third section of the novel and adds dramatic force to her eventual disillusionment. Just as the opening pages of Part II show Mrs. McCullers in her best celebratory voice, so the closing pages of the book reveal her ability to mourn for maturity as well as to praise it. At the beginning of Part III, the wedding ("unmanaged as a nightmare") is described in a half-dozen paragraphs and the remaining thirty pages deal with the accommodations of a girl now called Frances. At first, in the full flush of her disappointment, she is tearful and wickedly misanthropic, but after a comically abortive attempt to run away from home, she begins gradually to realize the childishness of her earlier dreams. Between herself and all the places she had so loftily dreamed of visiting, "there was a space like an enormous canyon she could not hope to bridge or cross. . . . She was back to the fear of the summertime, the old feelings that the world was separate from herself." Now, having parted with her fantasies, she begins to compromise like most other thirteen-year-old girls. She becomes close friends with Mary

Littlejohn (whom she ridiculed when she was Frankie), reads Tennyson, and plans at sixteen to take a leisurely trip around the world. Frances is a good deal more reasonable than F. Jasmine, but not altogether more attractive. In her pompous way, she corrects Berenice's diction; and in her preoccupation with Mary Littlejohn, she forgets the recently dead John Henry and seems unconcerned that Berenice will no longer work for the family. Without her spectacular and sparkling dreams, with her days filled with school and friendship, Frances seems just a bit too much like everyone else.

The Member of the Wedding is Mrs. McCullers' best book because it remains complete in itself — a small but undeniably affecting story of adolescent joy and frustration. The plot, limited to a few days in the life of a twelve-year-old girl, is more skillfully managed than the elaborate murder story in *Reflections in a Golden Eye*, or the haunting but ultimately mechanical quest pattern in *The Heart Is a Lonely Hunter*. The characters carry great conviction because Mrs. McCullers is wholly in command of their limited psychologies, and does not strain to suggest that they are darkly symbolic of more than themselves. Tonally, the novel is one of the few sentimental comedies in recent years to escape the charge of being maudlin; stylistically, it is the freshest and most inventive of her novels and stories.

In a recent survey, *Fiction of the Forties*, Chester Eisinger has traced the main flaw in *The Member of the Wedding* to "its focus on the child's self-centered world in which the macrocosm plays no part." But this, I think, is precisely the source of its strength. Throughout this essay, I have argued that Mrs. McCullers is fundamentally a master of bright and melancholy moods, a lyricist not a philosopher, an observer of maimed characters not of contaminated cultures. That she writes best of uncomplicated people in fairly straightforward narrative forms is proven positively by *The Member of the Wedding* and "The Ballad of the Sad Café," and negatively by the failure of her last full-length work of fiction. Published in 1961, after ten years of painful composition, *Clock Without Hands* tries to link the existential crisis of a man doomed by cancer to the sociological crisis of the South poisoned by racial strife. But because Mrs. McCullers was ill and working against her natural grain, the novel is deficient both in psychological intuition and cultural analysis.

The man condemned to die of leukemia is a forty-year-old druggist named J. T. Malone, whose final year in Milan, Georgia, 1953–54, provides the novel with its time scheme and organizational frame. Running parallel to Malone's story is the history of the town's leading family, the Clanes. At eighty-five, the former congressman, Judge Fox Clane, is a racist, voluptuary, and praiser of his own past; while his grandson, Jester, is a solemn adolescent of muddled but progressive inclinations. Both Clanes are haunted by the memory of the Judge's son and Jester's father, John, who committed suicide after the unsuccessful defense of a Negro accused of murdering the husband of a white woman with whom he had been intimate. For the Judge, the suicide represents a mysterious act of personal spite; for Jester, it is a puzzle he must solve in order to establish his own identity. An important clue to the puzzle is a blue-eyed Negro, Sherman Pew, a sullen poseur who insults white men but lives slavishly by the standards of bourgeois advertising. Jester, anxious to practice brotherhood, befriends Sherman; the Judge, aware that the boy is the illegitimate son of the Negro and the white woman, hires him as his secretary. The climax of the novel occurs when Sherman, stumbling on the truth about his ignominious origins, commits a series of outrages against the white community, drinking at a restricted fountain, watering the Judge's insulin injections, murdering Jester's dog, and renting a house in the white section of town.

A vigilante committee meets, but Malone, drawing the assassin's ballot, refuses from fear for his immortal soul to carry out the challenge. In his place, a mill foreman, Sammy Lank, proudly heaves two bombs through Sherman's window. Afterwards, at the point of murdering Sammy in vengeance, Jester learns not to be ruled by the lust for violence, and lets his hostage go. As the book ends, the Supreme Court announces school desegregation, Jester prepares to become a lawyer, Judge Clane tumbles into senility, and Malone quietly dies.

To anyone who remembers the daring symbolic design of *The Heart Is a Lonely Hunter*, the measured suspense in "The Ballad of the Sad Café," or the shrewd sense of motivation in *The Member of the Wedding*, *Clock Without Hands* must come as an unhappy reminder of a talent no longer at full strength. In none of her earlier books is the plot so clumsily managed, the pacing so tedious, the people so vacant, the symbolism so ineffectively contrived.

Take Malone, for example. At the start of the novel, he is the epitome of the common man, drab in thought, hesitant in action. When first given the death sentence, he refuses to face the truth, and looks for consolation in religion, mystery stories, and afternoon naps; but gradually, he wakes up to the emptiness of his entire life. It is here, however, that his creator fails him. Instead of providing Malone with heightened awareness and a language in which to express it, Mrs. McCullers continues to describe his dread as "amorphous" and his terror as "something awful and incomprehensible." If Malone has little credibility as an existential hero, Fox Clane and Sherman have even less as actors in a drama of racial conflict. Sodden with the worst illusions of the antebellum South, and anxious "to defend his womankind against the black and alien invader," the Judge at the start is a vigorous comic caricature. But by the third chapter, his endless ranting

against TVA, FHA, FDR, Bolsheviks in government, and Ne-
gresses at the Lincoln Memorial becomes tiresome and easy to
predict. In the light of his obvious political cunning, his plan
to redeem Confederate money is entirely implausible; and his
final collapse, during which he chants the Gettysburg Address
on the radio, is preposterous. Sherman, too, is given a set of contradictory emotions that never seem to live convincingly under
the same skin. Most often he is swaggering, truculent, and comically gullible, insulting Jester with infantile obscenities or drinking Lord Calvert's whiskey in hopes of becoming a "Man of
Distinction." When the Judge tells the boy about his scheme to
restore the financial health of the South, Sherman's lips and nostrils flutter, and he fiercely smashes the old man's fountain pen.
Yet, a moment later, after the Judge speaks of "polarities," Sherman writes the word down and thinks how he is "benefitting from
the Judge's vocabulary if nothing else." Given these absurdities,
it is impossible to believe in Sherman's role as the defiant young
Negro breaking community barriers by renting a house.

For these lifeless and improbable characters, Mrs. McCullers
seems to have had a symbolic intention. In a letter, written while
the book was still in manuscript, she spoke of Malone's white
blood cells crowding out the dark as "peculiarly a symbol of the
South." That Fox Clane is supposed to be "the South regenerate,"
Malone "the South finding its conscience at 11:59," and Sherman
a variety of the "social fantasy choking" the entire region was
noticed by the book's earliest reviewers; but neither they nor most
later readers found any part of the symbolism convincing.

Although *Clock Without Hands* is a disappointment, it can —
if viewed properly as an object lesson — direct us back to Mrs.
McCullers' earlier works and help us see their virtues more clearly.
In the past, a number of critics have sometimes taken her intentions in her novels as a measure of performance, and have evoked

the names of Tolstoi, Proust, and Faulkner to describe the range and quality of her achievement. Yet "The Ballad of the Sad Café" and *The Member of the Wedding* (the stories that will most likely last) demand comparison not with books by the prolific masters of world literature, but with works by three fine writers of a more moderate level of accomplishment: Eudora Welty, Katherine Anne Porter, and Flannery O'Connor. Like Carson McCullers, these contemporaries have by exploring the lives of isolated grotesques in twilight corners of the American South, produced a small body of fiction marked by eccentric originality, artistic finish, and a bleak poetic effect. Because of her hapless life and the limitations of her sensibility and vision, Mrs. McCullers' best work remains fixed on adolescent rather than adult stages of growth. For these and other reasons, she will most likely seem to posterity a less significant writer than Welty, Porter, or O'Connor; but she belongs by disposition and the solidity of her accomplishment in their company.

Selected Bibliography

The Writings of Carson McCullers

"Wunderkind," *Story*, 9:61–73 (December 1936). Short story.

The Heart Is a Lonely Hunter. Boston: Houghton Mifflin, 1940. Novel.

"Look Homeward Americans," *Vogue*, 96:74–75 (December 1, 1940). Sketch.

Reflections in a Golden Eye. Boston: Houghton Mifflin, 1941. Novel.

"Brooklyn Is My Neighborhood," *Vogue*, 97:62ff (March 1, 1941). Reminiscence.

"The Jockey," *Mademoiselle*, 17:15–16 (August 23, 1941). Short story.

"Night Watch over Freedom," *Vogue*, 97:29 (January 1, 1941). Patriotic tribute.

"We Carried Our Banners; We Were Pacifists, Too," *Vogue*, 97:42–43 (July 15, 1941). Reminiscence.

"Madame Zilensky and the King of Finland," *New Yorker*, 17:15–18 (December 20, 1941). Short story.

"Correspondence" (Letter of Manoel Garcia), *New Yorker*, 18:36 (February 7, 1942). Fictional exchange.

"A Tree. A Rock. A Cloud," *Harper's Bazaar*, 76:50ff (November 1942). Short story.

"The Ballad of the Sad Café," *Harper's Bazaar*, 77:72ff (November 1943). Story.

The Member of the Wedding. New York: Houghton Mifflin, 1946. Novel.

"How I Began to Write," *Mademoiselle*, 27:191ff (September 1948). Reminiscence.

"The Mortgaged Heart," *New Directions*, 10:509 (1948). Poem.

"When We Are Lost," *New Directions*, 10:509 (1948). Poem.

"Art and Mr. Mahoney," *Mademoiselle*, 28:120ff (February 1949). Sketch.

"Home for Christmas," *Mademoiselle*, 30:53ff (December 1949). Reminiscence.

"The Vision Shared," *Theatre Arts*, 34:28–30 (April 1950). Autobiography.

"The Sojourner," *Mademoiselle*, 31:90ff (May 1950). Short story.

"A Domestic Dilemma," *New York Post Magazine* (September 16, 1951), p. 10. Story.

The Ballad of the Sad Café. Boston: Houghton Mifflin, 1951. (Contains "The Ballad of the Sad Café," "Wunderkind," "The Jockey," "Madame Zilensky and the King of Finland," "The Sojourner," "A Domestic Dilemma," "A

Tree. A Rock. A Cloud," *The Heart Is a Lonely Hunter, Reflections in a Golden Eye*, and *The Member of the Wedding*.)

The Member of the Wedding. New York: New Directions, 1951. A play.

"The Dual Angel: A Meditation on Origin and Choice," *Botteghe Oscure*, 9:213–218 (1952). Poems.

"The Discovery of Christmas," *Mademoiselle*, 38:54ff (December 1953). Reminiscence.

"The Haunted Boy," *Botteghe Oscure*, 16:264–78 (1955); and *Mademoiselle*, 42:134ff (November 1955). Short story.

"Who Has Seen the Wind?" *Mademoiselle*, 43:156ff (September 1956). Short story.

"Stone Is Not Stone," *Mademoiselle*, 45:43 (July 1957). Poem.

The Square Root of Wonderful. Boston: Houghton Mifflin, 1958. Play.

"The Flowering Dream: Notes on Writing," *Esquire*, 52:162–64 (December 1959).

Clock Without Hands. Boston: Houghton Mifflin, 1961. Novel.

"A Child's View of Christmas," *Redbook*, 28:30 (December 1961). Reminiscence.

"The Dark Brilliance of Edward Albee," *Harper's Bazaar*, 97:98–99 (January 1963). Brief tribute.

"Isak Dinesen: In Praise of Radiance," *Saturday Review*, 46:28, 63 (March 16, 1963). Brief tribute.

"Sucker," *Saturday Evening Post*, 236:68–71 (September 28, 1963). An early story printed for the first time.

Sweet as a Pickle and Clean as a Pig. Poems. Boston: Houghton Mifflin, 1964. Children's verses.

"The March," *Redbook*, 128:64–65, 114–23 (March 1967). Short story.

"Hospital Christmas Eve," *McCall's*, 95:96–97 (December 1967). Sketch.

The Mortgaged Heart, edited by Margarita G. Smith. Boston: Houghton Mifflin, 1971. Posthumous collection of previously uncollected and unpublished materials.

Bibliographies

Stewart, Stanley. "Carson McCullers, 1940–1956: A Selected Checklist," *Bulletin of Bibliography*, 22:182–85 (April 1959).

Phillips, Robert S. "Carson McCullers: 1956–1964: A Selected Checklist," *Bulletin of Bibliography*, 24:113–16 (September–December 1964).

Stanley, William T. "Carson McCullers: 1965–1969: A Selected Checklist," *Bulletin of Bibliography*, 27:91–93 (1970).

LAWRENCE GRAVER

Biography

Carr, Virginia Spencer. *The Lonely Hunter*. New York: Doubleday, 1975.

Critical Studies

Baldanza, Frank. "Plato in Dixie," *Georgia Review*, 12:151–67 (1958).

Buchen, Irving H. "Carson McCullers, a Case of Convergence," *Bucknell Review*, 21:15–28 (1973).

Eisinger, Chester E. *Fiction of the Forties*. Chicago: University of Chicago Press, 1963. Pp. 243–58.

Emerson, Donald. "The Ambiguities of *Clock Without Hands*," *Wisconsin Studies in Contemporary Literature*, 3:15–28 (Fall 1962).

Evans, Oliver. *The Ballad of Carson McCullers*. New York: Coward McCann, 1966.

Felheim, Melvin. "Eudora Welty and Carson McCullers," *Contemporary American Novelists*, edited by Harry Moore. Carbondale: Southern Illinois University Press, 1964. Pp. 41–53.

Hassan, Ihab. *Radical Innocence*. Princeton, N.J.: Princeton University Press, 1961. Pp. 205–29.

"Human Isolation," *Times Literary Supplement* (London), 52:460 (July 17, 1960).

Kohler, Dayton. "Carson McCullers: Variations on a Theme," *College English*, 13:1–8 (October 1951).

Madden, David. "Transfixed Among the Self-Inflicted Ruins: Carson McCullers' *The Mortgaged Heart*," *Southern Literary Journal*, 5:137–62 (1972).

Phillips, Robert. "The Gothic Architecture of *The Member of the Wedding*," *Renascence*, 16:59–72 (Winter 1964).

Pritchett, V. S. "Books in General," *New Statesman and Nation*, 44:137–38 (August 2, 1952).

Schorer, Mark. "McCullers and Capote: Basic Patterns," *The Creative Present*, edited by N. Balakian and C. Simmons. New York: Doubleday, 1963. Pp. 79–109.

Smith, Simeon M. "Carson McCullers: A Critical Introduction." Ph.D. dissertation, University of Pennsylvania, 1964.

Vickery, John. "Carson McCullers: A Map of Love," *Wisconsin Studies in Contemporary Literature*, 1:14–24 (1960).

Weales, Gerald. *American Drama since World War II*. New York: Harcourt, Brace and World, 1962. Pp. 176–79.

Flannery O'Connor

M ARY FLANNERY O'CONNOR was born in Savannah, Georgia, on March 25, 1925. She was the only child of Regina L. Cline and Edward F. O'Connor, Jr. Both families were Roman Catholic. The Clines were a prominent family in the state, Regina Cline's father having been mayor of Milledgeville for many years.

Mary Flannery grew up as rather a solitary child until she attended parochial school. She loved pet fowl all her life. When she was five, an aunt gave her, as a curiosity, a bantam chicken that walked backwards, and it was this that led to her first national celebrity. The Pathé News people filmed little Mary O'Connor with her trained chicken, and showed the film around the country.

In 1938 Edward O'Connor was discovered to have disseminated lupus, an incurable disease in which the body forms antibodies to its own tissues. The O'Connors moved to Milledgeville, to the Cline house in the center of town. At Peabody High School, Mary Flannery was lively as well as studious. She wrote and illustrated books, and in her senior year she listed her hobby in the yearbook as "Collecting rejection slips." Among other pets she had a quail named Amelia Earhart and a tame goose; she rode horseback and made masonite jewelry. In 1941 Edward O'Connor died. Mary Flannery graduated from high school the next year, and enrolled in the Women's College of Georgia (then the Georgia State College for Women) in Milledgeville.

At college Mary Flannery majored in English and social science; she was art editor of the newspaper, editor of the literary quarterly, and feature editor of the yearbook. She wrote fiction for the literary quarterly, *The Corinthian*, but she thought of herself primarily as a cartoonist. In her senior year she submitted cartoons to the *New Yorker*, which encouraged her but never bought any.

She was graduated with an A.B. in 1945. One of her English teachers had submitted some of her stories to the Writers' Workshop of the University of Iowa, and she was awarded a Rinehart Fellowship at the Workshop. She now came to think of herself primarily as a fiction writer. In Iowa City she worked hard at writing, and continued to send out stories. The first one that sold appeared in *Accent* in 1946. In June of 1947 she received the degree of Master of Fine Arts in Literature. She stayed on at the university for another year, then went to Yaddo, where she began her first novel, *Wise Blood*, and later moved to an apartment hotel in New York. Four chapters of *Wise Blood* were published in *Mademoiselle, Sewanee Review*, and *Partisan Review* in 1948 and 1949. In New York, she became friendly with two other literary Roman Catholics, Robert and Sally Fitzgerald. When they bought a house in Ridgefield, Connecticut, in the summer of 1949, she moved out with them as their boarder, all the while continuing to work on *Wise Blood*.

Late in 1950 Flannery O'Connor became very sick; in Atlanta her ailment was diagnosed as disseminated lupus. She was pulled through with blood transfusions, and the disease was arrested with injections of a cortisone derivative, ACTH, then in the experimental stage. When Miss O'Connor was released from the hospital in the summer of 1951, she was too weak to climb stairs, so she and her mother moved to Andalusia, a dairy farm a few miles outside Milledgeville. There Mrs. O'Connor managed the farm, and Miss O'Connor, when her health improved in the fall, went back to writing, in a ground-floor room.

Wise Blood had been accepted for publication by Harcourt, Brace while Miss O'Connor was in the hospital, and it was published in 1952, to a chorus of praise and misunderstanding by some reviewers, outrage and misunderstanding by others. The daily routine at Andalusia became fixed. Flannery wrote in the mornings, then her mother drove them into Milledgeville to have the excellent lunch at the Sanford House. In the afternoons and evenings, if there were no visitors, she watched the fowl on the farm, read, or painted. The massive doses of ACTH weakened her bones; eventually her hip bones would not bear her weight. She used a cane at first, then from 1955 on she got around on aluminum crutches with arm supports.

Milledgeville liked Flannery O'Connor and was proud of her, but tended not to read her work and to be shocked and dismayed by what it did read. At least at first, many of the townspeople resented her fiction as a mockery of the Baptist and Methodist faiths. If she wanted to make fun of religion, a number of them felt, she should write about her own religion and make fun of *it*.

She kept up an extensive correspondence with a great many people, some of whom she never met. Any crank could write her and get a reply. A few of her letters have been published since her death, and they show her to have been an eloquent if often whimsical correspondent. In the same anti-intellectual spirit in which she sent Uncle Remus postcards to friends, she slipped readily into a folksy idiom: "I have done forgot," "them interleckchuls," and such.

Although Miss O'Connor disliked travel, and her crutches made it difficult to get around, she accepted all the lecture invitations that she could, even if they paid little or nothing. She always read her lectures word for word, and it is clear, now that several of them have been published, that they were very carefully composed, that they say exactly what she meant to say in exactly the words in which she meant to say it.

The special quality of her verbal humor, always delivered deadpan, is hard to describe. Perhaps it was Irish, but if so it was the corrosive Irish wit of Stephen Dedalus and his father, not the bejabers of stage Paddy. She took a sardonic pleasure in being photographed, grim and unsmiling, against the unpainted and dilapidated house of their Negro tenant farmers, and she remarked of the resulting photograph: "Looks like Sherman's just gone through." Of the Uncle Remus Museum in nearby Eatonton, the birthplace of Joel Chandler Harris, she said, "It's the only air-conditioned slave cabin in the United States." Of her trip to Lourdes: "I had the best-looking crutches in Europe." One year she gave her mother a jackass for Mother's Day, explaining it as "For the mother who has everything." She once told an interviewer that she always read "A Good Man Is Hard to Find" to college audiences because it was the only story of hers that she could read aloud "without busting out laughing."

A fair share of honors and awards came Flannery O'Connor's way during her lifetime. She received a Kenyon Review Fellowship in Fiction in 1953, and a renewal of it in 1954; a grant from the National Institute of Arts and Letters in 1957, and a grant from the Ford Foundation in 1959. Her stories won the O. Henry first prizes in 1957, 1963, and 1964. In 1962 she received an honorary D.Litt. from St. Mary's College, Notre Dame, and in 1963 a similar degree from Smith.

Early in 1964, while she was at work on an untitled third novel (a collection of stories, *A Good Man Is Hard to Find*, appeared in 1955; a second novel, *The Violent Bear It Away*, in 1960), Flannery O'Connor had to have an abdominal tumor removed. It proved benign, but the lupus became reactivated and her kidneys were affected. Miss O'Connor knew she was dying. She hoped only to finish enough stories for a book. By a marvel of the will, she did. She died early on August 3, 1964. *Everything That Rises Must Converge* appeared posthumously in 1965.

Shortly after the publication of *The Violent Bear It Away,*
Flannery O'Connor wrote to Sister Mariella Gable O.S.B., "I can
wait fifty years, a hundred years, for it to be understood." Her
reputation, here and abroad, was growing in the last years of her
life, and has greatly increased since her death. *Wise Blood* was
published in France (because of the dialect a feat of translation by
Maurice Coindreau) and was received as an important Existentialist novel. So far, the growing acclaim has not been accompanied by any comparable understanding of her meanings and
purposes. It is toward that end that the following pages modestly
aspire.

Flannery O'Connor's first novel, *Wise Blood* (1952), is a tragi-
comic account of the making of an anchorite in our unlikely time.
The young protagonist, Hazel Motes, called "Haze" (a haze in
the eyes, a mote in the eyes, a beam in the eyes?), loses his faith
while in the army, and becomes an apostle of negativism. He goes
from his native Eastrod (the rood in the East?), Tennessee, to a
city called "Taulkinham" that is obviously Atlanta, to preach
the "church of truth without Jesus Christ Crucified." He wears a
preacher's bright blue suit and a preacher's fierce black hat, but
the only sign he gives of his power is a mysterious "Take your
hand off me" to a policeman and a truckdriver (the *Noli me tangere* of the risen Christ in John's Gospel). As a result of Haze's
refusal to go along with a religion-faker who calls himself Onnie
Jay Holy (and is actually named Hoover Shoats), a man is hired
to dress up as Haze and replace him, and Haze eventually murders
the False Prophet, his *Doppelgänger*.

Another sort of antagonist is a boy named Enoch Emery, who
works as a guard at the city park, and has his own religious mystery: in fixed ritual stages he must daily have a sacramental milk-
shake and make suggestive remarks to the waitress, then visit the

zoo animals and make obscene comments on their appearance, finally go to the museum and pay his devotions to a mummy. These are Enoch's Stations of the Cross, as we note from the pun I have italicized: "We got to *cross* this road and go down this hill. We got to go on foot," Enoch tells Haze, but he does not know why. Eventually Enoch steals the mummy, which he thinks of as "the new jesus," and presents it to Haze, who smashes it. Enoch also reads the comics "every evening like an office." Eventually he finds his religious fulfillment dressed in a stolen gorilla costume, but it is as the apostle of the mummified "new jesus" that he functions in Haze's pilgrim's progress.

There is still another false prophet, a fake blind man named Asa Hawks who pretends to have blinded himself with lime to justify his belief in Redemption. Haze puts Hawks in the role of Elijah in his new faith, and expects "a secret welcome" from him. What he gets instead is Hawks's homely little fifteen-year-old daughter Sabbath Lily, who moves into Haze's bed, becomes the Madonna of the new jesus (she cradles the mummy in her arms, and addresses Haze as its "daddy"), and eventually turns into a monster of sexual voracity and heartlessness. She calmly watches as Haze improves on her father by *really* blinding himself with lime, then she as calmly deserts him.

The other important character in the novel, far more than a property or a symbol, is a high old rat-colored Essex automobile that Haze buys after he moves out of the room of a whore named Leora Watts. The Essex is Haze's religious mystery: It is Woman (the salesman asks him "would you like to get under and look up it?"), Ordination (Haze preaches No Jesus from its hood, as his grandfather had preached Jesus from the hood of his car in Haze's childhood), and Redemption ("Nobody with a good car needs to be justified," Haze tells Sabbath Lily, in the book's most wonderful line). Haze kills the False Prophet by running over him with the Essex, which then leaves, in a kind of Calvary sweat, "little bead-chains of water and oil and gas on the road"; when a policeman gets the Essex off the road by the simple expedient of pushing it over an embankment, Haze is left with no place to go but an inner Calvary of blindness, asceticism, and sacrificial death at the hands of the police.

The techniques for unifying this garish and diverse material include a heavy reliance on symbolism. The principal symbol that unifies (along with the mummy and the Essex) is the "wise blood" of the title. Enoch knows things "by his blood," because "He had wise blood like his daddy." He protests to Haze: "You think you got wiser blood than anybody else." Of course Haze *thinks* he has wise blood — the blood of the natural body that is his only reality — and he preaches "the church that the blood of Jesus don't foul with redemption"; but Haze, in the author's view, really *has* wise blood: the blood of his grandfather, the inherited vocation, that preaches *through him* Christ's Blood, shed to redeem.

Haze's "church of truth without Jesus Christ Crucified" is not only a body of doctrine, it is an important symbol. Here are some of its more striking tenets: "I don't say he wasn't crucified but I say it wasn't for you"; "Jesus is a trick on niggers"; "There was no Fall because there was nothing to fall from and no Redemption because there was no Fall and no Judgment because there wasn't the first two. Nothing matters but that Jesus was a liar"; "I believe in a new kind of jesus . . . one that can't waste his blood redeeming people with it, because he's all man and ain't got any God in him"; "I preach the Church Without Christ, the church peaceful and satisfied!" This is wonderfully funny, and a sharp mockery of secular rationalism, but on another level it is desperately in earnest, an indictment of the smug and secular Church today. This is made clear by a sly joke in a conversation between Haze and his landlady about his Church Without Christ: " 'Protestant?' she asked suspiciously, 'or something foreign?' He said no mam, it was Protestant."

Two principal strands of covert symbolism affirm what Haze denies. One is the oaths the characters use unconsciously. "Good Jesus," Enoch says. "My Jesus," Haze mutters, or "Sweet Jesus Christ Crucified." Sabbath Lily's explanation of why she is abandoning Haze gives us the book's deepest meaning in a brilliant pun: "She said she hadn't counted on no honest-to-Jesus blind man." The other is the rock-strewn landscape. When he was ten, Haze's guilt at seeing a naked woman in a tent show and picturing his mother in her place had led him to punish himself by walking with "stones and small rocks" in his shoes. Out driving the Essex, he sees a boulder on which is painted a call to repentance and "Jesus Saves." Later we are told: "Hazel Motes's face might have been cut out of the side of a rock" in his indifference to Enoch, and he ends the scene by throwing a rock at Enoch. Haze's duffel bag contains a Bible "that had sat like a rock in the bottom of the bag for the last few years." Blinded and chastising his flesh at the end, he lines his shoes with "gravel and broken glass and pieces of small stone." Eventually we recognize these stones, rocks, and boulders: they are tokens of the Rock, Peter's Church.

As this covert symbolism suggests, the development of the action is elaborately foreshadowed. One such motif is the general denial of Haze's denial of his vocation (from the negation of the negation, a wisdom). Hawks says "I can hear the urge for Jesus in his voice" and tells him "Some preacher has left his mark on you"; and Sabbath Lily tells Haze retrospectively, "I seen you wouldn't never have no fun or let anybody else because you didn't want nothing but Jesus!"

Haze's self-blinding is even more elaborately foreshadowed in the imagery, starting with the name "Hazel Motes," which opens the novel. Haze dismisses Hawks as "a blind fool," and rhetorically asks the first audience to which he preaches: "Don't I have eyes in my head? Am I a blind man?" Enoch sees the reflection of Haze's eyes in the glass of the mummy case as "like two clean bullet holes." Sabbath Lily tells her father why she likes Haze's eyes: "They don't look like they see what he's looking at but they keep on looking." When Haze drives out into the country with Sabbath Lily, the sky has "only one cloud in it, a large blinding white one with curls and a beard" (perhaps a little too patly God the Father). Haze tells Sabbath that his Essex is so superior because "It was built by people with their eyes open that knew where they were at," and by way of comment, the First Person of God turns into the Third, the Holy Ghost: "The blinding white cloud had turned into a bird with long thin wings and was disappearing in the opposite direction."

After Haze blinds himself, his landlady thinks: "Why had he destroyed his eyes and saved himself unless he had some plan, unless he saw something that he couldn't get without being blind to everything else?" At the end of the book, the landlady recognizes that she needs Haze: "If she was going to be blind when she was dead, who better to guide her than a blind man? Who better to lead the blind than the blind, who knew what it was like?" When she next sees him, he has been clubbed to death by the police. The landlady looks into his eyes "and the deep burned eye sockets seemed to lead into the dark tunnel where he had disappeared." As she stares, with her eyes shut, she sees him "moving farther and farther away, farther and farther into the darkness until he was the pin point of light" (this pinpoint of light had earlier been identified as the star over Bethlehem). Haze has been advancing "backwards to Bethlehem," in her words, and he has finally arrived there.

The organization of *Wise Blood* is thus a tight network of imagery, symbolism, and foreshadowing. The plot of the novel is much less tight, since the whole episode of Enoch and the gorilla suit is unrelated to Haze, and Enoch simply falls out of the book dressed as a gorilla. The language similarly shows that Miss O'Connor had not reached the stage of full control of her material. Some of it represents the perfect plain style of her later triumphs, but some of the tropes are so garish or elaborate as to be distracting, and thus ineffective. At one point, for example, Haze's face looks "like one of those closet doors in gangster pictures where someone is tied to a chair behind it with a towel in his mouth."

Perhaps the most remarkable thing about *Wise Blood*, in comparison with the later fiction, is its pervasive sexuality. Enoch prays to Jesus to help him escape from the woman who adopted him, and Jesus' answer to the prayer is the use of sex as aggression: "I went in her room without my pants on and pulled the sheet off her and giver a heart attact." The zoo animals that Enoch has to observe as a station of his cross represent sex as shameful: "If I had a ass like that," Enoch says prudishly of an ape, "I'd sit on it. I wouldn't be exposing it to all these people come to this park." One of the events that lead Haze to seduce Sabbath Lily involves sex as ludicrous: Leora Watts gets up one night while he is asleep and cuts "the top of his hat out in an obscene shape." Haze's sexual attachments in the novel are deeply perverse: a corrupt mother, a corrupt child, and an old Essex.

Wise Blood has been much misunderstood. If anything, the confusion was deepened in 1957, when the author printed her first public statement of her intentions, the essay "The Fiction Writer and His Country" in Granville Hicks's symposium *The Living Novel*. In it Miss O'Connor writes: "For I am no disbeliever in spiritual purpose and no vague believer. I see from the standpoint of Christian orthodoxy. This means that for me the meaning of life is centered in our Redemption by Christ and that what I see in the world I see in its relation to that." Her intentions were more specifically clarified in the tiny Author's Note to the second edition of *Wise Blood* in 1962, in which she describes the work as "a comic novel about a Christian *malgré lui*, and as such, very serious."

The problem is that the novel's Christian themes are put paradoxically, even negatively, the way Haze progresses to Bethlehem. One is Original Sin. In the army, Haze wants to lose his faith because he wants to escape from the knowledge of his fallen nature, "to be converted to nothing instead of to evil." He tells Hawks, "If I was in sin I was in it before I ever committed any," and he tells a waitress, "If Jesus existed, I wouldn't be clean." Another important theme is Affirmation by Blasphemy. Haze tells his sidewalk audience, "The only way to the truth is through blasphemy," and he reaffirms this doctrine against Onnie Jay Holy's principle, "If you want to get anywheres in religion, you got to keep it sweet." Haze later tells a boy at a filling station that "he had only a few days ago believed in blasphemy as the way to salvation, but that you couldn't even believe in that because then you were believing in something to blaspheme."

A third Christian theme of *Wise Blood* is Vocation. The landlady thinks of Haze, after he is blind, "He might as well be one of them monks . . . he might as well be in a monkery." Haze throws away his leftover money each month; he puts rocks in his shoes, and when the landlady asks him why, he says, "To pay," but he does not tell her what he is paying *for*, and it seems unlikely that he knows. When she discovers that he wears barbed wire around his chest, she tells him, "People have quit doing it." "They ain't quit doing it as long as I'm doing it," Haze answers. It is clear that he has founded a private monastic order, ascetic and penitential, and that the truth he formerly preached negatively he now witnesses to mutely, and will be martyred for. With no institution to channel its violence, in Miss O'Connor's view, his call can only destroy him.

Of the ten stories of *A Good Man Is Hard to Find* (1955), the three best, in my opinion, are "The Artificial Nigger," "Good Country People," and "The Displaced Person." "The Artificial Nigger" was Miss O'Connor's own favorite, and it makes impressive claims to be considered her best story. It tells of two backwoods Georgians, an old man named Mr. Head and his grandson Nelson, who go to the terrifying city for Nelson's first visit. The action of the story is their estrangement and reconciliation, but it is a readjustment as profound as that of the Conroys of Joyce's "The Dead." Nelson has never seen a Negro before, and the preliminary events of the story are encounters with real Negroes — first a huge Negro man on the train, wearing a yellow satin tie with a ruby stickpin, then an enormous Negro woman they meet on the street, whom Nelson inexplicably wants to hold him and mother him.

The dramatic crisis in the story is Nelson's running into an elderly white woman on the street, knocking her down and scattering her groceries. Mr. Head panics and re-enacts Peter's denial: " 'This is not my boy,' he said, 'I never seen him before.' " Nelson's subsequent hatred and contempt, and Mr. Head's guilt and shame, are wonderfully funny and moving, profoundly true and beautiful. Their reconciliation comes when they see, decorating a lawn, a shabby plaster statue of a Negro eating a watermelon. In the same voice, each exclaims: "An artificial nigger!" This communion transforms them magically, and they exchange identities: "Mr. Head looked like an ancient child and Nelson like a miniature old man." The artificial Negro is God's grace: "They could both feel it dissolving their differences like an action of mercy." Mr. Head has a moment of true repentance and charity, he and the boy are united in love, and the story is over.

The protagonist of "Good Country People" is the author's cruelest self-caricature: Joy Hopewell, hulking, thirty-two, a learned

Doctor of Philosophy. She has an artificial leg as a result of a hunting accident, she has changed her name legally from Joy to Hulga, she wears a yellow sweat shirt with a picture of a cowboy on a horse, and she is an atheist. When a simple-seeming country boy appears selling Bibles, she sets out to seduce him, and she appears for their date (in a perfect touch) wearing Vapex on the collar of her shirt, "since she did not own any perfume."

The Bible salesman appears to be another Hazel Motes, wearing the same bright blue suit and wide-brimmed hat, and protesting "I'm just a country boy." He turns out to be the False Prophet instead: when they are alone in the barn loft he reveals that his hollow Bible contains a flask of whiskey, a pack of pornographic playing cards, and a package of condoms. "You ain't so smart," he tells Joy-Hulga as he disappears down the loft trapdoor with her artificial leg, "I been believing in nothing ever since I was born!" It is the exposure of a fake Christian, but more significantly it is the exposure of a fake atheist, her intellectual pride and superiority revealed to be only ignorance and gullibility. Unfortunately, the story does not end where it should, with the symbolic defloration of the theft of the leg and the Bible salesman's reproof, but goes on for two paragraphs of superfluous irony.

"The Displaced Person" is the longest and most ambitious story in the book. In it a Polish Catholic refugee, Mr. Guizac, comes to work for Protestant Mrs. McIntyre, a widow who runs a dairy farm. He is the displaced person, but in the course of the complex tragic action, Mr. Shortley, the native hired man, becomes a displaced person when Mrs. McIntyre fires him, Mrs. Shortley becomes a displaced person when she dies of a stroke as they depart, Mr. Guizac becomes further displaced when the rehired Mr. Shortley carelessly allows a tractor to run over his spine, and Mrs. McIntyre herself becomes a displaced person at the end, collapsed, bedridden, and alone.

None of these melodramatic events, however, is the significant action of the story. The central figure in the story is a peacock, who enters in the first sentence, following Mrs. Shortley up the road, and exits in the last, when the priest feeds him breadcrumbs on his weekly visit to instruct the bedridden Mrs. McIntyre in the doctrines of his Church. The peacock is a traditional symbol of Christ's divinity and the Resurrection. In the story he functions as a kind of spiritual test: Mrs. Shortley never notices him; Mrs. McIntyre sees him only as "another mouth to feed"; her husband the late Judge had kept peacocks because "they made him feel rich"; the priest is overwhelmed by the peacock's beauty, and says of the spread tail, "Christ will come like that!"

As the peacock symbolizes Christ's divine nature, so the displaced person symbolizes His human nature. In the story's key conversation, Mrs. McIntyre says, in reference to Mr. Guizac, "He didn't have to come in the first place," and the absentminded old priest, mistaking her reference, answers, "He came to redeem us." Later, annoyed with all the religious talk, Mrs. McIntyre says indignantly to the priest, "As far as I'm concerned, Christ was just another D. P." But Mr. Guizac does more than embody Christ as he is displaced, suffers, and is slain. "That man is my salvation," Mrs. McIntyre had said earlier, in praise of Mr. Guizac's hard work, and the remark has Miss O'Connor's usual double meaning. "I am not responsible for the world's misery," Mrs. McIntyre tells Mr. Guizac later. But his death, in which they are all equally guilty, is redemptive for her insofar as it abases her pride and prepares her to accept the burden of the world's misery.

The other stories in the book are less impressive. The title story, "A Good Man Is Hard to Find," is a melodrama about a family casually wiped out by an escaped criminal called the Misfit, and in spots it is cruelly funny. "The River" is about a young boy who finds a symbolic baptism in drowning. Like *Wise Blood*, it relies heavily on the ironic use of profanity: "Well then for Christ's sake fix him," Harry's father says to the woman taking care of him, who does just that; "Healed of what for Christ's sake?" Harry's mother asks, unaware that the question contains its answer. The story is a little too pat, however, and the empty secular life of the parents is an unconvincing travesty. "The Life You Save May Be Your Own" is a slice of Tobacco Road, redeemed by Mr. Shiftlet's automobilolatry (the car represents an ideal marriage to him, as to Hazel Motes, and his destination is significantly "Mobile") and by a superb comic ending.

"A Stroke of Good Fortune" is the one markedly unsuccessful story in the book, a leaden tract against complacency and contraception. "A Temple of the Holy Ghost" is a portrait of the artist as a sardonic twelve-year-old girl, a Roman Catholic among rustics who identify Latin hymns as "Jew singing." "A Circle in the Fire" does not quite bring off its terror, but it has one moment of magnificent empathy, when the young girl sees the naked boys bathing in the woods, and thinks, not of how they look, but of how they *see*: "The trees must have looked like green waterfalls through his wet glasses." It is just this empathy that is lacking at the end, when she looks at her mother's face and sees it "as if it might have belonged to anybody, a Negro or a European or to Powell himself." Mrs. Cope has become a displaced person like Mrs. McIntyre, but she is never seen from inside as the boy Powell is. The remaining story, "A Late Encounter with the Enemy," is sharply satiric, of the deviled corsages of Hollywood as of the South's Confederacy cult, but it rises to distinction only in the incongruous final tableau: the old general's corpse sitting in the Coca-Cola line.

Her second novel, *The Violent Bear It Away* (1960), is Miss O'Connor's masterpiece. It tells the terrible initiation of a reluctant prophet. The adolescent protagonist is Francis Marion

---

Tarwater (his name is as richly symbolic as Hazel Motes's: Francis Marion is the "old swamp fox" of the Revolutionary War, tarwater is a discredited folk cure-all). He is recognizable by the author's usual sign of election, Jesus' *Noli me tangere*, early in the book. When the old Negro, Buford Munson, finds young Tarwater drunk and his great-uncle dead, Buford says, "He was deep in Jesus' misery," and young Tarwater replies, "Nigger . . . take your hand off me." The great-uncle, Mason Tarwater, was a mad prophet who made his living distilling bootleg whiskey, and kept "worthless black game bantams" as the old Judge kept worthless peacocks. The secular antagonist, George F. Rayber (raper?), young Tarwater's uncle and old Tarwater's nephew, is an ambiguous figure. He is Satanic, taking on, "like the devil," any look that suited him, but he is a *monk* of Satan, controlling the family curse of violence and madness in his blood ("he was the stuff of which fanatics and madmen are made") by "a rigid ascetic discipline," by rationality and good works. His mad barefoot pursuit of young Tarwater through the streets of the town is a penitential pilgrimage; more than Tarwater, *Rayber* looks "like a fanatical country preacher," and young Tarwater tells him perceptively (my italics): "It's *you* the seed fell in."

Rayber's idiot son, Bishop, is less a character than a sacrament: young Tarwater has been commanded by his great-uncle to begin his ministry by baptizing Bishop, and when he has the opportunity he compulsively baptizes and drowns him. The novel's other important character is Satan. He first appears as a skeptical voice in young Tarwater's drunken head, then as a vision of a friendly stranger in a panama hat; he returns as a voice to direct the drowning of Bishop; he appears in the flesh at the end of the novel to drug and rape young Tarwater in the final stage of his initiation into deranged prophecy.

The Violent, like *Wise Blood*, is tightly unified by symbolism.

The principal unifying symbol is burning. Evils "come from the Lord and burn the prophet clean," old Tarwater had told the boy; "even the mercy of the Lord burns." Young Tarwater imagines his return to the city after he receives his prophetic call, when "he would return with fire in his eyes." Old Tarwater once wrote a warning to Rayber: "THE PROPHET I RAISE UP OUT OF THIS BOY WILL BURN YOUR EYES CLEAN." After the old man's death, Tarwater burns their shack, intending to cremate the corpse in defiance of old Tarwater's fervent wish to be buried to await the Resurrection. On his way to the city, young Tarwater takes the glow of its lights to be the fire he set (a foreshadowing of his eventual return as a prophet). His eyes appear to Rayber to be "singed with guilt." (They foreshadow his madness, as Haze's eyes foreshadow his blindness.) A girl evangelist challenges Rayber as a damned soul and says, "The Word of God is a burning Word to burn you clean!" Young Tarwater burns himself clean in a secular sense after the rape by firing the woods where it occurred, but he has been burned clean in his great-uncle's sense too: his "scorched eyes" now look "as if, touched with a coal like the lips of the prophet, they would never be used for ordinary sights again." He then sets fire to his own woods, sees the fire he has set as the expected sign over his great-uncle's grave, "the burning bush," and hears God's command: "GO WARN THE CHILDREN OF GOD OF THE TERRIBLE SPEED OF MERCY." He sets his "singed eyes," in the book's last sentence, "toward the dark city, where the children of God lay sleeping." He is finally a prophet, and a madman.

A second important symbol, balancing judgment with mercy, is spiritual feeding. When old Tarwater got into his coffin to try it on for size, the boy saw "nothing showing but his stomach which rose over the top like over-leavened bread." The bread symbolized by the old man's belly is "the bread of life," Jesus, and young Tarwater decides that he is "not hungry for the bread of life." But when Rayber, in pursuing him through the city, sees him staring obsessively at a loaf of bread in a bakery window, Rayber thinks characteristically, "If he had eaten his dinner, he wouldn't be hungry." Young Tarwater tells a truckdriver who gives him a lift that he is hungry for real food; "I ain't hungry for the bread of life." Later he drinks the stranger's drugged liquor and remarks: "It's better than the Bread of Life!" Standing over his great-uncle's grave at the end, he has a vision of Mason Tarwater on the banks of the Lake of Galilee, eating the multiplied loaves and fishes, and he is "aware at last of the object of his hunger, aware that it was the same as the old man's and that nothing on earth would fill him." (As the old man's belly is the bread, his eyes are the fishes: "silver protruding eyes that looked like two fish straining to get out of a net of red threads"; "mad fish-colored eyes.")

The other important symbol in *The Violent Bear It Away* is Bishop, the holy idiot. Bishop's habitual toy is a trashbasket with a rock in it. He is able to make peanut butter sandwiches "though sometimes he put the bread inside." At one point Rayber realizes that young Tarwater is looking at Bishop but seeing "only a spot of light." These are all symbols we have noted before: Peter's Rock, the living Bread, the Star of Bethlehem. The woman who runs the resort where the murderous baptism occurs makes Bishop's sacramental nature explicit. When Tarwater drives Bishop away for touching him, she reproves Tarwater, "Mind how you talk to one of them there," and glares at him fiercely, "as if he had profaned the holy."

The structure of foreshadowing is more economical than that of *Wise Blood* and no less effective. Old Tarwater had warned his grand-nephew of the special dangers incurred by prophets: "'You are the kind of boy,' the old man said, 'that the devil is always going to be offering to assist, to give you a smoke or a drink or a ride, and to ask you your bidnis. You had better mind

how you take up with strangers.' " A salesman predicts of Tarwater, "He won't come to no good end." Rayber takes Tarwater
back to Tennessee because "He saw no way of curing him except
perhaps through some shock." Everything unfolds as prophesied:
the devil gives Tarwater a ride, the shock cures, the cure is a no
good end, at least in the world's eyes. Unlike that of *Wise Blood*,
the narrative structure of *The Violent* is perfectly shaped; there
are no loose ends like Enoch Emery. Here is *The Violent*'s magnificent first sentence: "Francis Marion Tarwater's uncle had
been dead for only half a day when the boy got too drunk to finish digging his grave and a Negro named Buford Munson, who
had come to get a jug filled, had to finish it and drag the body
from the breakfast table where it was still sitting and bury it in a
decent and Christian way, with the sign of its Saviour at the head
of the grave and enough dirt on top to keep the dogs from digging
it up." The novel unfolds the motifs of the opening sentence in-
exorably, from this first drunkenness to the final drugged drunkenness and transformation. Even the sodomic rape, not much
appreciated by the reviewers, is right and inevitable: it is at once
the ultimate violation of the untouchable anointed of the Lord,
a naturalistic explanation for the shaman's spirit possession, and
a shocking and effective metaphor for seizure by divine purpose.
(Yeats makes a similar use of rape in "Leda and the Swan.")

The book's language is sparse and functional. Old Tarwater's
instructions for his burial read like the best Twain ("Get two
boards and set them down the steps and start me rolling and dig
where I stop and don't let me roll over into it until it's deep
enough"). The tropes, however imaginative, are for the most part
economical and functional; for example, "The words were as
silent as seeds opening one at a time in his blood." Even a few
far-fetched ones, such as Rayber's eyes looking "like something
human trapped in a switch box," seem to justify themselves.

329

Finally there is the problem of the book's meaning. The chief clue is the title epigraph, Matthew 11:12, printed in very large type across the double title page: "From the days of John the Baptist until now, the kingdom of heaven suffereth violence, and the violent bear it away." This has been widely misinterpreted. The Authorized Version translates the last clause "and the violent take it by force," and the New English Bible reads "and violent men are seizing it." Its clear meaning is that the violent are enemies of the kingdom, capturing it from the righteous, as a sign of the imminent coming of the Messiah, the Christ. In this sense the Tarwaters are mad fanatics carrying away the kingdom from its lukewarm heirs, and Rayber is an equally mad fanatic preaching secular salvation. Rayber sees himself "divided in two — a violent and a rational self." Violence and madness are the curse in the family's blood, but Rayber succeeds in controlling them. The effect of the novel's events on young Tarwater is to extirpate the rational self instead, to burn away all reason and leave him entirely violent and mad.

It is in this extreme sense that young Tarwater is an allegory of the Church, which must lose the world to save it. Where *Wise Blood* is about Vocation along with several other mysteries, *The Violent* is wholly and centrally about Vocation and the prophet's necessary stage of resistance to Vocation (from Moses' pleading his speech defect to Jonah's taking flight). When old Tarwater said that if he died without baptizing Bishop, the baptism of Bishop would be "the first mission the Lord sends you," "the boy doubted very much that his first mission would be to baptize a dim-witted child." When his great-uncle tells of their freedom, young Tarwater feels "a slow warm rising resentment that this freedom had to be connected with Jesus and that Jesus had to be the Lord."

The analogy with Bible prophets is made again and again: "The old man compared their situation to that of Elijah and Elisha";

persecuted by Rayber, the old man is simultaneously "Jonah, Ezekiel, Daniel, he was at that moment all of them — the swallowed, the lowered, the enclosed"; arriving at Rayber's house, young Tarwater is similarly transformed: "His whole body felt hollow as if he had been lifted like Habakkuk by the hair of his head, borne swiftly through the night and set down in the place of his mission." When young Tarwater realizes his mission regarding Bishop, "He did not look into the eyes of any fiery beast or see a burning bush. He only knew, with a certainty sunk in despair, that he was expected to baptize the child he saw and begin the life his great-uncle had prepared him for."

In the book's boldest image, repeated after the drowning of Bishop, young Tarwater pictures himself "trudging into the distance in the bleeding stinking mad shadow of Jesus." He tirelessly insists to Rayber, of his great-uncle, "He ain't had no effect on me." The stranger's voice assures young Tarwater that he has not been called or received a sign, that all he feels are sensations, whereas Jonah's three days in the belly of the fish, "That was a sign; it wasn't no sensation." "The Lord speaks to prophets personally," the stranger adds, "and He's never spoke to you." But slowly, relentlessly, through denial and burning, murder and rape, Tarwater hears his call and responds, and in his madness he will preach the truth. Man is both vessel and instrument of divine purpose, and divine purpose is not answerable to human reason.

In *Everything That Rises Must Converge* (1965), the finest of the stories, to my taste, and the one least like anything Miss O'Connor (or anyone else) has done before, is "Parker's Back," the last story she wrote before her death. It tells of a young man named O. E. Parker whose only distinction is a passion for having himself elaborately tattooed. In what he believes is an accommodation to his wife's Fundamentalist piety, Parker has a Byzantine mosaic of a staring Christ reproduced on his back. He is then literally *christophoros*, Christ-bearing, "witnessing for Jesus" on his hide. Under this coloration Parker is transformed and reborn, resuming the Old Testament prophet names, Obadiah Elihue, that he has always concealed behind his initials, and suffering a Punch and Judy martyrdom as he passively allows his wife to punish his "idolatry" by beating him with a broom until "large welts had formed on the face of the tattooed Christ." The story is simultaneously uproarious and deeply moving, and the metaphor of tattooing — bloody, painful, indelible; garish, out of fashion, ludicrous — for the burden of Redemption is uncanny and perfect, a truly metaphysical conceit.

A long and ambitious story, "The Lame Shall Enter First," is impressive in a more familiar fashion. It is another look at the trio of Rayber, Bishop, and young Tarwater (in fact, according to Robert Fitzgerald's introduction to *Everything That Rises*, it uses material cut from *The Violent*). Superficially, the story is pathetic sociology: a well-meaning but unimaginative widower, Sheppard, neglects his son Norton, mainly because an older boy, Rufus Johnson, clubfooted and criminal, seems much more in need of help; the consequence is Norton's suicide. On a more perceptive level, Rufus is not a poor deprived cripple, but evil, demonic, a type of Satan; and Sheppard learns the reality of these entities to his cost. (This is Fitzgerald's reading in the introduction, encouraged by the statement in the story that finally Sheppard "saw the clear-eyed Devil, the sounder of hearts, leering at him from the eyes of Johnson.") But this is Sheppard's interpretation, not the author's. Miss O'Connor's own reading, I believe, is consistent with her radical Christian dualism and far more challenging: not Rufus but *Sheppard* is the type of Satan, taking over God's prerogatives in His assumed absence; and Rufus is the true prophetic voice of Judgment, saying of Sheppard "He thinks he's Jesus Christ!" and challenging him, "Satan has you in his power." (This is the read-

332

ing of Sister Rose Alice, in "Flannery O'Connor: Poet to the Outcast," in which she paraphrases the story's action as "The repulsive
good defeats the urbane evil.")

The third triumph in the book is "The Enduring Chill," a
devastatingly funny, if ultimately serious, story of a pretentious
young man whose dramatic coming home to die turns out badly.
The story mows down its targets with general ruthlessness: the
Church is wickedly satirized in a scatterbrained and irascible old
priest, blind in one eye and deaf in one ear; such secular "experience of communion" as racial integration comes off no better.
The symbols are masterly. When Asbury, the romantic invalid,
turns his head away in irritation from his mother's talk about the
dairy herd, he confronts "a small, wall-eyed Guernsey . . . watching him steadily as if she sensed some bond between them." When
he gets up to his room, there is a water stain on the ceiling that
looks like "a fierce bird with spread wings," with "an icicle cross-
wise in his beak." In the comic ending, the bond between Asbury
and the wall-eyed Guernsey is the discovery, by the local doctor
Asbury despises, that his supposedly fatal disease is only undulant
fever, caught from drinking unpasteurized milk; in the apocalyptic ending that follows the comedy, the fierce bird on the ceiling
is discovered to be the Holy Ghost, "emblazoned in ice instead of
fire," and, implacably, that terribly swift mercy descends upon
him.

The other stories are less impressive or are flawed in some fashion. The title story, "Everything That Rises Must Converge," has
a fine ending, Julian's "entry into the world of guilt and sorrow"
when his mother has a stroke occasioned by a Negro woman who
rose and converged with her. It is beautifully foreshadowed from
the story's first sentence, but the characters, a travesty segregation-
ist mother and a travesty integrationist son, are not adequate to
the finely structured action. "Greenleaf" takes another look at the

widow running a dairy farm. Here she is Mrs. May, "a good Christian woman with a large respect for religion, though she did not, of course, believe any of it was true." Her punishment is undergoing a rather Freudian Dionysiac mystery in which a scrub bull, "like some patient god come down to woo her," gores her to death "like a wild tormented lover." Unfortunately, the two worlds of Bacchic ecstasy and regional satire in the story coexist uneasily. "A View of the Woods" is a perfect comic story about a conflict between a grandfather and a nine-year-old granddaughter just like him, up to its natural ending after the first paragraph on page 80; then it falls into the unnecessary multiple death of Jacobean drama. The melodramatic "The Comforts of Home" travesties Miss O'Connor's familiar triad of parent-child-intruder, and is the one story in the book that seems to me a mistake from the beginning. "Revelation" is a marvelously funny apocalypse for the Laodiceans that goes on too long. "Judgement Day" is a reworking, shortly before Miss O'Connor's death, of an old story first written at Iowa in 1946, and is thus the only story in the book set outside Georgia. It is a magical and compelling account of the death and symbolic resurrection of an old Georgia man in New York City, made resonant by the author's sense of her own imminent death; only the Negro characters in it (perhaps part of the early material) fail to ring true.

In all her writing, Flannery O'Connor has certain preoccupations that seem almost obsessional. A few simple images recur so strikingly that every reader notices them: the flaming suns, the mutilated eyes, the "Jesus-seeing" hats, the colorful shirts. These images may be obsessive with the author, but they are used organically in the fiction. The sun in "A Circle in the Fire" is a symbol and specific foreshadowing of the boys' incendiary threat: "It was swollen and flame-colored and hung in a net of ragged cloud as if it might burn through any second and fall into the woods." The sunset in "Greenleaf" is another "swollen red ball," but as Mrs. May watches, "it began to narrow and pale until it looked like a bullet." It is narrow and pale to resemble the moon, since the bull first appeared to woo Mrs. May "silvered in the moonlight"; it looks like a bullet because the bull will soon come like a streak to penetrate her body, bull-bullet indeed.

A few recurrent symbols are more complex than these. One is the young preacher in bright blue suit and stern black hat. His principal embodiments are Hazel Motes and the False Prophet in *Wise Blood*, and the Bible salesman in "Good Country People," but we see traces of him everywhere: the bright blue suit on the preacher who introduces the girl evangelist who tells Rayber that he is a damned soul in *The Violent*; the stern black hat on the old man in "Judgement Day." These are not simply a uniform, but emblems: the blue suit glares with raw Fundamentalist fervor, the black hat represents what the old man's daughter dismisses as "a lot of hardshell Baptist hooey." The False Prophet dresses like Haze to steal his mission, but as a consequence of the transformation he dies an exemplary Christian death, confessing his sins and calling out "Jesus hep me"; the Bible salesman disguises himself to cheat the gullible, but instead he is instrumental in bringing Joy-Hulga to the beginnings of humility in humiliation.

The peacock is another complex symbol. It is central in "The Displaced Person," but it appears in many places: the innocent deaf girl in "The Life You Save May Be Your Own" has "eyes as blue as a peacock's neck," and learns to say only one word, "bird"; Joy-Hulga is "as sensitive about the artificial leg as a peacock about his tail"; the little girl in *The Violent* preaches "Silver and gold and peacock tails, a thousand suns in a peacock's tail," and Rayber thinks of her as "one of those birds blinded to make it sing more sweetly." As the peacock was a personal image of the Second Coming for the old priest and of wealth for the old Judge in "The Displaced Person," so it seems to have been a personal image of freedom and beauty (that is, of *art*) for Miss O'Connor. In an article, "Living with a Peacock," in *Holiday*, Miss O'Connor wrote: "My frenzy said: I want so many of them that every time I go out the door I'll run into one." Of this abundance, which in another aspect is God's grace, the deaf girl has only the useless beauty, Joy-Hulga only the vulnerability.

Another complex symbol can only be called, in acknowledgment of Miss O'Connor's debt, Georgia Snopesism. It is principally embodied in two families, the Shortleys in "The Displaced Person" and the Greenleafs in "Greenleaf," but there is more than a touch of it in the Pritchards in "A Circle in the Fire" and the Freemans who are the "good country people" of the story of that title. These families of tenant farmers usually include a man who is stupid, incompetent, and malevolent; a wife with "a special fondness for the details of secret infections, hidden deformities, assaults upon children"; and two or more mindless and voracious children. More than any other figures in Miss O'Connor's work, these Snopes families are social, even class, symbols (as are their Mississippi counterparts in Faulkner). They represent the southern poor white class seen as intrinsically vicious. In the stories, they murder Mr. Guizac and let the bull gore Mrs. May; in our newspapers, they have other victims.

As this suggests, not only do images and symbols recur, but fixed groupings of people recur, and certain figures in these fixed groups are consistently travestied. Fitzgerald's introduction to *Everything That Rises* refers to what he calls the "family resemblance" shown by many of the characters in the stories and novels, but this is less a matter of recurrent figures than of recurrent relationships. One is the duo of practical mother and dreamy child on a dairy farm. In "A Circle in the Fire" they are a "very small and trim" woman and a "pale fat girl of twelve"; in "Good Country People" they are a mother who "had no bad qualities of her own but she was able to use other people's in such a constructive way that she never felt the lack," and Joy-Hulga; and so on. This mother and daughter are complementary in a curious fashion: each is caricatured as seen by the other, the resourceful widow as smug and empty, the arty child as useless and affected. In the later stories of *Everything That Rises*, this pairing is varied. Mrs. May in "Greenleaf" has two sons, of whom only the younger is an intellectual, although the older manages to be equally unsatisfactory: he sells insurance, but it is "the kind that only Negroes buy." Mrs. Fox in "The Enduring Chill" similarly has two children, who between them compose the familiar character: Asbury has the artistic pretensions, his sister Mary George the scathing tongue. This last splitting is repeated in the fragment of the unfinished novel published in *Esquire* as "Why Do the Heathens Rage?"

A relationship that does not involve mutual travesty is one between a boy and his mother's brother or father. The first of these is Haze and his grandfather, the circuit preacher. In "The Artificial Nigger" this pair becomes Mr. Head and his daughter's son Nelson; in *The Violent* we get the complexity of young Tarwater and his mother's brother Rayber, Rayber and *his* mother's brother old Tarwater, with the two Tarwaters in the duplicated magical relation of mother's brother of a mother's brother to sister's son of a sister's son. In "A View of the Woods," the pairing becomes mother's father and *girl*. In "The Lame Shall Enter First," Rufus Johnson lives with his crazy grandfather (presumably his mother's father), until the old man goes off "with a remnant to the hills," to prepare against the destruction of the world by fiery flood. The point of this relationship is that the grandfather or uncle is the true father, and the grandson or nephew (however he resists it) is the true heir. This replacement of the father as authority by the mother's brother or father would be natural enough in the writing of an author whose father died in her childhood, but before settling for an autobiographical cause here we should notice that the mother's brother rather than the father as family authority is an important feature of primitive matriliny, and thus of much of our most resonant myth and legend.

The third set of characters is the trio of parent, child, and wolf cub, first exemplified by Rayber, Bishop, and young Tarwater in *The Violent*. We see it again in "The Lame Shall Enter First," with Sheppard, Norton, and Rufus Johnson, and less satisfactorily in "The Comforts of Home," with Thomas' mother, Thomas, and Star, the nymphomaniac girl the mother brings home. Travesty consistently accompanies this grouping, too, but here parent and child do not judge each other, but are both judged harshly by the outsider. Through Tarwater's eyes, we see Rayber as a blind fool and Bishop as a worthless idiot; through Rufus' eyes we see Sheppard as a blasphemous do-gooder and Norton as a spiritless nonentity. This is not so neat in "The Comforts of Home," since "Star Drake" is too preposterous a character to judge anyone; essentially, there we see the absurd gullibility of Thomas' mother's absolute faith in human goodness through his eyes, and we similarly reject Thomas' absolute lack of charity as evidenced by his behavior.

Half a dozen important themes run through all Miss O'Connor's work. One is a profound equation of the mysteries of sex and religion. When young Hazel Motes sees the naked woman at the carnival, his mother tells him "Jesus died to redeem you" as she switches him, and the two guilty mysteries merge inextricably in his mind. As the title of "A Temple of the Holy Ghost" (a Christian metaphor for the body) makes clear, the story is centrally concerned with this equation. The twelve-year-old girl protagonist is initiated into sexual mystery by her older cousins, who tell her of the hermaphrodite they saw at the carnival; at the same time she imagines herself a Christian martyr in a Roman arena; when the sun goes down "like an elevated Host drenched in blood" to end the story, it is the blood of menstruation and childbirth as well as of martyrdom and Christ's Passion. The neatest of these sex-religion equations is Mrs. McIntyre's reaction, in "The Displaced Person," to the priest's own equation of Christ and the peacock's tail: "Mrs. McIntyre's face assumed a set puritanical expression and she reddened. Christ in the conversation embarrassed her the way sex had her mother."

Another recurrent theme is change of identity, transformation, death-and-rebirth. Parker in "Parker's Back" is transformed by the tattoo, but most often in the fiction transformation occurs by renaming. Harry Ashfield becomes Bevel, who counts, in "The River"; Joy chooses a way of life by becoming Hulga in "Good Country People"; Hoover Shoats transforms himself into Onnie Jay Holy to run a fake religious radio program called "Soulsease"; Rayber tries to remake young Tarwater by calling him "Frankie"; even Parker needs a baptismal name change from O. E. to Obadiah Elihue to be fully transformed.

A theme of great power in the work is what might be called the perverse mother. When Leora Watts first goes to bed with Hazel Motes, she tickles his chin "in a motherly way," calls him "son," and calls herself "Momma." The mummy in the novel is not only a mock Christ child but a pun on "mommy," as a Freudian would guess from its place as the ultimate revelation of Enoch's Mystery cult. (This guess is supported in "Everything That Rises Must Converge" by Julian's picture of his mother, "shrunken to the dwarf-like proportions of her moral nature, sitting like a mummy.") Here are Joy-Hulga and the Bible salesman seducing each other in the barn loft: "His breath was clear and sweet like a child's and the kisses were sticky like a child's. He mumbled about loving her and about knowing when he first seen her that he loved her, but the mumbling was like the sleepy fretting of a child being put to sleep by his mother." Norton in "The Lame Shall Enter First" finds his dead mother in the sky through a telescope, but the only mother he finds in reality is death by hanging. Parker's mother "would not pay for any tattoo except her name on a heart, which he had put on, grumbling." Tarwater's mother, like Rayber's, was a whore, or so both Tarwaters are pleased to affirm.

Miss O'Connor's principal theme is what Walter Allen in *Esprit* excellently calls "a world of the God-intoxicated," pointing out that Rayber in his denial is as much intoxicated by God as are the Tarwaters. Miss O'Connor's male characters are God-intoxicated in a variety of ways. Those who have found their calling as preachers articulate the author's radical dualism. The preacher in "The River" challenges: "Believe Jesus or the devil! . . . Testify to one or the other!" Old Tarwater (and, we assume, Haze's grandfather) similarly rejects everything not Christ as anti-Christ. We see a youthful version of this figure in Rufus Johnson. Rejecting salvation from Sheppard, Rufus hisses: "Nobody can save me but Jesus." "If I do repent, I'll be a preacher," he says. "If you're going to do it, it's no sense in doing it half way." Sheppard sees him as "a small black figure on the threshold of some dark apocalypse." Rufus may continue to choose the devil, as Haze tried to do, or he may yet accept the call, as young Tarwater eventually does. The mark of election, the *Noli me tangere*, is on all three, but they are free to choose whether to preach the Word or, like Parker, mutely to witness it on their flesh.

One way that intoxication with God expresses itself, in short, is Satanism. The Misfit in "A Good Man Is Hard to Find" is a ruthless killer because "Jesus thown everything off balance." The Misfit preaches the same radical Christian dualism from a different pulpit: "If He did what He said, then it's nothing for you to do but thow away everything and follow Him, and if He didn't, then it's nothing for you to do but enjoy the few minutes you got left the best way you can — by killing somebody or burning down his house or doing some other meanness to him. No pleasure but meanness.'' The Misfit has chosen the second alternative, but he admits at the end of the story, after wiping out the harmless family, "It's no real pleasure in life." Rufus lies and steals, he tells Sheppard, because "Satan . . . has me in his power," and in the course of the story he succeeds in converting Norton to Satanism (and thus to suicide), since, as Sheppard recognizes (in the story's central irony) but cannot understand, "The boy would rather be in hell than nowhere."

Another form God-intoxication paradoxically takes is Rationalism. The first of these antagonists in Miss O'Connor's work is the enigmatic figure of Mr. Paradise in "The River," who comes to the healings to mock and to display his unhealed cancerous ear, but who always comes. He is a curious ritual figure, the ceremonial scoffer, the Bishop of Misrule, and his shepherd's crook as mock-pastor is the giant peppermint stick with which he tries to save Harry from his death. Rayber is a fuller treatment of the same figure. He too is a mock-pastor (he named his son "Bishop"), and when old Tarwater baptized young Tarwater as a baby, Rayber then blasphemously baptized him a second time on the buttocks. Rayber has a catcher-in-the-rye "vision of himself moving like an avenging angel through the world, gathering up all the children that the Lord, not Herod, had slain," its Eden "some enclosed garden . . . where he would gather all the exploited children of the world and let the sunshine flood their minds." Rayber turns off the girl evangelist's indictment by turning off his hearing aid, but in his case we know, thanks to analyses by young Tarwater and by the author, that he is not deaf to Christianity but so responsive to it that all his positions are counter-positions. Rayber's views caricature enlightened secular humanism by being stated as the negatives of Christian dogma, thus: "The great dignity of man," he tells young Tarwater, "is his ability to say: I am born once and no more."

If the male characters are all God-intoxicated, the female characters in Flannery O'Connor's fiction are mainly self-intoxicated. Smugness and self-satisfaction, often represented by women, is another important theme. Here is Mrs. Cope in "A Circle in the Fire" talking to Mrs. Pritchard: " 'Every day I say a prayer of thanksgiving,' Mrs. Cope said. 'Think of all we have. Lord,' she said and sighed, 'we have everything.' " The hoodlum boys who bring her to judgment state the truth she has forgotten: "Man, Gawd owns them woods and her too." Mrs. Cope, reciting all they have to be thankful for, "a litany of her blessings," becomes the monstrous comic figure of Mrs. Turpin in "Revelation." When she proclaims in the doctor's waiting room, "Thank you, Jesus, for making everything the way it is!" the Wellesley girl springs at her throat with a howl, throws a fit on the floor, and cries a revelation out of it, "Go back to hell where you came from, you old wart hog." This is a symbolic equivalent to the boys' judgment of Mrs. Cope, as the vision in which Mrs. Turpin sees the good Christians like herself in a hellfire in which "even their virtues were being burned away" is a symbolic equivalent to the boys' firing Mrs. Cope's woods.

In Flannery O'Connor's moral universe, in short, Hazel Motes may have backed himself into heaven, but fat Mrs. Turpin seems destined for hell. This dualism relates to another theme, the transvaluation of values in which progress in the world is retrogression in the spirit. When Mr. Shiftlet in "The Life You Save May Be Your Own" tells the old woman, "the monks of old slept in their coffins!" she replies, "They wasn't as advanced as we are." This is Miss O'Connor's standard joke. Old Tarwater speaks for the author when he tells the boy of Rayber's intention to give him "every advantage," and adds, "You have me to thank for saving you from those advantages."

It is thus necessary to imitate the monks of old, to deny the world, and Naysaying is another of Flannery O'Connor's major themes. "Flying is the greatest engineering achievement of man," Rayber says, and young Tarwater answers him, "I wouldn't give you nothing for no airplane. A buzzard can fly." Similarly, Mary Fortune denies that anyone has ever whipped her or ever could, although her grandfather has just seen her whipped; "I don't need no new shoe," Rufus Johnson insists to Sheppard, with his club-foot barely covered by the old torn shoe. These lying denials are a higher truth, the truth of the spirit that contradicts the weakness of the flesh.

Flannery O'Connor's meanings are not only Christian, they are Christian mainly in the mystic and ascetic tradition of St. John of the Cross ("Hence the soul cannot be possessed of the divine union, until it has divested itself of the love of created beings") rather than in the humanitarian tradition expressed in I John 4:20 ("If a man say, I love God, and hateth his brother, he is a liar").

Miss O'Connor is said to have been pleased when the London *Times* identified her as a "theological" writer. As a fiction-writing theologian, she seems the most radical Christian dualist since Dostoevski. There are two of everything in her work, one Christ's and one anti-Christ's. There are two wafers, and since Rayber rejects Christ's, "he felt the taste of his own childhood pain laid again on his tongue like a bitter wafer." There are two baptisms, the one old Tarwater gives and the one Rayber gives. There are two rivers in "The River," one "the rich red river of Jesus' Blood," the other the mundane river in which Mr. Paradise appears "like some ancient water monster." There are two fires in "A Circle in the Fire," one the fiery furnace in which the prophets dance, "in the circle the angel had cleared for them," the other set in the woods by the boys. The same two fires appear at the end of *The Violent*, when Tarwater raises himself from the ground, and "the burning bush had disappeared. A line of fire ate languidly at the treeline." There are two Hazes in *Wise Blood*, one a false prophet, and two young Tarwaters in *The Violent*, one of whom dissociates himself from the other as mad.

Miss O'Connor's subject is Vocation only in this radical dualist or tragic sense, that the way to sanctity is through the greatest sinfulness. She reported with pride to a friend that a young nun showed her full comprehension of *The Violent* when she said that she understood Tarwater perfectly: "He was struggling with his vocation. I've been through that — I know just how he felt and you did, too." The relationship between the two realms of experience, the young nun's spiritual struggle and Tarwater's criminal actions and passions, is analogical: murdering an idiot becomes a proper metaphor for Christian baptism, firing a woods a proper metaphor for Christian confirmation. In a time of desperate unbelief, in Miss O'Connor's view, the Christian sacraments must be understood to be equally desperate, and the language of desperation is violence and crime.

Two more thematic consequences of Flannery O'Connor's radical Christian dualism remain to be noticed. One is the False Christ. Hazel Motes says: "What do I need with Jesus? I got Leora Watts." When he leaves Mrs. Watts, the old Essex becomes his substitute Jesus. The car Mr. Shiftlet acquires by marrying and deserting the deaf girl is similarly a substitute Christ; when he finally gets it running "He had an expression of serious modesty on his face as if he had just raised the dead." Mr. Shiftlet explains his philosophy to the old woman: "The body, lady, is like a house: it don't go anywhere; but the spirit, lady, is like a automobile: always on the move." Thomas in "The Comforts of Home" and

Sheppard in "The Lame Shall Enter First" do not have false Christs, they *are* false Christs.

The remaining Christian theme is best put by St. Paul in I Corinthians 1:25, "Because the foolishness of God is wiser than men," and 3:19, "For the wisdom of this world is foolishness with God." The way to wisdom is through folly as the way to sanctity is through sin. Old Tarwater, taken to the insane asylum in a strait-jacket for his wild prophesying, is God's Fool, and young Tarwater's vision of following "the bleeding stinking mad shadow of Jesus" hinges on the same paradox: Jesus' way is mad only by "the wisdom of this world."

Protestant Fundamentalism is thus Miss O'Connor's metaphor, in literary terms, for Roman Catholic truth (in theological terms, this reflects ecumenicism). Why did she see through a glass darkly, rather than face to face? There are many answers, and no certain answer. One answer that she gave to interviewers, that Protestant Fundamentalism was the milieu in which she grew up, is not really satisfactory. True, there are not many Catholics in rural Georgia, but then there are not many (or any) Hazes or Tarwaters either. Miss O'Connor gave a deeper answer in an interview with Granville Hicks: "I'm not interested in the sects as sects; I'm concerned with the religious individual, the backwoods prophet. Old Tarwater is the hero of *The Violent Bear It Away*, and I'm right behind him 100 per cent."

In a letter to Sister Mariella Gable O.S.B., quoted in the memorial issue of *Esprit*, she wrote: "People make a judgment of fanaticism by what they are themselves. To a lot of Protestants I know, monks and nuns are fanatics, none greater. And to a lot of monks and nuns I know, my Protestant prophets are fanatics. For my part, I think the only difference between them is that if you are a Catholic and have this intensity of belief you join the convent and are heard no more; whereas if you are a Protestant and have it, there is no convent for you to join and you go about the world getting into all sorts of trouble and drawing the wrath of people who don't believe anything much at all down on your head. This is one reason why I can write about Protestant believers better than Catholic believers — because they express their belief in diverse kinds of dramatic action which is obvious enough for me to catch."

Whatever caused Miss O'Connor to choose Protestant Fundamentalism as her metaphor for Catholic vision, it was a brilliant choice. It gave her imagery that is naturally dramatistic, as she says, and, as she does not say, it freed her from the constraints of good taste — the young nun who identified her struggles with Tarwater's could not, as the protagonist of a novel, be made to undergo experiences comparable to his. The gains enormously outweigh the losses. If Flannery O'Connor, by choosing a tent revivalist subject matter, could not write such a portrait of serene saintliness as J. F. Powers' "Lions, Harts, and Leaping Does," in exchange she was spared the necessity of writing Powers' pious fables about the rectory cat. In any case, neither was in accord with her gifts or her temperament.

As a Catholic born and brought up in Georgia, Miss O'Connor always insisted, not only on her right to the imagery of southern Protestantism, but on its peculiar fitness for her as a Catholic. In a letter, she wrote: "Now the South is a good place for a Catholic literature in my sense for a number of reasons. 1) In the South belief can still be made believable and in relation to a large part of the society. We're not the Bible Belt for nothing. 2) The Bible being generally known and revered in the section, gives the novelist that broad mythical base to refer to that he needs to extend his meaning in depth. 3) The South has a sacramental view of life . . . 4) The aspect of Protestantism that is most prominent (at least to the Catholic) in the South is that of man dealing with God directly, not through the mediation of the church, and this is great for the Catholic novelist like myself who wants to get close to his character and watch him wrestle with the Lord."

Flannery O'Connor was a loyal Georgian and a loyal southerner, in her fashion. She was not only a southerner but a white southern lady. In one aspect this was an ironic stance. She told friends that she had not read *Lolita* because "White Southern ladies can't read such books," a remark she must often have heard about her own work. But it does not seem to have been an ironic stance in regard to the race question, on which Miss O'Connor maintained a consistent public silence. There are, however, curious symbolic statements in her work. "Her fiction does not reflect the social issues, particularly the racial problems, which beset the South during her lifetime," says John J. Clarke in *Esprit*. I think that it does, and more powerfully and truly than that of anyone else, but the expression is always implicit, covert, cryptic. As her mad prophets are metaphoric for Roman Catholic truth, so in a sense all the fierce violence in her work is metaphoric for violence done the Negro. This is most clear in *Wise Blood*, when ten-year-old Haze is trying to figure out what dirty mystery is going on in the carnival tent. We follow the sequence of his thoughts from "It's some men in a privy," to "maybe it's a man and a woman in a privy," to his sudden question to the barker: "Is it a nigger? . . . Are they doing something to a nigger?" (I would exchange many high-minded tracts on the Question for the insight in that progression.)

The Negroes in the stories are seen externally, as a conventional white southern lady would see them, with no access to their concealed sensibility, but occasionally one of them will say something (there are several such remarks in "The Displaced Person") that shows how much the author knows about that sensibility. Negroes in the fiction sometimes carry profound spiritual meaning, as in "The Artificial Nigger" or in the figure of Buford Munson in *The*

Violent. In several stories, and in the fragment of the unfinished novel, Negroes are images of fraternity. In the deepest sense, Harry in "The River," who goes to his death because he wants to *count*, or Norton in "The Lame Shall Enter First," who hangs himself because he wants to be *some*where, are symbols for Negro aspirations and frustrations; they are symbolic Negroes or "artificial niggers," in fact, and the author knew it.

Which brings us to the question of integration. Mr. Guizac, the displaced person, is a full integrationist out of desperation: he is trying to marry his sixteen-year-old Polish cousin to the Negro Sulk, to get her out of the refugee camps. It is this project, which Mrs. McIntyre characteristically describes as a match between a "poor innocent child" and a "half-witted thieving black stinking nigger," that leads to his fall from Mrs. McIntyre's favor and thus to his fate. Mr. Guizac's integrationist slogan is minimal: "She no care black. . . . She in camp three year." Insofar as he embodies Christ the Displaced Person, however, his implicit integrationist slogan is maximal: God died to redeem all mankind.

Integrationism is savagely travestied as sentimental and fatuous in Julian in "Everything That Rises Must Converge" and Asbury in "The Enduring Chill," but the opposing view is just as savagely travestied in their mothers. "They should rise, yes, but on their own side of the fence," Julian's mother says, and the title, as well as her stroke, is the rejoinder.

We understand the nature of Miss O'Connor's opposition to integration when we see Asbury think of smoking with the Negroes who work for his mother as "one of those moments of communion when the difference between black and white is absorbed into nothing." In Miss O'Connor's radical Christian dualism, this is a secular and thus a false communion, and integration in general is a secular and thus a false salvation. Whereas her friend Father Merton finds integration so deeply inherent in the Christian con-

348

cept of Incarnation that he regards any trace of racism in a Roman Catholic as automatically self-excommunicating, Miss O'Connor insists with Dostoevski that the only equality is to be found in the spiritual dignity of man, in the mystic communion of the Sacraments.

It is not easy to place Flannery O'Connor in a literary tradition. The writer to whom she is most indebted stylistically, Mark Twain, is never mentioned in discussions of her work, nor did she ever identify him as an influence, so far as I know. Yet if *The Violent Bear It Away* has any single progenitor, it is *Adventures of Huckleberry Finn*. Miss O'Connor's mature writing has very little to do with Faulkner or any of what is called "southern" literature. The writer who most influenced her, at least in her first books, is Nathanael West. *Wise Blood* is clearly modeled on *Miss Lonelyhearts* (as no reviewer noticed at the time), and contains many specific reminiscences of it. Hazel Motes has a nose "like a shrike's bill"; after he goes to bed with Leora Watts, Haze feels "like something washed ashore on her"; Sabbath Lily's correspondence with a newspaper advice-columnist is purest West; and all the rocks in *Wise Blood* recall the rock Miss Lonelyhearts first contains in his gut and then becomes, the rock on which the new Peter will found the new Church. The European writer Flannery O'Connor most profoundly resembles (in method, not in scale) is Dostoevski. Like him she created a deeply understood Enemy out of her own liberal and enlightened dreams. "Ivan Karamazov cannot believe," she wrote in her introduction to *A Memoir of Mary Ann*, "as long as one child is in torment" — no more can Rayber or Sheppard, she might have added.

It is surely too early to evaluate Flannery O'Connor's work or place it in our literature, but some beginnings can be attempted. Two points must be made immediately. The first is that despite the prevailing opinion, she was primarily a novelist, not a short story writer, and consequently her novels are better and more important than even the best of her stories. The second is that any discussion of her theology can only be preliminary to, not a substitute for, aesthetic analysis and evaluation.

The strengths of Flannery O'Connor's writing are those qualities in it that have been most disliked and attacked: the apocalyptic violence, the grotesque vision, the vulgarity. "Her novels suffer, I believe, from an excessive violence of conception," Warren Coffey wrote in *Esprit*, contrasting them with her stories. But it is precisely this violence in the novels — these murders and burnings, blindings and rapes — that is the heart of their imaginative power, as is murder in Dostoevski's novels. It is the violence of desperate Christianity, of the desperate and verbally inarticulate South, of a nation no longer quiet about its desperation. William Esty wrote scornfully, in *Commonweal*, of Flannery O'Connor's "cult of the Gratuitous Grotesque." Her fiction is grotesque, certainly, but never gratuitously so. For example, in the opening scene of "The Lame Shall Enter First," Norton eats a piece of chocolate cake spread with peanut butter and ketchup; when his father gets him upset, he vomits it all up in "a limp sweet batter." This is not only grotesque but thoroughly repulsive, and no less repulsive to the author, but it is entirely functional and necessary in the story: it perfectly symbolizes the indigestible mess of Sheppard's "enlightened" views, which Norton will similarly be unable to keep down. Flannery O'Connor herself answered the charge definitively in an unpublished lecture: "I have found that any fiction that comes out of the South is going to be considered grotesque by the Northern critic, unless it is grotesque, in which case it is going to be considered realistic." Nor is this merely a matter of the northern critic. All art, to the extent that it is new and serious, is shocking and disturbing, and one way of dismissing those truths that get through to us is as "grotesque."

We must not ignore the weaknesses of Flannery O'Connor's fiction. Her stories came to rely too often and too mechanically on death to end them. The deaths are ruinous to "A View of the Woods," and unnecessary in other stories. Her best stories — "The Artificial Nigger," "Good Country People," "Parker's Back" — neither end in death nor need to. One reason for her melodramatic endings seems to be theological. "I'm a born Catholic and death has always been brother to my imagination," Miss O'Connor told an interviewer in *Jubilee*, "I can't imagine a story that doesn't properly end in it or in its foreshadowings." It was one of her rare confusions of theology with aesthetics.

These endings result from a misjudgment in craft, as do those occasions — in "Good Country People" and "A View of the Woods" — in which she runs on past a story's natural finish. Other than these, the only fault in her fiction is a tendency to travesty. Caricature is a legitimate resource of art, and a magnificently effective one in her hands, but her caricature sometimes fell into over-caricature and lost its truth, so that we cannot believe in the existence of certain of her secular intellectuals or Negroes. If they are not people, they cannot function as symbols, since, as she says in the lecture on the grotesque, "It is the nature of fiction not to be good for much else unless it is good in itself."

Flannery O'Connor's fiction is a powerful example of what Kenneth Burke calls "symbolic action," functioning for the author as well as for the reader. The root meaning of "caricature" is "overload," and in this sense Miss O'Connor created characters and their dramatic oppositions by separating, exaggerating, and polarizing elements in herself. The Tarwaters and Rayber are the Yang and Yin of the author, each made extreme, in just the fashion that Stephen and Bloom are, or Ahab and Ishmael. These opposites held in tension externalize an inner war, but they do so dramatically and they progress to a dramatic resolution, in the process exorcising ambivalence and resolving doubt. "I have written a wicked book," Melville wrote to Hawthorne when he had finished *Moby-Dick*, "and feel spotless as the lamb." As Dostoevski could find all that was most detestable, Stavrogin and Smerdyakov, deep inside himself, so Miss O'Connor could find inside herself Hazel Motes, the blind fanatic, and Joy-Hulga, the spiteful atheist. And in finding them, in incarnating them in art, she rid herself of them. The stories are full of bitter hate *in order that* the author may be friendly and loving; the novels scream doubt and denial *in order that* the author may be devout and serene.

As this symbolic action transforms the author, so it transforms the reader. We undergo these terrible events, as horror-filled as Greek tragedy, to be purged and sweetened, even kept devout (in our different devotions). Few of Flannery O'Connor's readers, few even of her Roman Catholic readers, can share her desperate and radical Christian dualism, as she was fully aware. But it constituted a natural dramatism for fiction, as did Dostoevski's religion, and a fiction in no sense parochial. As a writer she had the additional advantage, as West did, of multiple alienation from the dominant assumptions of our culture: he was an outsider as a Jew, and doubly an outsider as a Jew alienated from other Jews; she was comparably an outsider as a woman, a southerner, and a Roman Catholic in the South. This is not to say that her views, or her alienation, produced the fiction; many have held more radical views, and been far more alienated, while producing nothing. Her gifts produced the fiction, but her situation gave them opportunities, and enabled her to exercise her intelligence, imagination, and craft most effectively. Her early death may have deprived the world of unforeseeable marvels, but she left us, in *The Violent Bear It Away*, parts of *Wise Blood*, and the best stories, marvels enough.

Selected Bibliography

Works of Flannery O'Connor

Wise Blood. New York: Harcourt, Brace, 1952.
A Good Man Is Hard to Find. New York: Harcourt, Brace, 1955.
The Violent Bear It Away. New York: Farrar, Straus, and Cudahy, 1960.
Everything That Rises Must Converge. New York: Farrar, Straus, and Giroux, 1965. (With an introduction by Robert Fitzgerald.)
"The Fiction Writer and His Country," in *The Living Novel*, edited by Granville Hicks. New York: Macmillan, 1957. Pp. 157–64.
"The Church and the Fiction Writer," *America*, 96:733–35 (March 30, 1957).
"Living with a Peacock," *Holiday*, 30:52 (September 1961).
Introduction to *A Memoir of Mary Ann*. New York: Farrar, Straus, and Cudahy, 1961, 1962.
Note on *The Phenomenon of Man*, by Pierre Teilhard de Chardin, *American Scholar*, 30:618 (Fall 1961).
"The Regional Writer," *Esprit*, 7:31–35 (Winter 1963).
"Why Do the Heathens Rage?" *Esquire*, 60:60–61 (July 1963).
"The Role of the Catholic Novelist," *Greyfriar*, 7:5–12 (1964).

Critical and Biographical Studies

Baumbach, Jonathan. "The Acid of God's Grace: *Wise Blood* by Flannery O'Connor," in *The Landscape of Nightmare*. New York: New York University Press, 1965. Pp. 87–100.
Browning, Preston M. *Flannery O'Connor*. Carbondale: Southern Illinois University Press, 1974.
Critique, Vol. 2, No. 2 (Fall 1958). (An issue jointly devoted to Flannery O'Connor and J. F. Powers, with a bibliography and articles on the former by Caroline Gordon, Sister M. Bernetta Quinn O.S.F., Louis D. Rubin, Jr., and George F. Wedge.)
Drake, Robert. *Flannery O'Connor: A Critical Essay*. Contemporary Writers in Christian Perspective. Grand Rapids: Eerdmans, 1966.
Driscoll, Leon, and Joan T. Brittain. *Eternal Crossroads, the Art of Flannery O'Connor*. Lexington: University of Kentucky Press, 1971.
Esprit, Vol. 8, No. 1 (Winter 1964). (A memorial issue.)

Farnham, James F. "The Grotesque in Flannery O'Connor," *America*, 105:277–81 (May 13, 1961).

Feeley, Kathleen. *Flannery O'Connor: The Voices of the Peacock*. New Brunswick: Rutgers University Press, 1972.

Ferris, Sumner J. "The Outside and the Inside: Flannery O'Connor's *The Violent Bear It Away*," *Critique*, 3:11–19 (Winter–Spring 1960).

Fitzgerald, Robert. "The Countryside and the True Country," *Sewanee Review*, 70:380–94 (Summer 1962).

Friedman, M. J. "Flannery O'Connor: Another Legend in Southern Fiction," in Joseph J. Waldmeir, ed., *Recent American Fiction: Some Critical Views*. Boston: Houghton Mifflin, 1963. Pp. 231–45.

Friedman, Melvin J., and Lewis A. Lawson, eds. *Added Dimension: The Mind and Art of Flannery O'Connor*. New York: Fordham University Press, 1966.

Gable, Sister Mariella, O.S.B. "Ecumenic Core in Flannery O'Connor's Fiction," *American Benedictine Review*, 15:127–43 (June 1964).

Gilman, Richard. "On Flannery O'Connor," *New York Review of Books*, 13:24–26 (August 21, 1969).

Gossett, Louise Y. "The Test by Fire: Flannery O'Connor," *Violence in Recent Southern Fiction*. Durham, N.C.: Duke University Press, 1965. Pp. 75–97.

Hart, Jane. "Strange Earth: The Stories of Flannery O'Connor," *Georgia Review*, 12:215–22 (Summer 1958).

Hawkes, John. "Flannery O'Connor's Devil," *Sewanee Review*, 70:395–407 (Summer 1962).

Hendin, Josephine. *The World of Flannery O'Connor*. Bloomington: Indiana University Press, 1970.

Hicks, Granville. "A Writer at Home with Her Heritage," *Saturday Review*, 45:22–23 (May 12, 1962).

———. "A Cold, Hard Look at Humankind," *Saturday Review*, 48:23–24 (May 29, 1965).

Howe, Irving. "Flannery O'Connor's Stories," *New York Review of Books*, 5:16–17 (September 30, 1965).

Hyman, Stanley Edgar. "Flannery O'Connor's Tattooed Christ," *New Leader*, 48:9–10 (May 10, 1965).

Joselyn, Sister M., O.S.B. "Thematic Centers in 'The Displaced Person,'" *Studies in Short Fiction*, 1:85–92 (Winter 1964).

McFarland, Dorothy Tuck, *Flannery O'Connor*. Modern Literature Monographs. New York: Ungar, 1976.

Malin, Irving. *New American Gothic*. Carbondale: Southern Illinois University Press, 1962. *Passim*.

Meaders, Margaret Inman. "Flannery O'Connor: 'Literary Witch,'" *Colorado Quarterly*, 10:377–86 (Spring 1962).

[Meyers], Sister Bertrande, D.C. "Four Stories of Flannery O'Connor," *Thought*, 37:410–26 (Autumn 1962).

Rose Alice, Sister, S.S.J. "Flannery O'Connor: Poet to the Outcast," *Renascence*, 16:126–32 (Spring 1964).

Solotaroff, Theodore. "You *Can* Go Home Again," *Book Week*, 2:1, 13 (May 30, 1965).

Spivey, Ted R. "Flannery O'Connor's View of God and Man," *Studies in Short Fiction*, 1:200–6 (Spring 1964).

Stelzmann, Rainulf A. "Shock and Orthodoxy: An Interpretation of Flannery O'Connor's Novels and Short Stories," *Xavier University Studies*, 2:1 (March 1963).

Stephens, Martha. *The Question of Flannery O'Connor*. Baton Rouge: Louisiana State University Press, 1973.

Stern, Richard. "Flannery O'Connor: A Remembrance and Some Letters," *Shenandoah*, 16:5–10 (Winter 1965).

Tate, Mary Barbara. "Flannery O'Connor: A Reminiscence," *Columns*, 2:1 (Fall 1964).

Vander Kieft, Ruth M. "Judgment in the Fiction of Flannery O'Connor," *Sewanee Review*, 76:337–56 (Spring 1968).

Walters, Dorothy, *Flannery O'Connor*. New York: Twayne, 1973.

355

ABOUT THE AUTHORS

About the Authors

MAUREEN HOWARD, a writer and teacher, is the author of the novel *Before My Time* and a contributor to the *New York Times Book Review*, *Ms. Magazine*, *Partisan Review*, and other magazines.

LOUIS AUCHINCLOSS is a prolific novelist and critic as well as a partner in a New York law firm. He also wrote the pamphlet *Edith Wharton* in the series of University of Minnesota Pamphlets on American Writers.

DOROTHY VAN GHENT, author of *The English Novel: Form and Function*, taught at several universities: Montana, Vermont, Brandeis, and Harvard.

RAY B. WEST, JR. has published poetry, fiction, and literary criticism. Now a professor emeritus of English at San Francisco State University living in Utah, he has taught American literature in several universities in the United States and abroad.

J. A. BRYANT, JR., Chairman of the Department of English at the University of Kentucky, is the editor of an edition of *Romeo and Juliet* and the author of *Hippolyta's View: Some Christian Aspects of Shakespeare's Plays* and *The Compassionate Satirist: Ben Jonson and His Imperfect World*. He also contributes to literary quarterlies and professional journals.

IRVIN STOCK, professor of English at the University of Massachusetts in Boston, is the author of *William Hale White (Mark Rutherford): A Critical Study* and has contributed articles on fiction to various literary quarterlies.

LAWRENCE GRAVER is Kenan Professor of English at Williams College and author of *Conrad's Short Fiction* and *Samuel Beckett*.

STANLEY EDGAR HYMAN taught at Bennington College and was a staff writer for the *New Yorker*. He was the author or editor of numerous books, including *The Promised End*. He also wrote another pamphlet in this series, *Nathanael West*.

INDEX

Index

INDEX

Macdermott, Macdougal (fictional character), 230–31, 247
McDowell, Frederick P. W., 75
MacLain, King (fictional character), 187, 188, 190–94 *passim*
McRaven, Laura (fictional character), 181–82, 183, 185–86, 187
Macy, Marvin (fictional character), 289–93 *passim*
Madame Bovary, 58
Mademoiselle, 312
"Magic," 124, 125
Mailer, Norman, 13
Making of Americans, The, 31
Malone, J. T. (fictional character), 304–6
"Man in the Brooks Brothers Shirt, The," 224–25
Mann, Erika, 267
Mann, Klaus, 267
Mansfield, Katherine, 160, 162
Manuscript (magazine), 167
"María Concepción," 18, 124, 125, 156
Marie, Queen of Romania, 55, 70
Mask of State: Watergate Portraits, The, 254
Mather, Cotton, 140, 163
Matisse, Henri, 32
Matisse, Picasso, and Gertrude Stein, 31
Matthew *11:12*, 330
Matthiessen, F. O., 161
Maupassant, Guy de, 69, 70, 277
Medina, 254
Medusa, 188
Meeker, Richard K., 67, 68
Melville, Herman, 29, 131, 159, 161, 162, 352
Member of the Wedding, The: theme and characterization in, 20, 295–304, 305; writing of, 268; success of, 270, 294, 303–4, 307; stage adaptation of, 270, 296, 297; symbolism in, 279–80; structure of, 294
Memoir of Mary Ann, A, 349

Memories of a Catholic Girlhood, 4, 23, 25–26, 218–21, 229
"Memory, A," 168–69
Men, portrayal of: by Glasgow, 8–9, 41–42, 44, 54, 58, 63, 66, 67, 73–74; by O'Connor, 20, 340–42; by McCullers, 21
Mercer, Mary, 272
Meredith, George, 38, 59
Merton, Father, 348–49
Mexico: Porter's literary use of, 122, 125–26, 129, 131, 150, 153, 157; Porter as resident of, 122, 140; Porter's articles on, 160
Milledgeville, Georgia, 311, 313
Miller of Old Church, The, 40, 50–51
Milton, John, 203
Miranda (fictional character), 163: as autobiographical character, 15, 123–24, 129; in "Pale Horse, Pale Rider," 15–16, 137–39, 152; in "Old Mortality," 16–18, 26, 129, 132–37, 147; in "The Grave," 123–24, 145–46; in "Noon Wine," 128; in *The Leaning Tower and Other Stories*, 139–49 *passim*; in "The Source," 142; in "The Circus," 144–45; in "The Old Order," 144, 156
Misérables, Les, 48
Miss Lonelyhearts, 349
Mississippi: Welty's roots in, 166–67, 204, 205, 210; Welty's literary use of, 168, 172, 173, 175, 181, 182–83, 186, 187, 194, 197, 206, 207, 209
Mississippi State College for Women, 167
Mitchell, Margaret, 42
Moby Dick, 159, 351
Moers, Ellen, 21
Morrison, Loch (fictional character), 190–91, 192
Mortgaged Heart, The, 266
Moss, Howard, 159
Motes, Hazel "Haze" (fictional character), 315–21 *passim*, 323, 325, 326, 327, 335, 337, 338, 339, 340, 342, 344, 347, 349, 352